Collective Bargaining and Wages in Comparative Perspective

Collective Bargaining and Wages in Comparative Perspective

Germany, France, The Netherlands, Sweden and the United Kingdom

Editor: Roger Blanpain
Guest editors: Thomas Blanke and Edgar Rose

Contributors
Kerstin Ahlberg
Brian Bercusson
Thomas Blanke
Niklas Bruun
Antoine T.J.M. Jacobs
Edgar Rose
Bernard Ryan
André Sobczak
Cristophe Vigneau

KLUWER LAW
INTERNATIONAL

A C.I.P. catalogue record for this book is available from the Library of Congress.

ISBN 90 411 2388 1

Published by:
Kluwer Law International
P.O. Box 85889
2508 CN The Hague
The Netherlands.
E-mail: sales@kluwerlaw.com
Website: http://www.kluwerlaw.com

Sold and distributed in North, Central and South America by:
Aspen Publishers, Inc.
7201 McKinney Circle
Frederick, MD 21704
USA

Sold and distributed in all other countries by:
Turpin Distribution Services Ltd.
Stratton Business Park
Pegasus Drive
Biggleswade
Bedfordshire SG18 8TQ
United Kingdom

Printed on acid-free paper

Printed in The Netherlands.

Table of Contents

LIST OF CONTRIBUTORS vii

FOREWORD ix

INTRODUCTION 1

1. Erosion or renewal? The crisis of collective wage formation in Germany 5
Thomas Blanke and Edgar Rose

2. France: The helping hand of the state 31
Christophe Vigneau and André Sobczak

3. The British case: before and after the decline of collective wage formation 49
Brian Bercusson and Bernard Ryan

4. The Netherlands: In the tradition of intersectoral pacts 89
Antoine T.J.M. Jacobs

5. Sweden: Transition through collective bargaining 117
Kerstin Ahlberg and Niklas Bruun

6. Ideas and suggestions. Input for the German debate 145
Edgar Rose

7. Outlook – Chances of European harmonization or coordination of collective wage formation 159
Thomas Blanke

ANNEX 169

List of Contributors

Kerstin Ahlberg, National Institute for Working Life, Sweden

Brian Bercusson, King's College, UK

Thomas Blanke, University of Oldenburg, Germany

Niklas Bruun, Swedish School of Economics and Business Administration, Finland

Antoine T.J.M. Jacobs, University of Tilbury, the Netherlands

Edgar Rose, University of Oldenburg, Germany

Bernard Ryan, University of Kent, UK

André Sobczak, Audencia Management School, France

Cristophe Vigneau, Université Paris 1, France

Foreword

Europe is growing. When the EU was founded in 1992 by the Treaty of Maastricht, it had 12 Member States. On 1 May 2004 this expanded to 25. This rapid expansion is creating enormous challenges for European integration.

At the moment, European unification means much more than the creation of equal conditions for markets and for competition. The signing of the European Constitution by the heads of government and state in October 2004 marked a milestone on the way to political and legal integration.

The effective realisation of the free movement of workers demands a deeper harmonization of working conditions and national systems of social security. During the 1990s, meaningful progress was made in this field owing to the strong commitment of the European Commission and strengthened by the structures of social dialogue. Remarkably, the core element of labour relations – wage determination – was excluded from harmonization. The present study is a response to this. Its aim is to analyse the prospects of building up structures of wage formation through collective bargaining and collective agreements in Europe.

The study complements a research project which was carried out under my supervision by Edgar Rose within the framework of the research network of Lower Saxony on 'Technological development and change in societal structures'. The basic assumption of this research project was that the institutional and legal framework of the German system of collective wage formation is under heavy pressure due to the challenges of internalisation ('globalisation'), decentralisation at the level of individual companies and individualisation. This has led to changes in the traditional system of collective bargaining, a development which is widely seen in the political and academic debate as a fundamental crisis of the system of concluding regional collective agreements on wages.

The aims of this international comparative report are twofold. First, we tried to find out whether the – arguably parallel – social, political and economic challenges to the systems of collective agreements in France, the United Kingdom, the Netherlands and Sweden would lead to crisis diagnoses and developments similar to those in Germany. If so, we expected that more homogeneous structures of collective bargaining would emerge which might improve the chances of creating structures of wage formation through collective bargaining and collective agreements in Europe. Secondly, we asked if the legal and institutional developments of the different national systems of collective bargaining constitute starting points for mutual learning in order to meet the new challenges. We took Germany as point of reference for this analysis: in our view, the German system of collective bargaining is undergoing particular problems and would therefore draw particular benefit from learning initiatives. We therefore asked the international experts not only to describe the problems arising in their own countries and the approaches to dealing with them but also to provide a critical commentary on our description of developments in Germany.

The reports from France (chapter 2: Christophe Vigneau and André Sobczak), the United Kingdom (chapter 3: Brian Bercusson and Bernard Ryan), the Netherlands (chapter 4: Antoine Jacobs) and Sweden (chapter 5: Niklas Bruun and Kerstin Ahlberg) which complement the German report (chapter 1: Thomas Blanke and

Edgar Rose), do not indicate – at least from a legal and institutional perspective – a 'bottom up' harmonization trend of this kind (chapter 7).

How this finding should be interpreted and what relevance it has for European prospects of wage formation through collective agreements at regional level remains open. For a precise answer, further research would be needed. It is possible that the social dimension of European unification is still not sufficiently advanced. Perhaps the emergence of a system of wage formation through collective agreements at European level can no longer be expected, owing to fundamental social and economic changes leading towards the erosion of such ideological and legal categories and concepts as 'dependent work', 'solidarity', 'subsidiarity' and 'social self-regulation' as preconditions of traditional collective bargaining structures at national level. In the final chapter we outline some preliminary interpretations of European prospects.

Consequently, this report does not end with a definitive result. However, it does lead towards a deeper understanding of the situation and an open question. The credit for this goes to the contributors. In the first place, this includes the authors of the national reports who also provided fruitful commentaries on our report on the German situation and took the time to participate in our two workshops. Credit also goes to all the other experts who participated in the workshops. I address particular thanks to the Hans-Böckler Foundation – Heide Pfarr, Ina Drescher and Martina Klein – and to the Hanse-Wissenschaftskolleg, Institute for Advanced Studies of the German *Länder* of Bremen and Niedersachsen in Delmenhorst – Gerhard Roth and Ingeborg Mehser – who graciously promoted the international part of the research project. Edgar Rose and the team at the Department of Labour Law at the Carl von Ossietzky University of Oldenburg – Bettina Graue, Peter Bleses, Claas Schwandt, Nina Decker and Christine Sell – gave indispensable aid in preparing and concluding this research project, most especially at the two workshops in Delmenhorst. Kerstin Ahlberg has given us enormous support in preparation of this edition in English and making contact with the editor and with the Swedish SALTSA programme by which this edition was generously supported: many thanks for this.

Thomas Blanke

Introduction: Transnational perspectives on the law of wage bargaining

Edgar Rose

For almost a decade, the traditional German system of collective wage bargaining has been considered to be *in crisis* by many lawyers[1] and most economists.[2] Indeed, in the 1990s a process of progressive erosion affecting the central institutions of the system could be observed. First of all, the decreasing membership of the bargaining partners on both sides was an alarm signal. Management strategies to abandon collective bargaining became widespread. The rate of employees covered by collective agreements was shrinking continuously. Year by year, it became more obvious that all parties concerned – employers, trade unions, the state – had not the capacity to resolve the growing difficulties of collective wage formation. Attempts to establish a national social pact failed. The concept of sectoral wage agreements in particular became problematic. The underlying idea of excluding lower-cost competition concerning wages between all relevant competitors in a branch began to lose its power to convince on open markets where almost everything can be produced for much cheaper wages beyond national borders. While the challenges of increasing competition on global markets, decentralizing management strategies and individualized employees put more and more pressure on the traditional sectoral bargaining system, the German social partners seemed to be constantly trapped in fruitless conflicts on how the system must be reformed.

This was the situation in Germany at the beginning of the *research project* that, between 2002 and 2004, formed the framework in which the contributions to this book were produced. The original idea was to mobilize international interventions in the deadlocked German debate. Two sources of international support were considered. First, we expected that there were similar problems in other European countries but more success in finding solutions. It might therefore be fruitful to listen to how problems had been managed in other systems in order to discuss what these foreign experiences could mean for the future of wage formation in Germany. Secondly, we assumed that helpful interventions may come from the European level where efforts to harmonize the national collective bargaining systems may have a future impact on the German system.

On the basis of these considerations we formulated *two bundles of questions*:

- Are there other European countries where the systems of collective wage formation are – or were – facing similar challenges to the German system? How do other national systems cope with those challenges and which solutions may be instructive also for the German situation?

1 See, e.g., Heinze (1997), p. 7; Raab (2004), p. 371.
2 See, e.g., Berthold/Stettes (2001); Schnabel (2004), p. 32.

- Do similar challenges imposed on many national systems of collective bargaining produce converging developments of national laws and institutions of wage formation? Does that facilitate the transnational coordination of wage bargaining in practice or, moreover, EU initiatives to harmonize national laws or even to create a legal framework for wage bargaining at the European level?

Particularly the first question had a decisive impact on our *selection* of the countries we included in our comparison. Only those countries qualified which are in a similar economic and societal situation to Germany: highly industrialized countries with export-oriented economies and developed collective bargaining and social welfare systems. We assumed that countries which do not meet these criteria are in such a different situation – for example, the new European member states in eastern Europe – that their experiences would not be applicable to the German case. Among the group of countries in a similar situation, however, it was reasonable to choose those which showed wide differences in order to make sure that there was a significant variation in the sample. So we opted for countries with strong (Sweden) and with weak (France) trade unions, with a high (France) and a low (United Kingdom) degree of state intervention in labour relations, and with a single channel (United Kingdom, Sweden) and with a dual channel (Netherlands) system of workers' representation. Moreover, we made sure that the 'three worlds of welfare capitalism' were represented in our sample:[3] the liberal (United Kingdom), the conservative (France) and the social democratic (Sweden) type of the welfare state.

As the core of the project's *research work* we asked experts from the four included countries – France, the Netherlands, Sweden and the United Kingdom – to give, first, a detailed report on the legal and institutional framework of collective wage formation in their countries, and second, a statement including judgements and suggestions in relation to the German case. A report on the German system and its current developments was given to the experts involved to enable them to discuss the German situation in detail. Chapter 1 of this book is a revised version of this German report. Chapters 2–5 are based on the four reports the experts presented in answer to our questions. All five chapters therefore touch on the same aspects of the topic in the same order.

Each country report starts – after an introduction – with an overview of *industrial relations* in the country concerned. For reasons of comparison and to facilitate transnational understanding, it was crucial to cover the whole institutional framework in which each system of collective wage formation is embedded. Then, as a second part, *the law* on collective wage formation is described in detail. Labour law plays a central role in all included countries to determine the procedures of wage formation: especially in France, the Netherlands and Germany; less so in the UK. Thirdly, all reports refer to the *current challenges* imposed on national collective bargaining systems. It is interesting to compare the different interpretations of what the current challenges are. High wage costs in a situation of increasing international competition, and management strategies trying to decentralise wage bargaining are frequently mentioned. The exception is the United Kingdom where all this happened much earlier and, at present, wage formation seems already to be perfectly decentralised. The fourth section of all reports concerns the *reactions* of the most important participants to the challenges described. This is where the strategies of the state, social partners and individual companies are specified in detail to allow a

3. See Esping-Andersen (1990), pp. 26–28.

discussion of which practices are not only successful in their original environment, but also applicable to other systems in other countries.

At this point, there is a break in the structure of all reports (except the German one which ends here). The perspective turns in order to compare each collective bargaining system with the *German case* in search of helpful observations from abroad. The idea was, as already mentioned, to use the knowledge and experience of international experts to break the deadlock of the German debate. First, the experts were asked to discuss differences and similarities between their home system and the German case. Then, they were required to identify – from their perspective – those aspects of the German system that generate specific strengths and vulnerabilities. Finally, the focus was put on central paradigms of the German debate in which the need for a more flexible and decentralised system of wage formation was taken for granted.

The four thought-provoking reports on wage formation in France, the Netherlands, Sweden and the United Kingdom go far beyond the original German research interests. They offer deep insights into how differently modern economies can adapt to the demands of globalisation. The ability to develop the systems of wage formation successfully in different national traditions making use of specific national resources is impressively described. That is why all this information is extremely valuable not only for the German debate, but internationally. To publish it in English was the logical move.

Besides, the German case itself was likely to interest an international public. Germany can serve as a *test case* of how national policymaking can benefit from foreign experiences. The research procedure was somewhat inspired by the Open Method of Coordination (OMC). This method – which now has a prominent place in the European Constitution – was invented for the European Employment Strategy and is now the method used for policy fields in which traditional European harmonization by 'hard law' is scarcely possible. Instead, the OMC promotes mutual learning between different national policymaking, identification of 'best practices' to inspire those who fall behind, and 'peer reviews' with transnational visits by experts to comment on foreign developments.[4] These elements of the OMC indeed played a role in our research concept in which wage formation in Germany was the test object.

The *test results* were ambiguous. On the one hand, the German debate can profit greatly from successful developments in other countries. Unquestioned 'truths' of German thinking were fruitfully challenged by the reports, ideas and inspirations from abroad (see Chapter 6): for example, the German belief that the legal regulation of collective bargaining in Germany was exceptionally restrictive proved quite simply to be wrong. On the other hand, national practices and institutional frameworks are so different, and the national strategies to overcome difficulties are so specifically based on the traditional strengths of each system, that there is usually no chance of determining 'best practices' that could serve as a model for direct implementation in other countries.

The same findings strongly affected our second bundle of questions because the answer was simply that there was 'no convergence'. Particularly when put under pressure, national strategies to overcome these problems do not lead to convergence of national laws and institutions of collective wage formation. Rather the opposite.

4. See also the suggestions of the High Level Group on Industrial Relations an Change in the European Union that recommended to apply the OMC to the transnational coordination of industrial relations (cf. High Level Group (2002), p. 37).

Each national strategy tends – or tended – to reinforce the specific competences to be found in that country, so that the disparities between systems became even deeper. There are some exceptions, however (see chapter 7).

What remains is to ask instead if there are other means or forces that may bring about a *Europeanization* of the laws and institutions of wage formation. In a brainstorming process we generated five theses on how Europeanization might occur in a 'bottom up' or a 'top down' scenario:

1. Similar socio-economic challenges may lead to converging system developments.
2. Transnational coordination of trade union wage policies may gradually generate a common European practice of wage bargaining.
3. Social dialogue in accordance with Art. 138, 139 EC Treaty may evolve into a legal platform for European collective wage agreements.
4. The forthcoming European Constitution may improve the legal base for collective bargaining at the European level.
5. The 'open method of coordination' applied to the law on wage bargaining may provoke a process of legal harmonization by mutual learning.

However, none of these paths will lead unerringly to a European framework of wage bargaining. Some assumptions – like the first one – simply prove false. These questions therefore remain open for further discussions, to which we like to contribute (see chapter 7).

REFERENCES

Berthold, Norbert, and Oliver Stettes (2001) 'Der Flächentarifvertrag – vom Wegbereiter des Wirtschaftswunders zum Verursacher der Beschäftigungsmisere', in Claus Ott and Hans-Bernd Schäfer (eds) *Ökonomische Analyse des Arbeitsrechts*, Tübingen: Mohr, pp. 1–29.

Esping-Andersen, Gøsta (1990) *The Three Worlds of Welfare Capitalism*, Cambridge: Polity Press.

High Level Group on Industrial Relations and Change in the European Union (2002), *Report*, European Commission (Directorate-General for Employment and Social Affairs) (http://europa.eu.int/comm/employment_social/publications/2002/ke4202472_en.pdf).

Heinze, Manfred (1997) 'Wege aus der Krise des Arbeitsrechts – Der Beitrag der Wissenschaft', in *Neue Zeitschrift für Arbeitsrecht* 14, pp. 1–9.

Raab, Thomas (2004) 'Betriebliche Bündnisse für Arbeit – Königsweg aus der Beschäftigungskrise?', in *Zeitschrift für Arbeitsrecht* 35, pp. 371–403.

Schnabel, Claus (2004), 'Letzte Chance für den Flächentarifvertrag', in *Wirtschaftsdienst* 84, pp. 32–39.

1. Erosion or renewal? The crisis of collective wage formation in Germany

Thomas Blanke and Edgar Rose

1. INTRODUCTION

The German system of collective wage formation is facing a number of serious challenges. According to many, the collective bargaining system has been in crisis since the mid 1990s. Indeed, acceptance of collective wage bargaining has decreased continuously in many respects, and its legitimacy is increasingly being questioned. Various aspects of this crisis are discussed in detail in Section 4. Before that, we look at how the German system has traditionally functioned (Sections 2 and 3). We identify its main characteristics, sources of stability and crucial points of vulnerability in order to understand how current challenges have been able to put it under pressure. The comments of other countries presented in the following chapters on the current problems of collective wage bargaining in Germany, including the question of whether successful ideas from abroad may also work well in the German environment, depend on some understanding of national differences concerning collective bargaining law, as well as cultures and traditions of industrial relations. Section 2, therefore, deals with 'Industrial relations in Germany' and Section 3 with the 'Legal framework of collective wage formation'. Having defined 'current challenges' in Section 4, in Section 5 we discuss the 'Reactions of the state, the social partners and enterprises' in coping with these challenges.

2. INDUSTRIAL RELATIONS IN GERMANY

There have been various attempts to describe the *basic features* of the German model of industrial relations and collective wage formation in the economic and sociological literature.[1] In the first place, every author emphasizes (i) the 'dual structure of interest representation' that consists, on the one hand, of collective bargaining between *trade unions* and employers' associations, mainly at the industry level, and on the other hand, of statutorily regulated codetermination at establishment level through *works councils*. The significance of another major characteristic is not disputed either, namely (ii) the 'high degree of juridification' caused by constitutional and statutory law and implemented by a large number of labour court decisions. There is less unanimity concerning the remaining basic characteristics of the German industrial relations system. The literature refers to such aspects as the

1. See, for example, Jacobi, Keller and Müller-Jentsch (1998), pp. 190–92; Müller-Jentsch (1995), pp. 13–8; Schmierl (2001), pp. 429–31.

high coverage rates of collective agreements, the high degree of aggregation and homogenisation of interests, and the relatively high degree of centralisation through agreements for whole sectors. These aspects are discussed here under the heading of (iii) 'centralisation'.[2]

2.1 Duality

There is no doubt that the dual structure is highly developed in the German system. Both branches of employee representation have a strong legal basis and a far-reaching influence over management decisions. In Germany, duality also means that there is a certain division of labour and other significant institutional differences between trade unions and works councils.

- *Trade unions* are organized at the industry level in order to negotiate sectoral agreements. Collective bargaining between trade unions and single companies is possible, but rare.[3] Usually there are no union representatives on the shop floor.[4] *Works councils* are elected at establishment level. They negotiate works agreements (*Betriebsvereinbarungen*) primarily for single establishments. The conclusion of a joint agreement for all the establishments of a company is an exception.
- Trade unions were founded voluntarily by workers and represent their membership. The bargaining power of trade unions derives from their members' ability to put economic pressure on employers, by going on strike if necessary. Works councils are elected by all staff members and represent the whole workforce of an establishment. They are not allowed to call for strike action. Their bargaining power derives from legal obligations imposed on the employer to seek agreement and, if negotiations fail, to comply with the decision of a mediation committee (*Einigungsstelle*).
- According to the traditional division of labour between both levels, the trade unions' main responsibility is to negotiate the *price of labour* defined by wage levels, wage structures and regulations determining the duration of working time. Additionally, a wide range of other working conditions may be regulated in collective agreements, such as duration of holidays, sick pay, or periods of notice in cases of termination. In fact, there are significant differences from industry to industry concerning subjects and provisions in more than 50,000 collective agreements.
- Works councils, on the other hand, have strong rights of codetermination concerning numerous details of *workplace organisation* and *workforce development*, such as working time arrangements, ways of monitoring employees' performance or conduct, occupational health and safety measures, and internal training programmes. They are also legally responsible for

---

2. In this we follow Schmierl (2001), pp. 429–31) who identifies three main characteristics: duality, high juridification and centralization.
3. About 3% of all firms have a company collective agreement (*Firmentarifvertrag*). Though, these firms cover nearly 10% of the workforce (cf. Data from IAB-Betriebspanel 2003).
4. In large firms of some traditional industry sectors (metal and chemical industry), there are special union representatives (Vertrauensleute), who are employees that are elected by their unionised colleagues. Their relevance, however, is continuously declining (cf. Wassermann 2003: 412 pp.).

negotiating social plans (*Sozialpläne*) in case of redundancies or other fundamental changes in enterprise organisation.

As a result of the features described, works councils are rather independent of trade union power. Vested with strong legal rights, they are able to represent employees' interests successfully in many cases without union support. As a result, some of them work without any contact with trade unions – some even exhibit more or less open hostility to trade union policies. However, most cooperate fully under conditions of mutual influence and benefit.[5] Usually, trade union candidates run successfully in works council elections. According to a number of surveys, between 60 and 75% of works councillors are unionized.[6] Moreover, works council members at important companies obtain influential positions not in management, but in the central committees of trade unions. Cooperation is therefore deep rooted. However, in cases of conflict, a works council is primarily responsible to the company employees who elected them.

Both trade unions and works councils play an important role in the German economy. However, their scope is limited. On average, *trade union density* had fallen to 24% of the (private and public) workforce by 2002.[7] There are wide variations from industry to industry. Works councils (or staff councils[8]) represent 57.8% of all employees in Western Germany and 49.6% of all employees in Eastern Germany (2001).[9] In private companies about 50% of employees are represented.[10] Almost the entire public sector is covered by staff councils. According to the Works Constitution Act, every establishment with at least five employees may elect a works council. Almost all large establishments with more than 300 workers have one, but small firms rarely do.

2.2 Juridification

Industrial relations in Germany are intensively regulated by law. The *Works Constitution Act* (*Betriebsverfassungsgesetz*) in particular, with more than 100 articles, is a very detailed catalogue of the rights and responsibilities of works councils. Much litigation is based on this statute. Even at the highest level, the Federal Labour Court (*Bundesarbeitsgericht*), an important decision is made concerning the rights of works councils almost every week. This high number reflects the fact that law is the main source of works council power. Not that most conflicts between works councils and management end up in court: many works councils, especially in large firms, do not need Labour Courts at all because management respects them and is willing to compromise. Knowing the strong legal

5. Müller-Jentsch (2003), p. 461, calls it a developed symbiosis.
6. Seventy-five per cent according to trade union data, 60% according to the Institute of the German Economy. Reported by Müller-Jentsch (2003), p. 461.
7. See Funk (2003), p. 18, Table 1. Union density is continuously declining, so it might be close to 20% in 2005.
8. Staff councils (*Personalräte*) are elected in the public sector on different, but similar legal grounds.
9. IAB Panel data reported by Müller-Jentsch (2003), p. 463.
10. Cf. IAB Panel data reported by Ellguth (2003), p. 194. It has recently been discovered that the exact number is not known. There are no official statistics. The trade union surveys that reported 40% representation of employees proved to be wrong because many small firms with works councils were not counted (see Ellguth (2003), p. 196).

rights of works councils, employers frequently prefer peaceful conflict management: instead of denying works councils their rights, they try to persuade them – for instance, that their proposals are required if the company is to remain competitive. Consequently, many works councils have developed into institutions of co-management. In many other firms, however, conflicts arise and ultimately the Labour Courts are called on to resolve them.

The other branch of the dual system, *collective bargaining*, is less regulated by statutory law. Nevertheless, litigation is almost as frequent as in the area of works council rights. One reason for this is that collective bargaining and the related right to strike are accepted as constitutional rights.[11] As a result, many collective bargaining cases become constitutional cases. On constitutional grounds, collective action law was created by the Labour Courts. Sometimes the Federal Constitutional Court also became involved. Because the right to strike was derived only from the bargaining rights of trade unions by means of judicial interpretation, it was limited to collective bargaining–related situations. Otherwise, there is no right to strike in Germany.

Important legal aspects of collective agreements, however, are regulated by German legislation. For instance, the parties that are eligible to engage in collective bargaining, many aspects of the binding effect of collective agreements (*Tarifbindung*) and an extension procedure are defined in the *Collective Agreement Act* (*Tarifvertragsgesetz*). In the past – perhaps 20 years ago – collective action cases dominated litigation. In recent years, however, most collective bargaining litigation has concerned the binding nature of collective agreements, generated by the large number of employers trying to get out of collective agreements. Besides conflicts of this kind, the Labour Courts have the task of interpreting the provisions of collective agreements in individual cases.

On the subject of juridification, we must cite one distinction that is rarely mentioned.[12] Industrial relations *procedures* in Germany are intensively regulated. Substantially, however, German law is still widely open to autonomous regulation by the social partners: no minimum wage and no working time legislation defining regular working time tie the hands of the collective actors.[13] Moreover, direct state intervention in order to intervene in collective wage conflicts (like legally obligatory mediation) is prevented by constitutional *collective autonomy*.

2.3 Centralisation

It is clear that industrial relations in Germany are not adequately described by the two characteristics mentioned so far. Further characteristics are less clear cut, however. Centralisation is frequently mentioned as another important aspect, but the existence of more than 57,000 collective agreements[14] seems to contradict any notion of

11. Collective autonomy and the right to strike are not explicitly mentioned in the Constitution. What is mentioned is the freedom to form coalitions: collective bargaining and collective action are inter preted as inseparably linked with that freedom. See Däubler (2003), pp. 29 and 41).
12. But cf. Müller-Jentsch (1995), p. 15.
13. Working time legislation is limited to aspects of health and safety, as a consequence of which 60 hours in a given week are legally possible (but with an overall average of 48 hours); however, collectively agreed regular weekly working time is usually between 35 and 40 hours.
14. Bundesministerium für Wirtschaft und Arbeit (2003), p. 5.

centrality. Indeed, compared to other European countries in which collective bargaining takes place at national level, Germany stands somewhere in the middle. The figure of 57,000 collective agreements, however, does not give an accurate impression.

Basically, sectoral agreements dominate the collective bargaining landscape in Germany. In 2002, there were 24,500 company agreements[15] which covered less than 10% of the workforce.[16] Moreover, a significant proportion of them merely concerned extension of the sectoral agreement to the firm (*Anschlusstarifvertrag*). Among 32,800 sectoral agreements 21,100 had only a secondary function related to an original agreement. However, there were still 11,700 original sectoral agreements which must be taken into account in any discussion of centralisation.[17]

The figure of 11,700 can be broken down as follows. More than 300 industries are distinguished, most of which negotiate at the level of groups of between 5 and 15 regions. The result is that Germany has nearly *1,500 units for sectoral bargaining purposes*.[18] Moreover, the issues regulated by collective bargaining are usually spread over five or six or even more single collective agreements. Additionally, there are extra agreements for different groups of employees (blue-collar, white-collar, trainees, and so on). As a result, it is not exceptional for one company to have to cope with 10 sectoral agreements or more, all concluded by the same union.

Still, the figure of 1,500 units for sectoral bargaining does not indicate high centralisation. Some industries and regions, however, are extremely small. Therefore, the vast majority of German employees work under the regulations of a few hundred sets of collective agreements. Even more important, there is a *high degree of coordination* between regions in certain industries. Usually, one or two regions lead the sectoral negotiations and the other regions follow, with little or no differences.[19] Traditionally, the metal sector also functions as a trendsetter for other industries. This kind of coordination is called pattern bargaining because most negotiations follow the patterns established by single bargaining units. However, that does not mean that most German sectoral agreements look the same. There are huge differences – especially between different industries – leading, for instance, to completely different payments for the same professions.[20]

Three considerations justify characterisation of the German system as centralized. First, the sectoral level still dominates. Second, there is almost no union competition: 90% of all unionized employees are members of sectoral organisations under the umbrella of the DGB. Third, the mode of coordination known as pattern bargaining results in a lot of standardisation within sectors and even some between different sectors. Nonetheless, if certain regions (for example, Eastern Germany) or certain industries have special needs, there is always room for the bargaining partners to react flexibly. Therefore, some authors speak of a *relatively* high degree of centralisation characterising the German system of collective wage formation.[21]

15. Bundesministerium für Wirtschaft und Arbeit (2003), p. 5.
16. IAB-Betriebspanel (2003).
17. All data from Bundesministerium für Wirtschaft und Arbeit (2003), p. 5.
18. All data from Bundesministerium für Wirtschaft und Arbeit (2003), p. 4, note 2.
19. See Bahnmüller, Bispinck and Weiler (1999), p. 10; Schmierl (2001), p. 430.
20. See Hassel (2002), p. 161.
21. Jacobi, Keller and Müller-Jentsch (1998), p. 191.

2.4 Conclusion

As a result of all three characteristics discussed so far, German industrial relations have been extremely *peaceful*, while nevertheless managing to achieve relatively *high wages* and working conditions acceptable to the majority of employees. The strike record indicates that the militancy of German employees is among the lowest in Europe.[22] This is not merely a consequence of legal restrictions on strike action, but also of the ability of works councils to resolve most conflicts peacefully on the shop floor. The successful conflict management of most works councils benefits from strong legal codetermination rights, but also from the division of tasks in the dual system that externalizes the most explosive subject – wages – to another level of conflict. Wage bargaining, which is the reason for almost all strikes in Germany, is not the task of works councils, but of trade unions. The trade unions prefer to carry out this task industry-wide with trend-setting negotiations (and perhaps strikes) in selected regions. Strong legal rights, duality and, finally, relatively centralized wage bargaining have contributed to the high degree of industrial peace historically. However, it seems that current developments and demands for the decentralisation of wage bargaining will cause significant problems in this environment.

3. LEGAL FRAMEWORK OF COLLECTIVE WAGE FORMATION IN GERMANY

Collective wage formation is the centrepiece of collective bargaining between trade unions and employers' associations in Germany. Collective bargaining law is therefore of the highest relevance to collective wage formation. Traditionally, works councils play a minor role in setting wages. In a period of ongoing decentralisation, however, this is being called into question. Works council rights and the rules governing conflicts between agreements made by trade unions and by works councils are becoming increasingly important. Finally, we shall discuss the impact of the individual law on collective wage formation.

3.1 Collective bargaining

3.1.1 Establishment of collective agreements

In Germany, no legal procedure forces any party to the negotiating table. There is neither a duty to bargain nor a right pertaining to one party that the other must start talks. Legally, constitutional collective autonomy includes both the right to bargain and to refrain from bargaining without state intervention. If an employer or employers' organisation refuses to negotiate, the common and legally accepted instrument available to trade unions is a call for strike action.

The most important legal restriction on collective bargaining determines the parties who are entitled to conclude collective agreements. According to the Collective Agreement Act (CAA), the employees' side must be represented by trade unions (Sect. 2, par. 1 CAA). Either trade unions and employers' associations or trade

22. On average, between 1998 and 2002 only 1.1 working days per year were lost per 1,000 employees because of strikes. Only Austria has lower rates in the EU (see Carley [EIRO TN0303110U] 2003).

unions and single employers can sign a legally valid collective agreement. The Federal Labour Court has developed a set of criteria defining a trade union:[23] it must be an employees' organisation with no significant employer membership and independent of the state, political parties and religious organisations. Moreover, a trade union must be strong enough to put pressure on its opponent to engage in real negotiations on collective agreements. As a result, some small employees' organisations have been denied the legal status of trade union by the Labour Courts, citing lack of members or organisational resources. For a number of reasons, works councils are not trade unions, and so their agreements with employers are not collective agreements (*Tarifverträge*), but works agreements (*Betriebsvereinbarungen*) which are defined in the Works Constitution Act (WCA) as a different legal form (Sect. 77 WCA).

3.1.2 The legally binding effect of collective agreements

According to German law, sectoral collective agreements are binding for those who are members – on both sides – of the contracting associations (Sect. 4, par. 1 with Sect. 3, par. 1 CAA). Exceptionally, the full legally binding effect can be extended to non-members merely by government decree (see section 3.1.3). Besides cases of extension, therefore, no legal obstacle prevents an employer bound to a certain agreement from paying those employees who are not organized in the contracting trade union less than the collectively agreed wages. Also in the case of a company agreement, the employer is obliged to apply collectively agreed provisions only to the trade union's membership. No legal provision forces the employer to treat non-unionized employees equally. In practice, however, virtually all employers choose not to make a distinction between unionized and non-unionized staff. Individual contract clauses – called '*reference clauses*' (*Bezugnahmeklauseln*) – ordering that all (or some) provisions of a collective agreement must be applied to that individual employment relationship, are widely used, particularly at companies bound by collective agreements. Almost all of them prefer equal treatment of all employees in order to take away any incentive to join a trade union. Even many companies not bound by collective bargaining use such individual contract clauses to standardize their employment conditions. However, individual contract clauses referring to collective agreements cannot create the full binding effect: in legal terms, individual labour law is authoritative in such cases. In an employment relationship in which collectively agreed wages are paid merely because of an individual reference clause, therefore, it is always possible to change the clause or replace it in favour of other employment conditions by individual agreement.

The *full binding effect* entailed by membership on the part of either party means that collective agreement provisions affect them *directly* and *compulsorily*. No additional agreement at the individual level is needed to compel implementation. Furthermore, any individual waiver of collective agreement rights is invalid. Deviations from collective agreement norms are permitted in just two cases (Sect. 4, par. 3 CAA): (i) deviations explicitly allowed in the collective agreement itself; (ii) deviations related to the 'favourability principle' (*Günstigkeitsprinzip*) according to which deviations in favour of employees are always permitted: even if the parties to the collective agreement decide that the collectively agreed standards shall include

23. See Peter (2003), p. 865.

not only minima but also maxima, individuals remain free to agree better conditions. In Germany, therefore, maximum standards in collective agreements are legally prohibited and void.[24]

Under German law the *after-effect* (*Nachwirkung*) of collective agreements relates to situations in which an old collective agreement expires without being replaced by a new one (Sect. 4, par 5 CAA). In such cases, the provisions of the old agreement must be applied until replacement by a new agreement. However, according to the dominant interpretation of German law, the replacing agreement need not necessarily be a collective agreement: an individual agreement may replace the after-effect of an expired collective agreement, even if it deviates to the detriment of the employee.[25]

To be distinguished from the after-effect is the statutory regulation in Sect. 3, par. 3 CAA which applies a so-called *binding after-effect* (*Nachbindung*). In German law, the binding effect of (sectoral) collective agreements commences with the conclusion of the agreement or with membership of a contracting association. However, it does not automatically end when membership ends. An employer (or employee) shall be fully bound to a collective agreement until it expires, even if membership is terminated beforehand. For example, collective wage agreements are usually made for one year: even if an employer leaves the contracting association the very next day after an agreement has been concluded, they will be fully bound by the agreement for the whole year.

As a result, employers trying to free themselves from a collective agreement by leaving the relevant association have two legal obstacles to overcome: (i) the full binding after-effect until expiry of the collective agreement and (ii) after-effect without time limitation but open to modification by means of other collective or individual agreements. For instance, Company X, which leaves a contracting association in June 2004, remains bound to the collective agreement concluded in January 2004 until the association agrees a replacement collective agreement in January 2005. Since it is not bound to the replacement agreement, however, Company X sticks with the terms of the old one (2004). These terms might remain subject to the after-effect for years if the employees do not agree to modification. As a consequence, wages are frozen at the level they stood at when the employer left the contracting association.

3.1.3 Extension procedure

According to Sect. 5 CAA, the German government – Minister of the Economy and Labour – may extend the full binding effect of sectoral collective agreements to all employment relationships in the industry and region for which the agreement was made. However, the government is not free to do so without the consent of a committee on which the social partners are equally represented. In addition, extension must meet certain criteria: it must be in the public interest and employers already bound by it must employ at least 50% of the workers in the relevant industry.

Use of the extension procedure has always been very limited. Particularly wage agreements have rarely been subject to extensions. In recent years their number has even decreased (see Section 4.2.2) because employers have increasingly refused to

24. See Deinert (2003), p. 1212.
25. See Bepler (2003), p. 1331.

support extensions. There is one exception, however: in the construction industry, consent of the social partners is no longer needed for the extension of minimum wage agreements, and extended wage agreements are in place all over the country.

3.2 Works council rights

According to the Works Constitution Act (WCA), works council rights vary, depending on the matter in question, from full codetermination to a simple right to be informed (for example, in relation to the company's economic affairs). As regards matters of personnel selection (hiring, promotion, training) there are limited veto rights, while full rights of codetermination apply to a wide range of social matters, such as working time arrangements or health and safety measures. *Codetermination* includes an obligation that the employer, before acting, must seek the consent of the works council. If negotiations fail, both sides may call for a mediation committee – on which both sides are equally represented and chaired by a neutral party – to decide the disputed question. The employer is legally bound by the committee's decision.

As already mentioned, the different responsibilities of trade unions and works councils are largely divided. Particularly at a time when decisions on working conditions are increasingly being decentralized to the company level, however, *conflicts of competence* may occur. In such cases, the Works Constitution Act clearly states that there shall be no codetermination by works councils insofar as an issue is completely regulated by collective bargaining (Sect. 87, par. 1 WCA). Frequently, additional regulations via codetermination are nevertheless possible because union contracts usually leave considerable room for shop-floor decision-making or explicitly allow modifications by means of agreements between employers and works councils.

As regards *wage formation*, works council competence is even more restricted.[26] Sect. 77, par. 3 WCA clearly states that wages cannot be regulated in works agreements by works councils. This article should be sufficient to prevent the principal role of the social partners in negotiating wages from being undermined by decisions made on the shop floor. Unfortunately, the legal situation is more complex in Germany because wages are explicitly a matter of codetermination under Sect. 87, par. 1 (10) WCA. This wage codetermination, however, is limited to the methods and criteria governing wage differentiation (wage structure). The Federal Labour Court has attempted to resolve these contradictory principles, decreeing first that the determination of *wage levels* shall be reserved for union (or individual) contracts, while second, matters of *wage structure* may be regulated between works councils and employers insofar as no final decision has been made by collective agreement. For instance, collective agreements usually allow different forms of remuneration: fixed pay or several forms of performance-related pay. The establishment's decision in favour of a given system and – in case of performance-related pay – in favour of a certain method and particular criteria is subject to agreement with the works council. Works councils may not, however, make agreements on particular sums or wage increase (or decrease) percentages. Only in areas in which collective wage formation is not customary may councils also reach agreement on wage levels.

Finally, it is absolutely illegal for works council agreements to deviate from collective agreements to the disadvantage of the employee, except where explicitly

26. For more details see Zwanziger (2003), p. 1349.

permitted. Such an agreement would be invalid for several reasons (see above). One reason is the *favourability principle* for collective agreements that allows deviations only in favour of the employee.

3.3 Beyond collective wage formation

Individual contract law related to wage formation also has a significant impact on collective bargaining. For example, employers attempting to free themselves from a union agreement must bear in mind that individual employment law too gives rise to a wide range of restrictions.

There is no statutory minimum wage in German individual employment law. However, a number of other restrictions on individual agreements on wage levels or wage flexibility derive from general contract law, general employment law, and anti-discrimination law. For instance, general employment law states that employees working *without a wage agreement* are entitled to the wages usual in that region and industry. This is important because this also applies if wage agreements are illegal and void.[27]

3.3.1 Moral minimum

Collective wage bargaining has a statutory floor in many countries: a clear and widely known minimum wage that provides orientation concerning what is acceptable as payment for low paid jobs. In Germany, there is nothing of the kind. However, wage agreements may be void if they fall short of a 'moral minimum'. Then, employees can claim a violation of bonos mores (*Sittenwidrigkeit*). This is the result of labour court efforts to apply elements of the civil usury law to wages. However, it remains unclear what the moral minimum might be.[28] Some courts declare that wage agreements below 50% of the wages normally paid for comparable jobs are illegal; others prefer 66%. Moreover, it is not clear how usual pay can be determined: comparable collective bargaining wages frequently serve as a standard. But not all courts agree on that.

Some authors call this a judicial minimum wage.[29] However, the 'moral minimum' lacks the legal clarity and common knowledge characteristic of a statutory minimum wage. Furthermore, it clearly does not serve as a floor for collective bargaining because it takes the results of collective bargaining as a legitimate norm. Even 50 or 66% of extremely low collectively agreed wages is legally permitted.

3.3.2 Equal pay

There is a general legal obligation on German employers to treat employees equally. This is regarded as an underlying principle of employment law as a whole and has been shaped by numerous court decisions, although it is also treated in statutory law (for example, equal treatment of part-time workers). The general principle of *equal*

27. See Preis (2004), p. 1540.
28. See Preis (2004), p. 1541.
29. Hanau 2000: 1254.

treatment should not be confused with special anti-discrimination rights (see below). It is applied to many questions of wage differentiation in an increasing number of cases.[30] The principle of equal treatment therefore provides employees with a good opportunity to get individual wage agreements reviewed by a Labour Court.

Wage claims on the grounds of equal treatment, however, are not often successful because courts give considerable latitude to 'objective grounds' (*sachliche Gründe*) as justification for unequal treatment. Sometimes plaintiffs are successful: for instance, in the former GDR, a local-born employee was paid less for the same work than employees hired from the western part of Germany. The employer's justification was that employees with a good knowledge and experience of a market economy were needed. However, the Federal Labour Court[31] could not find any real grounds for holding the performance of the East German employee to be less valuable than that of his western counterparts. Equal treatment was ordered.

The European anti-discrimination regulations under Article 141 EC (former Article 119) concerning the principle of *equal pay for male and female workers* for equal work or work of equal value was implemented as a provision of the German Civil Code (Sect. 611 par. 3 Civil Code). There has been considerable successful litigation on discrimination against part-time workers, who are usually female. Unfortunately, other issues of gender-based wage discrimination remain unresolved. The most important task seems to be to determine what *work of equal value* means because there is still a high degree of gender segregation in the German labour market. Frequently, men and women are *not* doing the same work: they have different jobs that are not easy to compare in terms of 'equal value'. Usually, work done mostly by men is better paid.

Hitherto, complaints demanding equal pay for work of equal value have rarely been brought before the Federal Labour Court. In one recent case an attempt was made to enforce the principle of equal pay also in relation to very different jobs. A female social worker in the public service sector claimed that she was doing work of equal value in comparison with technicians receiving better pay under the relevant remuneration scheme. Her most telling argument was that both groups have to have a comparable university diploma in applied science. However, the complaint was unsuccessful. As in other cases concerning work of equal value, the court delivered a very long and complicated statement of its reasons, explaining that the plaintiff had taken the wrong groups for comparison. The Court stated that,[32] beside technicians and social workers, several other groups had the same category of diploma and, like social workers, they all earned less than technicians, although in most of these groups women were a minority. As a result, the Court held that the share of women in the discriminated-against group was not significantly higher than in the better-off group. In sum, female plaintiffs claiming equal pay for work of equal value have not had much success in Germany.

Equal pay litigation, then, is mostly unsuccessful. However, that does not mean that equal pay norms have had no impact on wage formation. Employers take the view that it is worth taking equal pay norms seriously in order to avoid a judicial review of their whole remuneration system, which might arise from complaints on equal pay grounds that are quite easy to file. Many employers prefer to adhere to collective agreement provisions because the results of collective bargaining on wage

30. See in detail Rose 2003.
31. See BAG, 15 May 2001, Betriebs-Berater (2001), 2166.
32. See BAG, 10 December 1997, *EzA* No. 22 § 612 BGB.

differentiation are generally accepted as fair by the courts, while individually agreed wages are strictly scrutinized under equal pay regulations.

3.3.3 Wage flexibility

A new debate has emerged concerning how much economic risk employers may transfer to employees by flexible wage agreements. In practice, two contractual *variable pay* arrangements are widespread.

First, employers often reserve the right to cut wages. In the opinion of the Federal Labour Court such contractual clauses are legal to the extent that wages are not protected by collective agreements. However, a good reason (*billiges Ermessen* or 'reasonably exercised discretion') is required if the employer uses such a clause to cut the regular monthly wage: otherwise, only supplementary annual benefits such as 'Christmas pay', if provided under a '*reservation clause*', may be cut. If there is no such contractual clause, the only legal way of cutting individually agreed wages without mutual agreement is a so-called '*Änderungskündigung*' or 'dismissal with the option of altered conditions of employment'. Under the *Protection against Dismissal Act,* an employee may file a complaint against such a dismissal. Labour Courts strictly scrutinize whether 'altered conditions' are socially justified.

Second, an increasing number of employers are implementing systems of variable wages such as *performance-related* or *profit-related* pay. There are almost no legal restrictions on such systems insofar as the 'moral minimum' mentioned above is not violated. In the debate on the issue, however, it has been suggested that another principle of employment law be applied, namely that the employer must carry the company and economic risk (*Betriebs- und Wirtschaftsrisiko*) attaching to variable pay systems. That could mean, for instance, that under a system of performance-related pay business problems may not be taken as grounds for reducing wages. It might also mean that payments related to company results must be restricted to a minor part of an individual's total wage.

However, notions have not been implemented in individual employment law in terms of the explicit statutory provisions or court decisions. In contrast, collective agreements do regulate performance-related pay systems, usually rather strictly. The desire to have more scope to introduce variable pay might therefore constitute another reason why an employer might wish to withdraw from collective bargaining.

4. CURRENT CHALLENGES TO THE GERMAN SYSTEM

There is empirical evidence that the German system of collective wage formation is undergoing significant structural change. Since 1995 the share of employees whose terms and conditions of employment are regulated by collective agreements (sectoral and company agreements) has fallen from about 82% (1995) to 70% (2002) in Germany (West).[33] At the same time, the legal framework of the collective bargaining system has come under considerable pressure. In an increasing number of cases, conflicts have been brought before the Federal Labour Court which has frequently had to decide on complaints against employers trying to free themselves from a collective agreement.

33. Data from IAB-Betriebspanel, reported by Kohaut and Schnabel (2001 and 2003).

Various legislative proposals have been introduced in order to allow wage reductions below collectively agreed levels. So far, all of them failed, in the wake of which 'opening clauses' were concluded as part of industry-wide collective agreements in which certain criteria and procedures were defined allowing agreement on wage cuts below the sectoral level at individual companies.

Behind these facts lie challenges generated by far-reaching economic and societal change. We shall look first at such *megatrends* as globalisation and individualisation, followed by a description of particular aspects of the *decreasing acceptance* of collective wage formation in Germany.

4.1 Megatrends

The German debate focuses on four general developments that are of great importance for the development of collective bargaining.[34]

1. A structural economic change is taking place characterized by a *decline in manufacturing industry* and an expanding service sector. It is accompanied by a growing share of small firms, including one-person firms, and by a decentralisation of company structures, also in traditional industries. The problem with small units in relation to collective wage formation is that the smaller an establishment is, the less likely is it that there will be a works councils or adherence to collective bargaining.
2. New *information and communication technologies* have penetrated working life almost completely. One consequence of this is that new forms of work organisation arose in the 1990s in order to stimulate workforce motivation, flexibility and creativity by means of 'job enrichment' in contrast to the extreme division of labour implemented previously by Taylorist rationalisation strategies. In Germany, the most prominent work concept became 'group work' defined as delegation of decision-making to work groups or teams. Collective representation may be replaced in part (or even undermined) by the direct participation of groups or individuals.
3. In an increasingly *individualized society*, both developments mentioned above correspond to the preferences of many employees who seek opportunities for self-employment or direct participation at the workplace. Moreover, these developments are generating a growing demand for more wage flexibility and new forms of performance-related wage differentiation that do not fit the traditional remuneration systems of collective agreements.
4. The strongest pressure on the traditional system of wage formation, however, is coming from the *internationalisation of markets*, the growing number of cross-national companies and, with reference to the European level, from demands for legal harmonisation. Falling transaction costs for the worldwide flow of information, capital, services and products are intensifying international competition. Lower wage costs in other countries are enabling competitors to undercut prices. As a result, national companies are trying to transfer some production lines to other countries, or at least are threatening staff or trade unions with plans to internationalize production or services if wage cuts are not accepted.

34. See Funk (2003), p. 16f; see also Dombois (2001), p. 131f, Schroeder (2003), pp. 149ff, and Schmierl (2001), p. 433.

In relation to collective wage formation, all four megatrends are generating demands for *decentralisation* from the sectoral to the company level. Single companies wish to be more flexible and independent of sectoral provisions. Their international position may require rapid adaptation to changing conditions. Their internal strategies for coping with post-Taylorist work may be too specific to be regulated industry-wide: contemporary forms of performance-related pay – for example, dependent on individual target-setting procedures – may be hard to implement under sectoral control.

4.2 Declining acceptance of collective wage formation

Data from recent surveys reveal that the scope of collective bargaining decreased slowly but constantly from 1995 to 2000. At the same time, the governmental extension procedure for collective agreements was applied less frequently. In addition, diminishing support for collective wage formation is apparent, with growing criticism from economists and political parties. On the political level, there is a broad consensus that the system of sectoral agreements must be made more flexible to meet economic exigencies.

4.2.1 Coverage of collective bargaining

Before we consider the coverage rates of German collective agreements we must look at the different ways in which employees may be covered. As already mentioned (3.1.2), basically only trade union members can be covered with fully binding effect.[35] On average, 24% of the German workforce is unionized (in 2002).[36] However, not all unionized employees work in companies bound by collective agreements. As a result, only about 20% of all employees are fully covered. At the same time, as mentioned above, employers bound by collective agreements pay collectively agreed wages not only to union members, but also to the rest of their workforce without any differentiation. In 2003, 46% of all employers (in western Germany) were bound, employing 70% of all employees. In the eastern part, 54% of all employees are covered (see Table 1).[37] It is likely that in most of these companies individual 'reference clauses' are used, resulting in full application of collectively agreed provisions to all employees. These figures therefore provide the most reliable picture of the scope of collective wage bargaining.

Another 16% (west) or 24% (east) of employees work at firms *not bound* by collective bargaining, but which adhere to the terms of collective agreements anyway.[38] In such firms 'reference clauses' are also often included in individual contracts guaranteeing the application of collectively agreed norms. However, in contrast to bound companies, the extent to which their 'reference clauses' include all the provisions of the relevant collective agreements is less clear. No precise figures are available. However, many of these firms clearly use 'reference clauses' with

35. The only other way of obtaining the fully binding effect is by government extension.
36. See Funk (2003), p. 18.
37. IAB-Betriebspanel 2003.
38. IAB-Betriebspanel 2003.

exceptions, since there is no legal obstacle to doing so. Also widely used are employment contracts that define a limited set of working conditions individually and refer to collective agreements for all other issues not explicitly mentioned. In such cases, wages in particular are likely to deviate from collective agreements.

In any case, the influence of collective bargaining extends far beyond the members of signatory trade unions and employers' associations. Table 1 presents the full range of affected employees: only 14% in the west and 22% in the east work in firms that make no use of collective agreements at all.

Table 1 Percentage of employees working at firms that are bound to, or make use of, or make no use of collective agreements in 2003 (%)[38]

	Germany (west)	**Germany (east)**
Employees at firms that		
are bound to *sectoral collective* agreements	62	43
are bound to *company collective* agreements	8	11
are not bound, but agree individually with employees to (partly) *adopt the conditions* of sectoral collective agreements	16	24
make *no use* of collective agreements	14	22

Development of the coverage rate is most reliably indicated, however, by the share of employees working at firms bound by collective agreements. Figure 1 presents the fall in the coverage rate for *sectoral bargaining* in the western part of Germany.

Figure 1 Employees working at firms bound by sectoral collective agreements in western Germany (%)[40]

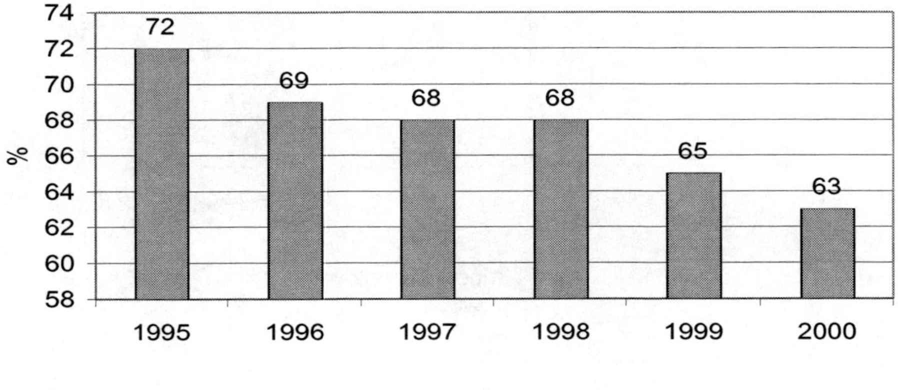

39. Data from IAB-Betriebspanel surveys carried out annually and involving more than 15,000 interviews.
40. Data from IAB-Betriebspanel surveys carried out annually and involving more than 15,000 interviews (see Kohaut and Schnabel 2001 and 2003).

Figure 1 shows, the number of employees working for employers bound to sectoral agreements fell between 1995 and 2000, from 72% to 63%.[41] Since then, the proportion has stabilized. In the territory of the former GDR, the share of employees working at firms bound by sectoral bargaining is much lower, and also shrinking: for example, from 51% in 1998 to 43% in 2002.

Industry-wide sectoral agreements are typical of the German system. Company agreements cover companies employing 8–11% of the national workforce. More precisely, the share of employees working in companies covered by company agreements is almost stable in the west of Germany (about 8%). It is higher in the area of the former GDR (about 11%).[42] We do not really know what kinds of company agreement are hidden behind these figures. Some have special contents reflecting the needs of the individual company. Other company agreements take the form of so-called 'joining collective agreements' (*Anschlusstarifverträge*) which have no content at all apart from a single clause declaring that the regulations of the sectoral agreement must be applied to the company.

Figure 2 shows that the coverage rate is much higher among large companies than among small ones. Most large companies are organized in employers' associations which conclude sectoral agreements. The smaller a company is, the less likely is it to be a member of an employers' organisation. So, the decrease in coverage can be explained in part by the rising number of small firms with a rising share of all employees.

Figure 2 Percentage of employees working at firms bound by sectoral collective agreements in western Germany (by size of firm)[43]

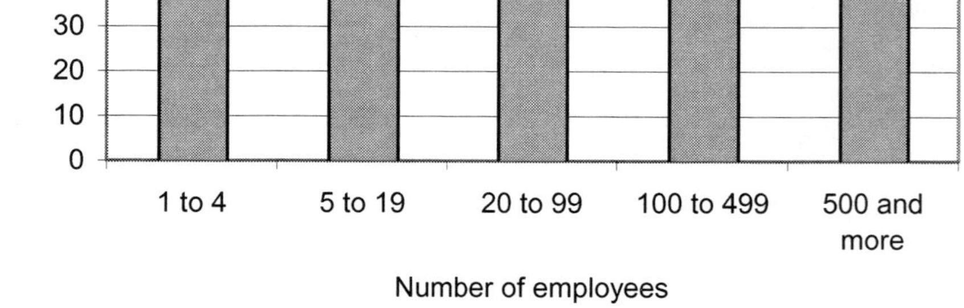

41. The number of bound companies fell from 53% (1995) to 43% (2003).
42. Cf. IAB-Betriebspanel 2003.
43. Data from surveys of the IAB-Betriebspanel carried out each year with more than 15 000 interviews.

4.2.2 *Decreasing use of extension*

While the use of collective wage agreements by individual contract clauses is of considerable empirical significance, their extension by governmental decree is not. Such decrees – for legal details see Section 3.1.3 – are not particularly rare: about 100 cases a year are reported. However, in 2002, out of 57,600 registered collective agreements only 522 were extended. Furthermore, a 1997 survey reveals that only 163 of 558 collective agreements subject to governmental decree were related to wages.[44] These wage agreements bound an additional 700,000 employees, about 2.5% of all employees.

The number of extended wage agreements has fallen rapidly over the last ten years.[45] In the early 1990s, the extension of wage agreements played a dominant role in 10 sectors (including retail, construction, cleaning, hairdressing, and other services). In 2002, this had fallen to only five sectors. In the retail sector the extension of wage agreements became almost impossible because the employers did not cooperate in the relevant committee. As a result, the extension procedure in Germany may be regarded as in crisis:[46] just when coverage rates are shrinking because of decreasing membership of associations, the state is becoming less and less able to counteract the process by extension because employers are ceasing to cooperate with the extension procedure. The construction industry is something of an exception in this respect: coverage through extension has increased since 1999 because minimum wage agreements may be extended without the employers' approval.

4.2.3 *Diminishing political and business support*

The German system of collective wage formation has been subjected to severe criticism by economists since the 1980s. Rising unemployment has led to demands to deregulate the system of sectoral wage agreements. Economists argue that the sectoral rigidities of wage formation hinder the adaptation of wages to the needs of enterprises and markets. From this point of view, an overpriced workforce leads to a situation in which many jobs cannot generate enough profit to cover their cost and must therefore be eliminated. This analysis became dominant in the German economic debate in the 1990s.[47] It was proposed, first, that the social partners should be forced to open up collective agreements to concessional bargaining by works councils, and second, that the use of the statutory extension procedure should be subjected to more restrictive legal criteria.

On the political level, the economists' proposals were widely discussed. However, all attempts to transform them into law have so far failed. Recently, the political pressure seems to have become overwhelming because all political parties have come to hold that sectoral agreements in their current form are too restrictive and a hindrance to employment policy. The Liberals (FDP) and the Christian Democrats

44. See Iwd (1998), volume 6, p. 2.
45. See Kirsch (2003), p. 411.
46. For example, Kirsch (2003).
47. See Deregulierungskommission (1991), Monopolkommission (1994) and Sachverständigenrat (2002).

(CDU/CSU) have formulated legislative proposals that would allow works councils or two-thirds majorities of the workforce to decide on wage cuts below collectively agreed wages. The 'favourability principle' should be reinterpreted in such a way that employment protection can be brought forward as justification of lower wages. Prominent members of the government parties have declared the system of collective wage formation in Germany detrimental to employment. SDP Chancellor Schröder demanded in 2003 that the social partners must voluntarily open up collective agreements to the concessional bargaining of works councils (opening clauses). Otherwise the legislator would have to act.

The crisis of collective wage formation in Germany is a result not only of decreasing coverage rates, but also of a loss of support from politicians and experts for the central idea underpinning sectoral bargaining, namely that strictly binding agreements are required in order to avoid social dumping.

5. REACTIONS OF THE STATE, SOCIAL PARTNERS, AND ENTERPRISES IN GERMANY

German political and economic institutions have reacted to the crisis of collective wage formation in different ways. On the state level, Labour Courts have inevitably been called upon to address numerous conflicts arising from employers trying to get out of collective bargaining, while legislation has remained broadly paralysed. The social partners reacted by opening up sectoral agreements to limited decentralisation. Finally, enterprises have developed flexible remuneration systems inside and outside collective agreements.

5.1 State

5.1.1 Increasing Labour Court activity

Since the 1990s, legal obstacles preventing employers from getting out of collective bargaining have been widely discussed in Germany. The Federal Labour Court has heard a rising number of cases concerning whether employers are bound to union agreements any longer.

So far, there have been three main paths along which this 'flight from collective agreements' (*Tarifflucht*) has taken place:

1. The employer renounces membership of the employers' association which signed the sectoral collective agreement from which the employer wishes to free himself. As already mentioned, there are two statutory provisions that prolong the binding effect of a union agreement beyond membership of the association. First, every employer who was a member of a contracting association at the time of conclusion of the collective agreement remains bound until the agreement ends, regardless of whether membership is terminated in the meantime. Second, after a collective agreement has ended, its regulations remain effective until they are replaced by a new agreement: the so-called 'after-effect' (Nachwirkung). During this 'after-effect' period, however, the employer may replace these regulations by individual agreements. Wage cuts are therefore possible if employees accept them. Among many cases on such issues, the

Federal Labour Court[48] had to decide whether or not employers could replace 'after-effect' regulations by a new collective agreement with another union. The court declared that a replacement agreement must be binding for both sides. A new collective agreement would replace regulations only for employees who are members of the contracting union. In consequence, there is no way of reducing wages by leaving the employer's association and seeking out a 'cheap' union willing to agree to low wages because this union usually has no members in the company.

2. Transfer of the company, or part of it, to another employer, one not bound by collective agreements (or bound by different agreements with a lower wage level). However, statutory regulations (based on Directive 77/187/EEC, now Directive 2001/23/EC) similar to those already mentioned prevent wage cuts in most cases. The collectively agreed wages which the transferor (= old employer) had to pay are transformed into conditions of the individual contract with the transferee (= new employer). They cannot be replaced by different regulations pertaining to the individual contract before at least one year has passed. The collective agreements of the transferee, however, may replace these conditions. However, the Federal Labour Court[49] again restricted such replacement of transformed conditions to cases in which both sides – transferee and employees – are bound by the collectively agreed regulations of the new employer.

3. The employer does not renounce collective bargaining completely. The intention is merely to pay wages below the level of the union agreement in order to survive a commercial crisis without redundancies. In order to achieve this, a so-called 'alliance for work' (*betriebliches Bündnis für Arbeit*) is entered into at company level. Usually, the employer negotiates with the works council to determine the wage concessions the employees will accept in return for employment protection. This would clearly be illegal if it happened without the approval of the parties to the collective agreement. In practice, it often works because no one files a complaint. In one prominent case (the 'Burda case'), the Federal Labour Court[50] had to decide whether the union was allowed to bring an action against such concessional bargaining. In this case there was no official agreement between employer and works council. Instead, it was merely agreed that every employee sign an individual concession agreement with the employer. The court's judgement was clearly in favour of collective bargaining, stating that the union had the right to take the company to court in order to prevent actions undermining the binding effect of collectively agreed wages, even if all the employees accepted the wage cut individually.

   In another judgement made the same day, however, the Labour Court[51] pointed out a legal path to working conditions below collectively agreed minimum standards. On this path, works council and employer may agree on wages below the level of the union agreement. However, before this may come into effect the approval of both contracting associations is needed. Strikingly, the court did not require a general 'opening clause' as part of the collective agreement subject to deviation. Instead, the contracting associations may allow deviations from collectively agreed conditions at any time and in

48. See BAG, 28 May 1997, NZA 1998, p. 40.
49. See BAG, 30 August 2000, NZA 2001, p. 510.
50. See BAG, 20 April 1999, NZA 1999, p. 887.
51. See BAG, 20 April 1999, NZA 1999, p. 1059.

favour of any single employer, no matter what the original union agreement says.

Not all Federal Labour Court decisions were in favour of employees trying to prevent the loss of protection under collective agreements. Generally, however, the Court became a stabilising factor in the system of collective wage formation. In conflicts concerning the binding effect, the court raised legal obstacles for employers trying to get out of collective bargaining. At the same time, controlled paths to more flexibility inside collective bargaining were prepared.

5.1.2 Legislative activities

Legislation was paralysed by strong forces that clearly wished to break up the German system of sectoral wage formation in favour of concessional bargaining on the shopfloor level. Political supporters of the traditional system had to work hard merely to preserve the status quo. Legislative action to stabilize the system was very rare, but at least two legislative developments should be mentioned.

First, a new statutory regulation on temporary agency work in 2003 created a situation in which almost all agencies became bound by collective agreements. Under the new law temporary agency workers can claim the same working conditions, including wages, as the workforce of the user firm.[52]

In Germany, traditionally both the user firm and the agency profit from the lower wages paid to temporary workers compared to those at the user firm.

Equal pay at the user company would considerably reduce the benefits of this employment form for both companies so an exemption from equal treatment provided in the new statute came into widespread use: lower wages are possible if concluded in collective agreements between unions and agencies. Since then, the temporary agency sector, which previously had had no collective bargaining, became intensively covered by collective agreements in a matter of months.

Second, in several *Länder* so-called 'collective bargaining loyalty laws' (*Tariftreuegesetze*) were passed limiting public contracts concerning public transport or construction work to contractors offering collectively agreed working conditions.[53]

5.2 Social partners: flexibility by collective bargaining

In the 1980s it was unambiguously the case that all employers bound to an industry-level collective agreement had to pay the same wages, without exception. Now, in most wage agreements various exceptions are explicitly regulated. Originating in the German reunification process, these regulations – called 'opening clauses' (*Öffnungsklauseln*) – spread from east to west. In this way employers' and employees' associations reacted to criticism that collective agreements are not flexible enough to meet the needs of individual companies. One result of this seems

52. In Germany, as in other European countries, the temporary agency worker has only an employment contract with the agency while he or she is actually working at the user firm. Wages are therefore paid by the agency.
53. The legal problems affecting such laws are discussed by Kämmerer and Thüsing (2003).

to be that political proposals to enforce flexibility by means of statutory opening clauses have been rejected, though they are still on the political agenda (see 4.2.3).

Sometimes, opening clauses in collective agreements provide for special negotiations between trade unions and employers' associations if companies claim that the wage standards of the sectoral agreement will lead to lay-offs. Since 2004, this has been the case in the crucial metal sector.[54] Usually, however, opening clauses allow employers and works councils to negotiate on limited deviations from collectively agreed standards. If explicitly regulated in the union agreement, works councils may conclude works agreements (*Betriebsvereinbarungen*) on wage levels. In almost all opening clauses, however, there are criteria, limits or procedures designed to ensure that the conditions of the union agreement prevail. Four kinds of opening clause are distinguished by Schnabel:[55]

1. Hardship clauses: at the request of a company claiming to be in serious economic difficulties (usually on the basis of specific criteria) the parties to collective bargaining negotiate if (and by how much) wages may be reduced.
2. Opening clauses with veto rights: employers and works councils negotiate on deviations from the collective agreement. However, whether their agreement comes into effect depends on the approval of the collective bargaining signatories.
3. Opening clauses without veto rights: without veto rights works agreements between employers and works councils do not need the approval of the collective bargaining signatories. However, limits are generally applied, such as a maximum of 10% below the collectively agreed wage level.
4. Small-enterprise clauses: provisions of some collective agreements allow small firms to reduce wages below the general standard.

About 10% of German companies (mostly larger firms) make use of opening clauses to deviate from the wage standards of collective agreements. A recent survey indicates that management and works councils have developed 'alliances for work' in 23% of all companies with more than 20 employees. In more than 40% of such alliances, wage cuts are exchanged for job security. Most of them use opening clauses in collective agreements.[56]

5.3 Wage flexibility at the company level

Wage cuts are not the only response of companies under pressure. The wage structure is also subject to change in many cases. Since the early 1990s, many German companies have been undergoing a process of post-Taylorist reorganisation. In the last years of the decade, the focus of the debate shifted from organisational issues to the remuneration system. There is no clear trend towards a single concept of modern work, but rather a great variety of organisational models. Some companies have experimented with relatively innovative post-Taylorist forms of work organisation; others have introduced more conservative models with few changes from the Taylorist division of labour. Tendencies towards a 'return to Taylorism' are also being

54. See Bispinck (2004), p. 240.
55. Schnabel (1998), p. 89.
56. The data are reported in Massa-Wirth and Seifert (2004), p. 249.

reported. The old forms of remuneration, however, are now widely condemned by employers as no longer appropriate.

Old remuneration systems such as piece work gave workers an incentive to remain highly inflexible in a particular job with a limited range of activities. Modern systems are expected to encourage more flexibility (for example, job rotation), higher quality work and more creativity. Many companies have changed their remuneration systems – or intend to do so – in order to implement different forms of performance-related or profit-related payments. One system frequently recommended by management consultants has three layers:

1. flat basic payments that may be identical to the part of wages protected by collective agreements;
2. additional performance-related pay that may be defined by performance appraisals (*Leistungsbeurteilungen*) or, highly recommended these days, by target-setting agreements (*Zielvereinbarungen*) that determine certain performance targets related to certain bonus payments for an individual or a group of employees;
3. profit-related pay in various forms, such as annual or monthly bonuses related to business results or employees' financial participation in the form of employee shares or share-options.

Recent surveys show that the remuneration policy of many firms is undergoing considerable change.[57] About 20% of all surveyed firms have made significant modifications to their wage systems (performance-related pay 18%, profit-related annual bonuses 25%). Bonus payments related to target-setting agreements are now a widespread form of performance-related pay for whitecollar workers (about 18% of all firms). For blue-collar workers premium pay, often determined by a performance appraisal system, has become important (18% of all firms).

Some firms abandon collective bargaining in order to obtain the flexibility required to implement modern remuneration systems. However, most try to remain with collective bargaining and implement performance-related and profit-related pay above the wage level of collective agreements or in areas in which the collective agreement is not very precise.[58] In sectoral collective agreements there are usually precise regulations on piece work. However, for other forms of performance-related pay, there is often just a rough framework of – mostly procedural – rules. Companies use – more or less correctly – the space provided by such frameworks to install modern remuneration schemes. Works councils are widely involved in this process.

5.4 Results

In Germany, the character of sectoral wage formation is changing in many ways. The wages agreed in sectoral agreements are partly losing their function as strict minimum standards.

- This is indicated, first, by the diminishing coverage rate of sectoral wage agreements, although the influence of sectoral bargaining is still considerable.

57. See Bahnmüller (2001), p. 147.
58. See Bahnmüller (2001), p. 167.

Even for most companies not covered directly, the wage regulations of sectoral agreements are relevant as the most important orientation point. In western Germany, for example, collective wage formation still affects more than 80% of all employees.

- Second, the efforts of the social partners to stabilize sectoral bargaining lead to more flexible regulations that allow additional bargaining on the company or establishment level. Trade unions and employers' associations agree increasingly on opening clauses. Employers and works councils are using the space left by sectoral regulations more and more intensively. In most cases it is a mutual process in which employees obtain job protection for wage concessions. Especially if wages are cut below collective agreement standards, the employer usually has to offer long-lasting job security, supported by considerable investment.

As a result, the number of exceptions from wage standards fixed by collective bargaining is growing significantly. However, they remain deviations from what is still the standard: the dominance of sectoral bargaining remains basically intact as the main source of wage standardisation in almost all areas.

There are additional sources of stability in the German system. On constitutional grounds, the Labour Courts have in many cases protected the traditional system by enforcing the law restrictively. Constitutional collective bargaining autonomy (*Tarifautonomie*), therefore, remains a significant feature of German law stabilising the system. Moreover, it has deterred attempts to legislate inroads into the binding force of collective bargaining. However, even strong legal instruments cannot stop the erosion of acceptance which has characterized collective wage formation for many years.

The other feature that may stabilize the German system is the dual structure of worker representation. Representation at the establishment level has long been the domain of strong and independent works councils. Therefore, it is no surprise that their tasks and competences are growing in times of decentralisation. In recent decades it has become common practice to leave many legislative and collective regulation problems to works agreements. Now this seems to be happening to wage regulation. However, it would be more than just another step in the same direction if works councils were to obtain full control over wage bargaining. Generally, works councils lack the bargaining power to achieve fair and well accepted wage agreements. Without the right to call for strike action, they would have to look for other ways to put pressure on employers in wage conflicts. Their traditional advantage of being little involved in the annual struggle for better wages would be lost.

As a result, both sectoral standardisation and peaceful co-management on the shop floor may disappear. For the moment, however, the sectoral standards prevail in most cases.

The new opening clauses and other features of modern sectoral agreements leave a lot of room for shopfloor decision-making by management and works councils. Usually, however, the scope for deviations from sectoral agreements is carefully defined by collective bargaining and the final decision on wage cuts must be made at the sectoral level by the social partners. Whether this kind of control is sufficient to preserve the dual character of the system is not yet clear. Some commentators see the dual structure as the Achilles heel of the system, while others stress the opportunities the dual structure offers for a well organized form of decentralisation. Further experience will show who is right and who is wrong.

6. CONCLUSIONS

In the current crisis of collective wage formation in Germany there are signs of both erosion and renewal. At the heart of the problem is the dual system of employee representation. The crucial question is whether decentralisation – or, more precisely, the shift of competences from trade unions to works councils – is possible without breaking the dominance of sectoral bargaining. In that case, the change may help to achieve new stability in the collective bargaining system. On the other hand, the lost societal consensus on the benefits of collective wage formation, with strong opposition from both economists and politicians, is a constant threat to the future of collective bargaining autonomy. The next change of government will probably suffice to institute further erosion of collective bargaining as a political goal.

REFERENCES

Bahnmüller, Reinhard (2001), *Stabilität und Wandel der Entlohnungsformen*, München und Mering: Hampp.

Bahnmüller, Reinhard, Reinhard Bispinck and Anni Weiler (1999), Tarifpolitik und Lohnbildung in Deutschland, WSI Discussion Paper No. 79, Düsseldorf: Böckler.

Bepler, Klaus (2003), Kommentar zu §4 TVG – V. Die Nachwirkung von Tarifverträgen, in Wolfgang Däubler (ed.), *Kommentar zum Tarifvertragsgesetz*, Baden-Baden: Nomos, p. 1287–338.

Bispinck, Reinhard (2004), Kontrollierte Dezentralisierung der Tarifpolitik – Eine schwierige Balance, in *WSI Mitteilungen* 57: 237–45.

Bundesministerium für Wirtschaft und Arbeit (2003), *Tarifvertragliche Arbeitsbedingungen im Jahr 2002*, Bonn: BMWA.

Carley, Mark (2003), *Entwicklungen im Bereich des Arbeitskampfes – 1998–2002*, Dublin: European Foundation for the Improvement of Living and Working Conditions, http://www.eiro.eurofound.eu.int/about/2003/03/update/tn0303110u.html.

Däubler, Wolfgang (2003), Einleitung B. – Verfassungsrechtliche und völkerrechtliche Garantien der Tarifautonomie, in Wolfgang Däubler (ed.), *Kommentar zum Tarifvertragsgesetz*, Baden-Baden: Nomos, p. 28–61.

Deinert, Olaf (2003), Kommentar zu § 4 TVG – IV. Das Günstigkeitsprinzip, in Wolfgang Däubler (ed.), *Kommentar zum Tarifvertragsgesetz*, Baden-Baden: Nomos, p. 1208–87.

Deregulierungskommission (1991), *Schlussbericht: Marktöffnung und Wettbewerb*, Gutachten für die Bundesregierung, Bonn.

Dombois, Rainer (2001), Collective bargaining and employment regulation in Germany – the erosion of industry-wide collective bargaining and new need for differentiated regulation patterns, in Mateo Alaluf and Carlos Prieto (eds), *Collective Bargaining and the Social Construction of Employment*, Brussels: ETUI, pp. 131–64.

Ellguth, Peter (2003), Quantitative Reichweite der betrieblichen Mitbestimmung, in *WSI Mitteilungen* 56: 194–9.

Ellguth, Peter, and Susanne Kohaut (2004), Tarifbindung und betriebliche Interessenvertretung: Ergebnisse des IAB-Betriebspanels 2003, in *WSI Mitteilungen* 57: 450–4.

Funk, Lothar (2003), Der neue Arbeitsmarkt und der Wandel der Gewerkschaften, in *APuZ* B 47–48: 14–22.

Hanau, Peter (2000), §63 Entgelthöhe, in Reinhard Richardi and Otfried Wlotzke (eds), *Münchener Handbuch zum Arbeitsrecht*, 2nd ed., München: Beck, pp. 1253–60.

Hassel, Anke (2002), A New Going Rate? Co-ordinated Wage Bargaining in Europe, in Philippe Pochet (ed.), *Wage Policy in the Eurozone*, Brussels: Lang, pp. 149–76.

IAB-Betriebspanel (2003), Tarifbindung der Betriebe und Beschäftigten in West- und Ostdeutschland 2003, in Ellguth and Kohaut (2003), p. 451 (Tables 1 and 2).

Iwd (1998), Allgemeinverbindlichkeit – Ein zweischneidiges Schwert, in *Iwd – Informationsdienst des Instituts der deutschen Wirtschaft Köln*, Vol. 6, pp. 2–3.

Kohaut, Susanne, and Claus Schnabel (2001), Tarifverträge – Nein Danke!? Einflussfaktoren der Tarifbindung west- und ostdeutscher Betriebe, Nürnberg: Universität Erlangen, Lehrstuhl für Arbeitsmarkt- und Regionalpolitik, Discussion Paper No. 08.

Kohaut, Susanne, and Claus Schnabel (2003), Zur Erosion des Flächentarifvertrags – Ausmaß, Einflussfaktoren und Gegenmaßnahmen, in *Industrielle Beziehungen* 10: 193–219.

Jacobi, Otto, Berndt Keller and Walther Müller-Jentsch (1998), Germany: Facing New Challenges, in Anthony Ferner and Richard Hyman (eds), *Changing Industrial Relations in Europe*, 2nd ed., Oxford: Blackwell, pp. 190–238.

Kämmerer, Axel, and Gregor Thüsing (2003), Neue Wirkungen des Tarifvertrags: Möglichkeiten eines Tariftreuegesetzes, in Gregor Thüsing (ed.), *Tarifautonomie im Wandel*, Köln: Heymanns, pp. 213–38.

Kirsch, Johannes (2003), Die Allgemeinverbindlicherklärung von Tarifverträgen – ein Instrument in der Krise, in *WSI Mitteilungen*, pp. 405–412.

Massa-Wirth, Heiko, and Hartmut Seifert (2004), Betriebliche Bündnisse für Arbeit mit begrenzter Reichweite? in *WSI Mitteilungen* 57: 246–54.

Monopolkommission (1994), *Mehr Wettbewerb auf allen Märkten*, 10. Hauptgutachten 1992/93, Baden-Baden: Nomos.

Müller-Jentsch, Walther (1995), Auf dem Prüfstand: Das deutsche Modell der industriellen Beziehung, in *Industrielle Beziehungen* 2: 11–24.

Müller-Jentsch, Walther (2003), Mitbestimmungspolitik, in Wolfgang Schroeder and Bernhard Weßels (eds), *Die Gewerkschaften in Politik und Gesellschaft der Bundesrepublik Deutschland*, Wiesbaden: Westdeutscher, pp. 451–77.

Peter, Gabriele (2003), Kommentar zu § 2 TVG, in Wolfgang Däubler (ed.), *Kommentar zum Tarifvertragsgesetz*, Baden-Baden: Nomos, pp. 863–929.

Preis, Ulrich (2004), Kommentar zu § 612 BGB, in Thomas Dieterich, Rudi Müller-Glöge, Ulrich Preis and Günter Schaub (eds), *Erfurter Kommentar zum Arbeitsrecht*, 4th ed., München: Beck.

Rose, Edgar (2003), Die Pflicht des Arbeitgebers zur Gleichbehandlung beim Entgelt, in Jürgen Klusmeyer, Ulrich Meyerholt and Peter Wengelowski (eds), *Umwelt – Arbeit – Bildung*, Oldenburg: BIS, pp. 229–61.

Schnabel, Claus (1998), The Reform of Collective Bargaining in Germany: Corporatist Stability vs. Firm Flexibility, in Reiner Hoffmann et al. (eds), *The German Model of Industrial Relations between Adaptation and Erosion*, Düsseldorf: Böckler.

Schroeder, Wolfgang (2003), Die Transformation einer bundesdeutschen Basisinstitution – oder: warum Bob Dylan Recht hatte ..., in *PROKLA* 33: 147–58.

Schmierl, Klaus (2001), Hybridisierung der industriellen Beziehungen in der Bundesrepublik – Übergangsphänomen oder neuer Regulationsmodus?, in *Soziale Welt* 52: 427–48.

Sachverständigenrat (2002), *Zwanzig Punkte für Beschäftigung und Wachstum*, Jahresgutachten 2002/03, Stuttgart: Poeschel.

Wassermann, Wolfram (2003), Gewerkschaftliche Betriebspolitik, in Wolfgang Schroeder and Bernhard Weßels (eds), *Die Gewerkschaften in Politik und Gesellschaft der Bundesrepublik Deutschland*, Wiesbaden: Westdeutscher, pp. 405–28.

Zwanziger, Bertram (2003), Kommentar zu § 4 TVG – VII. Tarifvertrag und betriebliche Regelungen, in Wolfgang Däubler (ed.), *Kommentar zum Tarifvertragsgesetz*, Baden-Baden: Nomos, pp. 1349–77.

2. France: The helping hand of the state

Christophe Vigneau and André Sobczak

1. INTRODUCTION

The industrial relations system in France is characterized by strong state intervention. As a result, relations between management and labour have always been conceived with the help or under the auspices of a third actor: the state. This also applies to wage formation. However, the role of the state appears rather marginal in determining wage levels. Under French law collective bargaining is the main source of wage regulation. In particular, sectoral collective agreements determine occupational wage levels for each industry. If we compare the French situation with the German one, we see that both industrial relations systems are experiencing similar trends, such as the decentralization of collective bargaining towards the company level, mainly at the behest of the employers. However, this phenomenon raises different problems and has different consequences in France and Germany, in accordance with the different features of their respective industrial relations systems.

2. INDUSTRIAL RELATIONS IN FRANCE

Industrial relations are relations between trade unions and employers' organizations. The French system of industrial relations may be considered as highly regulated by the state, and so as characterized by a narrow conception of collective autonomy. The state has always played a crucial role in promoting collective bargaining or in compensating for the absence of an effective industrial relations system. This state intervention concerns not only (i) the definition of the actors, but also (ii) the content and (iii) the legal effects of collective agreements.

2.1 The actors

The industrial relations system in France is characterized by the division of both the employers' organizations and the trade union movement. French employers are represented by four different organizations at national level: the umbrella organization MEDEF,[1] representing both employers' and business/trade interests, coexists with a separate organization for small and medium-size enterprises (CGPME[2]), as well as two organizations representing particular sectors, namely agriculture (FNSEA[3]) and craft work (UPA[4]). Since the transformation of the former

1. Mouvement des Entreprises de France.
2. Confédération Générale des Petites et Moyennes Entreprises.
3. Fédération Nationale des Syndicats d'Exploitants Agricoles.
4. Union Professionnelle Artisanale.

CNPF into MEDEF in 1998, the latter aims to represent every company in France, but many small and medium-size companies prefer what they see as the more entrepreneurial approach of CGPME to MEDEF's managerial approach.[5] However, a number of sectoral organizations and companies are members of both organizations.

Turning to the trade unions, the existing division was recently augmented by the creation of new trade unions (SUD,[6] UNSA[7]), mainly in the public sector and composed of former members of the five historical trade unions (CGT, CGT-FO, CFDT, CFTC, CGC). This emergence of new trade unions which are particularly strong in some public companies (SNCF, PTT) may be interpreted as a trend towards the corporatist organization of workers. The trade union movement is also characterized by strong ideological diversity. Some are greatly influenced by communist ideas (CGT), others by socialist (CFDT), Christian (CFTC) or anarchist ideologies (CGT-FO). Nevertheless, the emergence of new unions reflects the radicalization of a fringe of the trade union movement. In this context, the trade union movement in France appears highly divided and, as a consequence, relatively weak. Industrial relations in France remain highly adversarial, which derives from the revolutionary tradition of an important part of the trade union movement.

This division greatly reduces the collective power of trade unions in France, which represent on average only 9% of the workforce (less than 5% in the private sector). In this context of fragmentation and low representativeness, the state plays a central role in defining the industrial relations actors. More precisely, the law regulates which trade unions are allowed to conclude collective agreements.[8] However, the statutory rules on collective agreements both explain and cause this division. According to French labour law, collective agreements are agreements concluded between one or more employers and one or more representative trade unions.[9] Furthermore, 'representative trade union' means 'actor in tripartite social dialogue at national level'. Representativeness is assumed for all unions affiliated to the five major national confederations declared representative by government decree in 1966.[10] All other unions must prove their representativeness. Judges must take into account their membership, independence, contributions, experience and number of years in existence, as well as their stance during the period of Occupation in the Second World War.[11] A valid collective agreement signed by a trade union organization is applicable to all workers in the relevant area.

Until the 2004 Act on social dialogue and professional training,[12] the legal principle was that it was sufficient that one trade union affiliated to one of the five major national confederations signed a collective agreement at the sectoral or the company level, even if this union represented only a minority of workers at the relevant level. The act adopted in 2004 does not eliminate this rule but does introduce important changes.[13] In particular, the new regulation promotes a collective

5. Bunel (1998).
6. Solidaires, Unitaires, Démocratiques: union mainly present in the public sector and especially the French national railway company (SNCF) and the post office (La Poste).
7. Union Nationale des Syndicats Autonomes: union mainly present in public administration.
8. Article L. 132-2 Code du travail.
9. Yannakourou (1995).
10. Arrêté du 31 mars 1966: CGT, CGT-FO, CFDT, CFTC, CGC.
11. Article L. 133-2 Code du travail.
12. Projet de loi relatif à la formation professionnel et au dialogue social.
13. Ray (2004), Teyssié (2004).

bargaining system based on a majority requirement. A majority of trade unions is required in some situations to prevent a collective agreement signed by a minority of trade unions from entering into force. This also applies to attempts to oppose a national cross-sectoral agreement. Only a majority of the trade unions recognized as representative at national level may oppose the entry into force of a collective agreement signed by a minority of trade unions. In this sense, the new system maintains the possibility for a single trade union to conclude a collective agreement, but such a collective agreement may be declared null and void if a majority of trade unions opposes it. The 2004 Act also established the majority principle at sectoral and company level. However, at these levels the majority may be either for (positive majority) or against (negative). The 2004 Act leaves it to management and labour to conclude a framework agreement at sectoral level whereby they determine the validity of sectoral collective agreements. If they choose to adopt the negative majority mechanism, only a majority of trade unions recognized as representative in the sector may oppose a collective agreement. However, the framework agreement may also decide to evaluate the majority at the moment of the conclusion of the sectoral collective agreement. Here, the entry into force of a collective agreement depends on the signature of trade unions representing the majority of workers within the sector. Two ways of calculating this majority are foreseen in the Act: (i) based on the results obtained by each trade union at the last elections or (ii) through a special consultation of the workers concerned. Labour and management may also determine the validity of collective agreements signed at company level. They must choose at sectoral level between a positive and a negative majority. The majority, either negative or positive, is calculated on the basis of the results obtained by trade unions in the first round of the elections. In sum, the new regulation bases the system of collective bargaining on the majority principle. Doubtless, the 2004 Act will have an impact on French trade unions. It will increase the power of the biggest trade unions and eventually reduce the division of the trade union movement.

The reform also reconsiders the monopoly of trade unions within social dialogue. In France, the conclusion of collective agreements has so far been a monopoly of the trade unions.[14] As in Germany, however, there is a dual channel of interest representation within companies, with trade unions on the one hand and elected works councils on the other. The creation of trade union sections regrouping all employees that are members of the same union is authorized in all French companies. These trade union sections have no legal personality, but they are allowed to collect membership fees during working time, to distribute leaflets at the beginning and the end of the working day[15] and to organize a meeting once a month outside working time.[16] In companies with 50 employees or more, each representative trade union may appoint a union delegate whose role is to conclude collective agreements with the employer.

Workforce delegates who may be elected in companies with 10 employees or more, or works councils that may be created in companies with 50 employees or more are in principle not authorized to conclude collective agreements. Works councils are mainly entitled to be informed and consulted about different aspects of company management. They are also in charge of social activities within the company. An agreement concluded between the employer and the works council is

14. Morin (1998).
15. Article L. 412-8 Code du Travail.
16. Article L. 412-10 Code du Travail.

currently considered to be an atypical agreement that has less legal weight than collective agreements.[17] In fact, the employer may decide to terminate it unilaterally as long as he announces his decision in good time. Therefore, the dual system in France appears to be stronger than in Germany. This exclusive power to negotiate collective agreements raises serious problems, given the weak presence of trade unions at company level, especially in small and medium-size companies. The shop floor has long been neglected by the trade union movement which opted for a centralized system of industrial relations. Therefore, the intersectoral and sectoral levels have long dominated collective bargaining in France.

In order to nurture collective bargaining at company level, since 1982 the state has imposed an annual obligation to negotiate on specific issues. Since 1995 there has also been the possibility for elected representatives of the employees and a worker empowered by representative trade unions to sign collective agreements. In 1998 and 2000, the working time acts also made this possible. The 2004 Act on social dialogue and professional training has extended these possibilities to all matters.[18] However, these options are available only in companies in which there is no trade union representation. Furthermore, the validity of such agreements depends on different conditions. Agreements signed by elected representatives must be ratified by a national commission composed of representatives of labour and management. Agreements concluded by a worker empowered by a trade union must be ratified by the community of workers within the company, by referendum. With these mechanisms the 2004 Act ends the monopoly of trade unions on concluding collective agreements. As the Constitutional Court held in 1996,[19] trade unions have only a natural vocation to bargain and sign collective agreements. This means that in the absence of a trade union, other bodies may conclude collective agreements.

2.2 Content

Legislation gives wide scope to collective bargaining. The social partners may conclude collective agreements on working conditions in general and on workers' social guarantees.[20] Therefore, collective bargaining is given large competence to regulate the situation of employees at the workplace. However, the content of collective agreements is strongly determined by the so-called '*principe de faveur*'.[21] This principle defines the relationship between statutory rules, collective agreements and employment contracts. According to this principle, expressed in different articles of the French Labour Code, collective agreements must not derogate from statutory rules except for the benefit of workers. One may easily understand the crucial role and scope of this principle in defining the content of collective agreements. In this context, statutory rules are conceived as minimum standards which may be improved by a collective agreement. This principle prevents any downgrading of statutory regulations by collective agreements. It may be considered as a structural principle governing the system and inspired by the specific *ratio* of labour law.

The 2004 Act on social dialogue has greatly reduced the scope of the favourability principle between collective agreements at different levels. In fact, the reform

17. Freyria (1988).
18. Borenfreund (2004).
19. Conseil Constitutionnel, 6 November 1996, *Droit social* (1997), p. 31.
20. Article L.132-1 Code du travail.
21. On this principle, see Jeammaud (1999) and Bocquillon (2001).

authorizes company agreements to derogate to sectoral agreements whether more or less favourably for the worker, unless the sectoral agreement expressly prohibits such a derogation.[22] Therefore, the sectoral agreement no longer constitutes a set of basic rights for company-level agreements. The 2004 Act has radically changed how conflicts between levels of bargaining are resolved. This reform seems to go beyond even the German opening clauses insofar as the latter must merely *allow* derogations, whereas derogations will become the rule in France unless the sectoral agreement prohibits them. In other words, collective agreements signed at branch level will have binding effect only insofar as that is foreseen in the agreement. Nevertheless, the reform of social dialogue excludes the possibility of derogating in a less favourable direction on wages, whether it concerns minimum wages or wage categories. In this situation the previous mechanism still applies: collective agreements signed at company level may derogate to agreements signed at branch level only in favour of the workers.

2.3 Legal effect

The legal effect of collective agreements is defined by statutory rules. In common with their German colleagues, French labour lawyers consider that collective agreements have a dual character. In Germany, one distinguishes between the contractual part and the normative part; in France the view is that at the moment of their conclusion collective agreements are contracts, but when they are applied they are treated as regulations.[23] In French labour law, a collective agreement has normative effect if the employer has himself signed the agreement or is affiliated to the employers' association which signed it.[24] In such companies all the workers are covered by the collective agreement, whether they are union members or not,[25] which is certainly not an incentive for French workers to join unions.

However, the problem of the legal scope of collective agreements is generally solved by the widespread use of the so-called extension procedure. As in other European countries, a procedure enables the Minister of Labour to extend the application of collective agreements at the sectoral level to all the companies in this sector even if they are not members of the employers' organization party to the agreement,[26] so reinforcing the normative character of collective agreements. Extension is decided upon through an executive order from the Minister of Labour after consultation with the National Commission on Collective Bargaining.

Not all collective agreements may be extended. Only collective agreements covering a wide range of provisions dealing both with individual and collective labour law, such as classifications, wages and rights of unions and works councils,[27] may be extended. This condition is intended to give the widest possible effect to the extension procedure. Furthermore, in order to be extended, a sectoral or cross-sectoral agreement, and its riders and appendices, must have been negotiated and agreed by a committee composed of the representatives of the employers'

22. Article 37 of the Law introducing new article L. 132-23 Code du Travail. On this, see Souriac (2004).
23. Pélissier, Supiot and Jeammaud (2002), p. 863.
24. Article L. 135-1 Code du travail.
25. Pélissier, Supiot and Jeammaud (2002), p. 893.
26. Pélissier, Supiot and Jeammaud (2002), p. 946.
27. The complete list of 13 clauses that must figure in the agreement can be found in Article L. 133-5 Code du travail.

associations and trade unions concerned[28] and chaired by a representative of the Ministry of Labour. All representative unions and employers' organizations must be invited to this commission; otherwise the procedure may be annulled by the administrative courts.[29]

The extension procedure can be initiated by the signatories to the agreement. In general, one of the final clauses of the agreement provides that the parties may ask that the text be extended. The initiative may also come directly from the Minister of Labour, but this is very rare. The extension procedure starts with consultation with the National Commission on Collective Bargaining, which gives a reasoned opinion on the clauses the Minister may want to exclude from extension. In practice, the National Commission cooperates closely with the agreement signatories. Unions and employers' associations may oppose extension if the agreement: has not been signed by all representative organizations; does not contain all the provisions defined by law; or does not cover all professional categories. Such opposition must be undertaken by at least two representative organizations. The Minister of Labour may then decide to halt the procedure or to proceed to a second consultation of the National Commission. Even if the opposition continues, the Minister is not bound by the recommendation of the National Commission. However, he must exclude from the extension procedure those provisions of an agreement that might contravene existing legislation.

The Minister's decision to extend the collective agreement must be published in the Official Journal, opening a period of 15 days during which comments may be made by unions and employers' associations, as well as other persons. The executive order granting extension enters into force only after this period. Like any executive order, it can be challenged before an administrative court on the ground of abuse of power.

In contrast to Germany, the Minister of Labour in France has the option of a so-called 'enlargement procedure'. By this procedure, the minister may decide to apply a collective agreement concluded elsewhere to sectors or areas in which there is no union and/or employers' association entitled to engage in collective bargaining.[30] In other words, a collective agreement is made binding for another economic sector or another geographical area outside the agreement's original scope. Decisions of this kind may be made only if the National Commission on Collective Bargaining is not opposed to an enlargement. Both extension and enlargement are very effective, and have brought the rate of employees covered by collective agreements to over 95%.

As in Germany, there are significant debates in France on the duration of collective agreements. Most collective agreements in France are concluded for an indefinite period. Such agreements may come to an end either because they are replaced by a new agreement or because one party decides to terminate them. In both cases, such agreements may continue to have some effects. Two problems may be distinguished: the replacement and the termination of collective agreements.

According to French labour law, social partners bound by a collective agreement have to meet at least once a year to bargain on wages.[31] Collective agreements

28. Article L. 133-1 Code du travail.
29. Conseil d'Etat, 20 May 1988.
30. Article L. 133-12 Code du travail.
31. At sectoral level: Article L. 132-12 Code du travail; at company level: Article L. 132-27 Code du travail.

concluded for an indefinite period might be revised on this occasion.[32] As in Germany, only the unions that signed the initial agreement, or which decided to adhere to it later on, are entitled to sign replacement agreements. In France, however, it is sufficient that only one of the unions which signed the initial agreement signs the new agreement, as long as this union is recognized as representative.[33] Nevertheless, the unions representing the majority of the company's workers (those which obtained the votes of more than half the workers authorized to vote at the last election of the works council) can oppose the revision ('*droit d'opposition*').[34] Since 2004 the revision of collective agreements must respect the majority principle in either its positive or its negative sense.

On the principle that it must always be possible to terminate permanent legal partnerships, collective agreements concluded for an indefinite period can be terminated at any time ('*dénonciation*').[35] If all the employers or all the unions decide to terminate such an agreement, French labour law obliges the social partners to open new negotiations within three months.[36] The former agreement remains in effect until the conclusion of a new agreement, up to a maximum of one year. Beyond this period, if no new agreement has been signed the employees retain their individually acquired benefits ('*avantage individuel acquis*').[37] Such benefits shall not apply to employees taken on at a later date. Also excluded are benefits which do not correspond to an already established right but only to a possible benefit. Regarding collective agreements concluded for a definite period, their duration is limited to a maximum period of five years.[38] On expiry, the same procedure is applied as in case of cancellation of a collective agreement with no fixed term.

3. LEGAL FRAMEWORK OF COLLECTIVE WAGE FORMATION IN FRANCE

According to French labour law, the payment of a wage to the worker is one criterion of an employment contract. The notion of wage ('*salaire*') is the subject of a debate among French labour lawyers.[39] There are two main approaches. First, one can adopt a purely contractual perspective and consider that the wage is compensation for the work done by the worker. The duty to pay the wage to the worker derives from the employment contract which determines its amount and structure. The wage must therefore correspond to the accomplished work, independently of the worker's personal needs or those of their family. However, French labour law has a wider definition of the wage, including all the benefits the worker receives from their employment. To the contractual wage is added not only additional payments by the employer, but also amounts paid by third parties, such as tips and even wage substitutes paid by public authorities or social security. This definition therefore goes far beyond the contractual framework and confirms that in France the conclusion of an employment contract in itself furnishes the worker with a set of statutory

32. Vachet (1993); Morin (1993).
33. Article L. 132-7 Code du travail.
34. Article L. 132-7-II Code du travail
35. Article L. 132-8 Code du travail
36. Article L. 132-8, paragraph 5, Code du travail.
37. Article L. 132-8, paragraph 6, Code du travail; Dockès (1993); Despax (1990).
38. Article L. 132-86, paragraph 2, Code du travail.
39. Hennebelle (2001).

entitlements, defined not only by the employment contract itself, but also by collective agreements and by legislation.

To a certain extent, French labour law may be taken to recognize the notion that the purpose of wages is to provide their recipient with a living, because the principle 'whoever works has the right to receive fair and satisfactory remuneration' has constitutional weight.[40] Rules governing wage formation are considered to achieve 'economic equilibrium' and 'social justice'.[41] This equilibrium is organized on the basis of a legal construction made up of statutory rules, collective bargaining and individual contracts. A minimum wage is fixed by the state. Collective bargaining and individual contracts may improve on this statutory minimum wage. Wage formation in France is therefore embedded in a particularly strict framework composed of rules from (i) collective law and (ii) individual law.

3.1 Collective wage formation and the favourability principle

Collective wage formation is governed in France by the '*principe de faveur*', according to which in case of conflict between different norms the one that is the most favourable to the worker shall prevail.[42] Although this principle was seriously weakened in other areas of labour law by the 2004 Act on social dialogue,[43] it has been clearly maintained concerning both the minimum wage and wage categories.[44] Collective agreements may not in particular derogate *in peius* to the provision contained in the collective agreement signed at branch level. There is therefore nothing similar to German opening clauses. Nevertheless, it must be recognized that the increasing possibilities of reducing workers' rights defined at a higher level by so-called derogative agreements – particularly in respect of working time – may have an indirect impact on collective wage formation.

According to the favourability principle, wage determination in France by employment contract must respect the minima which are fixed either (a) by legislation or (b) by collective agreements.

a) Existence of a legal minimum wage

In France, wage levels were at first determined only by collective bargaining. Only in 1950 was a statutory minimum wage established ('*salaire minimum de croissance*') which had to be observed in all sectors and in all employment contracts.[45] The aim was to ensure the lowest paid workers a purchasing power guarantee and participation in the economic development of the nation.

The amount of the legal minimum wage also depends upon price evolution and economic growth:[46]

1. The minimum wage is indexed in relation to the national price index on

40. Déclaration universelle des droits de l'Homme.
41. Sellier (1990).
42. Pélissier, Supiot and Jeammaud (2002), p. 139.
43. Projet de loi relatif à la formation professionnel et au dialogue social.
44. New Article L. 132-23 Code du Travail.
45. Savatier (1997).
46. Article L. 141-3 Code du travail.

consumer goods. When consumer prices rise by at least two per cent, the minimum wage must be raised automatically by the same proportion.[47]

2. The minimum wage may be raised each year in July by the government after consultation of the National Committee for Collective Bargaining, given that it must increase by at least as much as half of the increase of the workers' purchasing power.[48] The recommendation of the social partners is in no way binding for the government which takes its decision based on political reasons.

Since the introduction of the 35-hour week in 2000, there have been two different hourly minimum wage levels because the government decided that the reduction of working time must result neither in a fall in the purchasing power of minimum-wage earners already on a 35-hour week nor in an automatic pay rise for those still working a 39-hour week (which would have brought about an 11.3% increase in the hourly cost of the minimum wage). A different minimum wage therefore exists for people who are still working a 39-hour week (and to whom the old mechanisms still apply) and for those who are now on a 35-hour week. A guaranteed monthly wage is now applied to the latter, with increases on the basis of inflation and half any rise in purchasing power of blue-collar workers' basic monthly pay. In order to merge the two levels of minimum wage, different wage rises are fixed by the government for the two categories of worker. In 2004, the rise in the minimum wage was particularly high (5.8%) for the minority of workers who are still working a 39-hour week, but most recipients saw a much lower rise (2.1%), of no more than inflation in some cases.

Since 1 July 2004, the minimum wage has been fixed at 7.61 euros per hour, which corresponds to 1154.18 euros per month for a person working 35 hours a week. Each rise in the minimum wage has a direct impact on the lowest wages because, according to the '*principe de faveur*', it must be respected even if a collective agreement at the sectoral or company level fixed a lower wage. More generally, given the overall weakness of collective bargaining in France, the minimum wage is an essential element of protection for a significant proportion of employees. In 1998, 2.5 million employees (12.5% of the working population) were paid the minimum wage, 50% more than in 1994. Nevertheless, even if the relatively high minimum wage tends to reduce earnings inequality, it does not lead to uniform earned income. First, its increase affects only the lowest wages and in no way leads to an automatic increase in all wages. Second, not all the elements that make up annual income (such as overtime or seniority premiums) are taken into account when setting the minimum wage.

b) Collective bargaining on wages

Collective bargaining on wages has always been very important. Since 1950, the Minister of Labour's option to extend the application of a collective agreement at the sectoral level to all companies in the sector has been subordinated to the inclusion of wage provisions in the agreement.[49]

In France, there are two kinds of agreement: classification agreements and wage agreements.

47. Article L. 141-3 Code du travail.
48. Article L. 141-4 Code du travail.
49. Article L. 133-5 Code du travail.

1. Classification agreements
   At the industry or sectoral level, the social partners conclude agreements that fix different wage categories based on qualifications. For organizations already bound by a collective agreement, there is even a legal obligation to meet and to negotiate at least once every five years to examine whether classifications should be revised.[50] At the company level, the employer then allots each employee a wage category.
2. Wage agreements

Sectoral level agreements
In France, collective bargaining on wages traditionally takes place at the sectoral level. Social partners who are already bound by a collective agreement at sectoral level even have a legal obligation to meet at least once a year to negotiate on wages.[51] The minimum fixed by these sector-wide agreements must be respected in individual employment contracts. This means also that revised collective agreements shall apply to employees whether they want it or not: refusal might be a ground for dismissal because no modification of the contract has taken place.[52] On the other hand, if the collective agreement is terminated without being replaced by a new one, the wage will be considered as an individually acquired benefit which is integrated into the employment contract.

Recommendations of employers' associations
Surprisingly, according to a decision of the French Supreme Court of June 1999,[53] a one-sided recommendation on wages issued by an employers' association is binding on its members if its terms are clear and precise.

Company agreements
Since 1982, collective bargaining on wages has also been institutionalized at the company level. Under the *Code du travail*,[54] employers in companies where there is at least one union must hold a collective bargaining round on wages every year.

According to the '*principe de faveur*', company agreements must respect the minima fixed by the sectoral-level agreement, but they may modify the wage structure. In fact, company agreements can distribute wage increases in different ways, as long as the global wage increase in the company is at least as large as the one in the sectoral agreement.[55] In this case, unions can oppose the agreement as long as they represent the majority of employees (that is, those which obtained the votes of more than the half the workers eligible to vote at the last works council election).[56]

50. Article L. 132-12 Code du travail.
51. Article L. 132-12 Code du travail.
52. Soc., 27 June 2000, *Bull.civ.*, n°247.
53. Soc., 29 June 1999, *Bull.civ.*, n°308; De Quenaudon (1997).
54. Article L. 132-27 Code du travail.
55. Article L. 132-24 Code du travail.
56. Article L. 132-26 Code du travail.

3.2 Wage flexibility and principle of equal treatment

The French '*principe de faveur*' guarantees that workers will be paid at least the minimum wage fixed by law or by collective agreements. Employment contracts may not set a wage below these minima. Furthermore, French labour law guarantees workers a certain wage stability. The employer cannot impose a modification of the employment contract, whether it concerns the amount or the structure of the wage, without obtaining the agreement of the worker.[57]

As in Germany, however, French labour law allows forms of variable pay, as long as the minima fixed by the legislator or by the bargaining partners are respected.

In French labour law, companies with 50 employees or more have an obligation to develop employee financial participation schemes which must be negotiated with the unions ('*participation*').[58] French legislation mentions other collective forms of profit-related pay ('*intéressement*'),[59] that may be adopted on a voluntary basis, but these are all additional payments that can in no way go below the minima fixed by the law or by collective agreements.

The same rule applies to forms of variable pay introduced by the employment contract. The courts accept target-setting clauses in employment contracts as long as the minima are respected. Moreover, the courts take the view that annual targets are negotiated between worker and employer and are not unilaterally imposed by the latter. Finally, the target must be reasonable and, taking into account the general economic situation, achievable.

Finally, wage flexibility must be compatible with the principles of (i) non-discrimination and (ii) equal pay in conformity with EU law.

a) Anti-discrimination rights

French labour law contains important anti-discrimination rights and facilitates the employee's pursuit of such rights by specific rules regarding the burden of proof. Under French law, any discrimination on grounds of sex, nationality, political opinion, age, union affiliation or sexual orientation is prohibited. This concerns the selection of candidates for a job, but also wages and training. Any decision taken in violation of this principle is considered null and void[60] and may lead to criminal sanctions.[61]

As at the EU level, French labour law endeavours to make it easy for employees to pursue their rights, holding that it is not the task of the worker to prove discrimination: the employee need only allege different treatment amongst workers doing the same job. It is then up to the employer to present an objective and legitimate justification for this different treatment. An employer must therefore provide an objective reason for wage differentiation. Furthermore, French labour law allows trade unions and NGOs not only to assist workers, but also to act in their place.[62]

57. Soc., 28 January 1998, Dr. soc., 1998, p. 533 comment G. Couturier.
58. Article L. 442-1 Code du travail.
59. Article L. 441-1 Code du travail.
60. Article L. 122-45 Code du travail.
61. Article 225-2 Code pénal.
62. Article L. 122-4-1 Code du travail.

b) Equal pay

French labour law has long recognized the principle of equal pay for male and female workers.[63] This includes the basic wage as well as all other benefits paid for work done. As at the EU level, the principle of equal pay applies not only to equal work, but also to work 'of equal value'. Work of equal value is defined by the French *Code de Travail* as work that implies comparable knowledge, recognized by a diploma, skills resulting from experience, responsibilities and physical burden. Despite this legal definition, as in Germany there has been litigation in order to determine what work of equal value means.

According to the Supreme Court, it is permissible to pay lower wages to female workers if they have a lower physical work load[64] or if they are less versatile.[65] On the other hand, the Court recently stated that the employer cannot prove absence of discrimination on the ground of sex by showing that similar wage differences exist among male workers.[66]

In a very important decision the French Supreme Court decided that the principle of equal pay for male and female workers is an application of the more general rule 'same work, same wage'.[67] Consequently, employees in identical situations must receive the same remuneration. It is up to the employer to prove that the difference in treatment is lawful.

4. CURRENT CHALLENGES TO THE FRENCH SYSTEM

As in Germany, the French system of collective wage formation is under increasing pressure linked to the relatively high cost of labour. Despite the recent period of growth, the French unemployment rate is still among the highest in the European Union. Consequently, collective bargaining on wages is facing some difficulties, especially at the sectoral level. These difficulties do not concern the number of collective agreements, although the number of collective agreements at the sectoral level has fallen slightly over the last few years (from 897 in 2001 to 884 in 2003). Indeed, thanks to the extension and enlargement procedures, the rate of employees covered by collective wage agreements has increased significantly, from 86.4% in 1985 to 93.4% in 1995.

The problem lies with the content of these agreements. Provisions on wages are still the main subject dealt with by collective agreements, at both the sectoral level (47% of agreements contain provisions on wages) and the company level (42% of agreements, excluding those on employee financial participation). At the company level, the number of agreements concerning wages is increasing quite rapidly. However, since the 1990s wages fixed by collective agreements at the sectoral level have increased very slowly, even more slowly than the legal minimum wage. As a consequence, in more than 80% of French sectors, collective agreements contain minimum wages below the legal standard at least for those with the lowest qualifications.[68] Of course, due to the favourability principle, these collective

63. Article L. 140-2 Code du travail.
64. Soc., 18 March 1981, *Bull.civ.*, n°229.
65. Soc., 31 May 1988, *Dalloz*, Informations rapides, p. 219.
66. Soc., 28 November 2000, *Bull.civ.*, n°395.
67. Soc., 23 October 1996, *Droit social*, 1996, p.1016, comment A. Lyon-Caen.
68. Haag, Lozier and Ughetto (2002).

agreements have no effect on the amount of money paid to the worker. They only allow the employer to compensate the difference between the collective and the legal minimum by different forms of variable pay.

5. REACTIONS OF THE STATE, SOCIAL PARTNERS AND ENTERPRISES IN FRANCE

Compared to its German counterpart, the French system of collective wage formation resists economic pressure relatively well. Even if there seems to be a wide consensus to reinforce the role of the social partners and of collective bargaining, the existence and even the regular increase of the legal minimum wage is not really contested by different governments. Of course, this does not mean that the French system is not changing. The most important change is perhaps the transformation of collective bargaining. First, more and more collective agreements are linking wages to other issues, especially working time, the objective being to obtain wage moderation in exchange for flexibility and working time reduction. Second, there have been some changes concerning the conclusion of collective agreements which tend to weaken the traditional monopoly of trade unions. These changes were mostly introduced by the state, which is consistent with the important role it plays in the French system of industrial relations.

5.1 Changes introduced by state intervention

In order to fight high unemployment, French governments since the 1990s have tried to reduce the cost of labour. As nobody dares to question the legal minimum wage, the approach has been to reduce companies' social contributions for employees on the lowest wages. Recent French governments have also linked wage evolution and the reduction of working time in order to moderate increasing labour costs. The introduction of the 35-hour week,[69] for example, provided an opportunity not only to organize companies in a more flexible way, but also to freeze monthly wages, even if the hourly wage increased. More generally, working time legislation has been used by French governments to make important changes in the collective bargaining system, not directly in relation to wage formation, but having an effect on it.

a) Collective wage formation

Since the beginning of the 1980s, there has been a shift in collective bargaining from the sectoral level to the company level. This is partly linked to the legal obligation for companies to bargain at least once a year on wages and working time,[70] but also to the pursuit of greater flexibility. This shift is also favoured by the possibility – in particular cases – of concluding company agreements which favour the workers less than agreements at the sectoral level ('*accords dérogatoires*'),[71] even if this

69. Law of 19 January 2000; *Droit social*, 'Le temps après la loi Aubry II', numéro spécial, mars 2000; *Droit social*, 'Le projet de loi Aubry II', numéro spécial, décembre 1999.
70. Article L. 132-27 Code du travail.
71. Le Goff (2002), p. 435.

possibility is limited to working time and still excluded as regards wages.[72] With the 2004 Act on social dialogue, the possibility for a collective agreement signed at company level to derogate from provisions established by sectoral collective agreements becomes the rule. However, wages remain among the few exceptions for which derogations are permitted only for the benefit of workers.

Another important change concerns the actors entitled to conclude collective agreements. In a context of falling trade union membership, the lack of unions at company level – especially in small and medium-size enterprises – is a major problem. In this context, a growing number of companies are concluding agreements with the works council, although in France these are not considered as collective agreements, but as atypical agreements ('*accords atypiques*').[73] The legal weight of these agreements is reduced because courts associate them with 'unilateral commitments' ('*engagement unilateral*'),[74] which means that they may be cancelled by unilateral decision of the employer. This explains why such agreements are rarely used in relation to wages.

They are quite common in the field of working time: agreements with the works council are even explicitly authorized by the law introducing the 35-hour week. Of course, these 35-hour agreements concluded at the company level often also deal with wage issues. In fact, French legislation does not guarantee employees whose working time is reduced that their monthly wage will be maintained, but leaves it to the social partners at company level to determine whether there will be financial compensation. In many cases, agreements with the works council lay down compensation for low wages (based on state assistance), but also freeze or moderate wages for a given period, a new phenomenon in a system based on annual bargaining rounds. In fact, the 35-hour-week reform has given the employers the opportunity to introduce greater flexibility in working hours but also to moderate pay rates.

Such agreements challenge the '*principe de faveur*' insofar as it is not really clear whether they benefit workers or not. They create a trade off between the social partners ('*accords donnant-donnant*').[75] This explains why the legislation demands that such agreements be confirmed by a majority vote of the workers. By the way, the legitimacy of agreements concluded by trade unions which represent only a small part of the workers in a company is more and more coming into question,[76] even among union leaders. So far, however, except for the 35-hour agreement,[77] the principle remains that the signature of one union recognized as representative at the national level is sufficient to make the agreement compulsory for all the workers in the company.

b) Individual wage formation

Apart from the reduction of social contributions for low wages, there have been no major changes in French law on individual wage formation. One might mention the

72. The possibility mentioned above to adapt the wage structure of a sectoral agreement at the company level is in fact not considered to be an '*accord dérogatoire*' because the global amount paid to the workers is at least as large as that laid down in the sectoral agreement.
73. Freyria (1988); Vachet (1990).
74. Soc., 5 June 2000, *Bull. civ.*, n°208; Supiot (1992); Dockès (1994).
75. Pélissier, Supiot and Jeammaud (2002), p. 875.
76. Pélissier, Supiot and Jeammaud (2002), p. 129.
77. Article 19 V, law of 19 January 2000.

reinforcement of the legislation against discrimination which transposes the principles of the relevant European directive.[78]

5.2 Changes due to collective bargaining

Linked to state intervention in the field of working time, there have also been changes in collective bargaining on wages. In fact, there is a tendency in collective bargaining to link wages to employment and working time.[79] At the company level, for example, many collective agreements try to compensate for a reduction of working hours by wage moderation over several years, a new model in France where wage bargaining traditionally takes place every year.

Another important change is the reduction of the difference between wages fixed by sectoral-level agreements and those fixed by company agreements.[80] Whereas at the beginning of the 1990s sectoral-level wages were about 20% lower than company-level wages, the difference had almost vanished by the end of the 1990s.

To summarize, the French system of collective wage formation is evolving in order to adapt to economic and social pressures, but no fundamental changes have emerged. Neither the important role played by the public authorities nor the '*principe de faveur*' which establish a clear hierarchy of norms in labour law, and particularly in the field of wages, are really under challenge. It seems that the French system is resisting external pressure much better than, for example, the German system. This stability is so entrenched that there does not appear to be great demand for change among the major French actors in labour relations. Having been particularly reluctant to accept the introduction of the 35-hour week, even the employers seem to prefer more flexibility than reduction of the minimum wage or profound changes to the system of collective wage formation.

6. FRANCE AND GERMANY: DIFFERENCES AND SIMILARITIES IN COLLECTIVE WAGE FORMATION

6.1 Important differences

One major difference in the legal framework of collective wage formation is the absence of a minimum wage in Germany. In France, there has been a legal minimum wage since 1950. More generally, the role of the state in wage determination appears much more important in France than in Germany. By contrast, the German system appears exclusively based on strict collective autonomy. A good example of this is the statutory requirement imposed on employers by French law to open negotiations at the sectoral and company levels. The periodicity of this obligation to open negotiation is defined by law.

Another difference worth mentioning is the crucial role played in Germany by the metal industry in determining wages at national level. Certainly, the metal industry is much more important in Germany than in France.

78. Law of 16 November 2001.
79. Haag, Lozier and Ughetto (2002), p. 146.
80. Haag, Lozier and Ughetto (2002), p. 152.

Concerning differences in respect of industrial relations, the French system differs from the German in that it does not give works councils the power to negotiate at company level. Collective bargaining is a monopoly of the trade unions. In our opinion, this has a significant impact on wage formation: above all, it prevents sectoral wage competition.

German codetermination is obviously another a major difference between French and German industrial relations law. Since codetermination applies only to large companies and it is mainly small companies that do not apply sectoral collective agreements it is worth asking whether codetermination prevents wage reductions on the part of employers.

Another difference is the importance of the region in Germany as a level of collective bargaining. It would be interesting to know whether this level of negotiation has an impact on wage determination.

The power and structure of the trade union movement are further important differences between France and Germany. The weakness and divisions which characterize trade unions in France have a great deal to do with the role of the state in collective labour law. Trade unions are usually not in much of a position to negotiate wages at company level.

6.2 Important similarities

In both France and Germany sectoral collective agreements play a decisive role in wage determination. However, also common to both countries is strong demand from employers to decentralize wage negotiations.

From an economic point of view, in both France and Germany there is strong pressure on wages. Wages are becoming a key issue, often linked to working time reduction. The reduction of working time must be related to the very low wage increases during the 1990s. Another common trend is the employers' desire to differentiate wages between employees. These practices must be strictly controlled since it may lead to indirect discrimination against certain categories of worker.

In both France and Germany it is possible to extend collective agreements. However, in contrast with Germany most sectoral agreements in France are extended by decree of the Minister of Labour.

7. STRENGTHS AND VULNERABILITIES OF THE GERMAN SYSTEM FROM A FRENCH POINT OF VIEW

The lack of stability of the German system may derive from the fact that hardly any use is made of extension. However, it has not been established that this administrative procedure renders collective agreements more stable.

In a way, the German system of wage formation may have more survival potential, mainly because it appears more flexible than the French system. Obviously, the corollary of such flexibility is that it may go against the workers' interests. The French system, mainly because the role of the state is more important, does not involve strong trade unions ensuring the protection of workers. In other words, the equilibrium reached by the German system appears weak but is also more flexible. The French system is doubtless more rigid, mainly because of different substantive or procedural rules articulating the different levels of wage formation.

The strength but also the weakness of the German system lies in the fact that wage formation is regulated mainly by the social partners. The German system is likely to survive on condition that a relative consensus exists on wages between management and labour. It also implies strong representativeness on the part of the employers' organization. In this sense, the current crisis will put the German conception of collective autonomy to the test.

8. DECENTRALIZATION AND GROWING FLEXIBILITY IN GERMANY FROM A FRENCH POINT OF VIEW

France and Germany are facing the same process of decentralization of wage formation, mainly at the behest of the employers. This trend appears quite dangerous in a context of weak trade union representation at company level. Nevertheless, the process is taking different forms and raising different problems in the two countries. From a French perspective, flexibility seems inherent in the German wage formation system: legal elements are absent which might control or orientate the decentralization process but would also make it more rigid. In fact, the problems seem more related to the conditions of decentralization than to the process of decentralization itself. In France, in contrast, criticisms come mainly from employers and concern the elements which make the system more stable (statutory minimum wage, favourability principle, extension procedure) and prevent decentralization from becoming detrimental to workers. In consequence, decentralization is not necessarily perceived as bad for employees as long as the legal rules governing the relationship between statutory law, collective bargaining and individual contracts are respected. For example, although France is facing the same phenomenon of wage cuts by virtue of company-level agreements, the structuring elements of wage formation reduce the scope of these collective agreements. It is precisely these structuring rules which are at stake in the current reform of collective bargaining in France.

9. CONCLUSIONS

Hitherto, one of the main differences concerning collective wage determination in France and in Germany has been the role of the state and the social partners. In France, the state has not hesitated to support collective bargaining between trade unions and employers, especially at the enterprise level, by introducing a duty to bargain or by making financial support dependent on the conclusion of a collective agreement, for example within the framework of the 35-hour week. Nevertheless, the reform of the regulations on collective bargaining adopted in May 2004 is likely to introduce profound changes in French labour law and reduce the differences with the German system. Even if, in the area of wages, the reform maintains the favourability principle between collective agreements at company and sectoral level, the possibility – under certain conditions – of concluding agreements with the works council may have an impact on collective wage determination and increase the pressure on the trade unions. France and Germany face the same challenge: trying to avoid wages becoming the criterion of competition between companies within the same sector. What is at stake is ultimately the historical unifying function of working conditions realised by labour law.

REFERENCES

Bocquillon, Fabrice (2001), Que reste-t-il du principe de faveur?, *Droit Social*, p. 255.
Borenfreund Georges (2004), La négociation collective dans les entreprises dépourvues de délégués syndicaux, *Droit Social*, p. 606.
Bunel, J. (1998), Le patronat français, in Jacques Kergoat et al., *Le monde du travail*, La Découverte, p. 401.
De Quenaudon, René (1997), Nature et régime d'une recommandation patronale, *Dalloz*, p. 50.
Despax, Michel (1990), Le maintien des avantages individuels acquis en matière de rémunération, *Droit Social*, p. 156.
Dockès, Emmanuel (1993), L'avantage individuel acquis, *Droit Social*, p. 826.
Dockès, Emmanuel (1994), L'engagement unilatéral de l'employeur, *Droit Social*, p. 227.
Freyria, Charles (1988), Les accords d'entreprise atypiques, *Droit Social*, p. 43.
Haag, Antoine, Françoise Lozier and Pascal Ughetto (2002), L'impact des systèmes de négociation collective sur l'évolution des salaires: le cas de la France, 1990–1998, in C. Yakubovich (ed.), *Négociation collective des salaires et passage à la monnaie unique. Une comparaison Allemagne, Espagne, France, Italie*, Cahier Travail et Emploi, Paris: La Documentation française, p. 142.
Hennebelle, Diane (2001), *Essai sur la notion de salaire*, PU Aix-Marseille.
Jeammaud, Antoine (1999), Le principe de faveur. Enquête sur une règle émergente, *Droit Social*, p. 115.
Le Goff, Jacques (2002), *Droit du travail et société. Les relations collectives de travail*, Rennes: Presses universitaires de Rennes.
Morin, Marie-Laure (1993), La signature des accords collectifs: à propos de la réforme de la procédure de révision, *Revue de Jurisprudence Sociale*, p. 74.
Morin, Marie-Laure (1998), Des titulaires du droit à la négociation collective, *Droit Social*, p. 21.
Pélissier, Jean, Alain Supiot and Antoine Jeammaud (2002), *Droit du travail*, 21e éd., Paris: Dalloz.
Savatier, Jean (1997), Les minima de salaires, *Droit Social*, p. 575.
Sellier, François (1990), L'évolution des règles sur les salaires dans le système français de relations professionnelles, in *Les systèmes de relations professionnelles*, Editions CNRS, p. 81.
Ray, Jean-Emmanuel (2004), Les curieux accords dits 'majoritaires' de la loi du 4 mai 2004, *Droit Social*, p. 590.
Souriac M.-A. (n.d.), L'articulation des niveaux de négociation, *Droit Social*, p. 579.
Supiot, Alain (1992), La réglementation patronale de l'entreprise, *Droit Social*, p. 215.
Teyssié, Bernard (2004), La négociation des conventions et accords collectifs après la loi n° 2004 du 4 mai 2004, *Dalloz*, p. 2060.
Vachet, Gérard (1990), Les accords atypiques, *Droit Social*, p. 620.
Vachet, Gérard (1993), La révision des conventions et accords collectifs, *Droit Social*, p. 134.
Yannakourou, Stamatina (1995), *L'Etat, l'autonomie collective et le travailleur. Etude comparée du droit français et italien de la représentativité syndicale*, Paris: LGDJ.

3. The British case: before and after the decline of collective wage formation

Brian Bercusson and Bernard Ryan

PART 1: THE BRITISH SYSTEM OF COLLECTIVE WAGE FORMATION

1. INTRODUCTION

Wage formation in Britain – as currently constituted – is quite different from that of many other European countries. Continental systems of industrial relations may be facing challenges to a traditional system of collective wage formation and the possibility of fundamental changes to that system. In the British case, however, such a scenario applies more directly to the period from the mid-1960s to the late 1980s than to the current context. That a fundamental change took place – based on a marked reduction in trade union influence and a related increase in business flexibility – is not in doubt. Contemporary debates concern instead the possibility of revitalising trade unionism and collective bargaining.

For that reason, the first part of this chapter starts somewhat further back in time. The discussions of both the system of industrial relations (section 2) and the legal framework of collective wage formation (section 3) begin with the traditional system as it existed in the mid-1960s, and then chart subsequent developments. This part of the chapter concludes with a discussion of the prospects for trade unionism and collective bargaining, and of possible legal policies to that end (section 4).

2. INDUSTRIAL RELATIONS

2.1 Pressure on the traditional system

Within the British system of industrial relations, regulation of the terms and conditions of employment depends primarily upon the recognition of trade unions by employers for collective bargaining purposes. It is estimated that roughly 60% of employees were covered by national collective agreements through the 1950s and 1960s, and that coverage then increased to a peak of 76–78% in the mid-1970s.[1] The statutory wages councils were a secondary system of collective wage formation.

Note: In contrast to the contributions on France, the Netherlands, and Sweden, the present chapter is divided into two parts. Part I was written by Bernard Ryan and includes a report on the British system of collective wage formation corresponding to sections 1 to 5 of the other contributions. Part II was written by Brian Bercusson: corresponding to sections 6 to 8 of the other contributions, it includes comments on the German case from a British point of view.

1. S. Milner, 'The Coverage of Collective Pay-setting Institutions in Britain, 1895–1990', *British Journal of Industrial Relations* 33 (1995), pp. 70–90, Table 2.

These were tripartite bodies, made up of worker representatives, employer representatives and independent members, which adopted legally binding orders concerning terms and conditions of employment in less-organized sectors. It is estimated that in the mid-1960s wages councils covered 3.5 million employees (or 15%), and that their coverage had declined to 2.75 million employees (or 13%) by 1984.[2] Overall, it is estimated that the percentage of employees who were covered by national collective bargaining and/or wages councils peaked at 84–85% in the mid-1970s.[3]

Pressure for change in the British industrial relations system in the 1960s and 1970s was primarily a consequence of economic pressures. The focus tended to be on comparatively high rates of inflation, but there was also pressure to raise comparatively low levels of productivity. Union power in a context of full employment was thought to be implicated in these difficulties, both as a cause of inflationary pressure and as an explanation of the failure to enhance productivity by the ending of restrictive practices.[4] These pressures led to repeated attempts to implement incomes policies (both voluntary and statutory) between 1962 and 1979. The apparent failure of incomes policies in turn led to pressure for fundamental reform in the law governing industrial relations.[5] By the 1980s and 1990s, the economic pressures on the industrial relations system were of a different kind. 'Compositional' effects, from a decline in established industries (especially mining and manufacturing) and in established patterns of employment (male, full-time, permanent) led to a corresponding reduction in the extent and influence of trade unionism.[6] Greater international competition in much of the private sector, and financial constraints in the public sector, contributed to pressure for change in industrial relations.

Government policy was a second, largely autonomous, source of pressure on the traditional system. Conservative governments under Thatcher (1979–1990) and Major (1990–1997) were generally sceptical of trade unionism and collective bargaining, and fostered change in industrial relations through the reform of collective labour law (discussed below). Moreover, their neoliberal policy outlook favoured change in industrial relations through the promotion of economic internationalization, deregulation in labour and other markets, and the tightening of financial discipline throughout the public sector.

In any event, throughout the 1980s majority public opinion was either sceptical of trade unions or accepting of them in only a weakened state. Gallup data show that trade union popularity reached its lowest point in the years 1975–1979, before increasing again as unions grew weaker in the 1980s. There was also extensive support for Conservative reforms of collective labour law in the years from 1979. Marsh has argued that this pattern showed public support for a 'bound and gagged' form of trade unionism.[7] Even in 1996, the British Social Attitudes Survey (BSAS) found little support among employees (23%) for the proposition that unions had 'too

2. *Ibid.*, p. 78.
3. *Ibid.*, Table 2.
4. See Royal Commission on Trade Unions and Employers' Associations ('Donovan'), Report, Cmnd. 3623 (1968), Chapters 4 and 6.
5. See generally C. Crouch, *The Politics of Industrial Relations* (2nd ed., Fontana, 1982).
6. F. Green, 'Recent Trends in British Trade Union Density: How Much of a Compositional Effect?', *British Journal of Industrial Relations* 30 (1992), pp. 445–58.
7. D. Marsh, 'Public Opinion, Trade Unions and Mrs Thatcher', *British Journal of Industrial Relations* 28 (1990), pp. 57–65.

little power', as against 15% who thought unions had 'too much'.[8] More generally, it is widely believed that support for trade unionism and collective bargaining has been weakened by changes in social attitudes.[9] On this view, British society has become less solidaristic and more individualist and consumerist, with a consequent unwillingness to participate in, or to tolerate, collective action in the employment sphere. It has been suggested that the underlying explanations of such a change include a less marked social stratification, greater affluence, changed employment patterns and technological change.[10]

Change in industrial relations

The combination of economic pressures, government hostility and changes in social attitudes led to progressive, yet fundamental, changes in the British system of industrial relations. Evidence for change is provided in particular by the more or less continuous decline in the level of trade union membership since 1979. One set of membership figures, available throughout the period being considered here, is that provided by trade unions to the Certification Officer. A second – for the years from 1989 – is based upon the Labour Force Survey. The two sets of figures are together presented in Table A1 in the Appendix. They show a cumulative fall of around 45% in the absolute level of UK trade union membership, from 13 million in 1978 to perhaps 7.35 million by 2003. That corresponds to a fall of 46% in union density among employees in Great Britain – from about 53% in 1978 to about 29% in 2003.

When one looks behind these aggregate figures, moreover, an even worse position emerges for the unions. In the first place, there is a strong secular trend of decline, with a fall in union density on one or other measure in each year since 1978. Second, the fall in trade union density has been pervasive, having occurred in every sector and for every significant personal or occupational characteristic. Third, private sector trade unionism is at a particularly low level: only 18% according to the 2001 LFS, as against 59% in the public sector.[11] Fourth, there are a growing number of persons who have never been a trade union member: up from 28% in 1983 to 48% in 2001, according to the BSAS.[12] Finally, the evidence suggests that it is particularly young workers who are not joining trade unions, with the BSAS finding that trade union density declined from 50% in 1983–5 to 34% in 1999–2001 among those 25 and over, but from 38% to 15% among those under 24.[13] All of these considerations point to the underlying weakness of trade unions.

8. A. Bryson and S. McKay, 'What About the Workers?', in R. Jowell, J. Curtice, A. Park, L. Brook, K. Thomson and C. Bryson (eds), *British Social Attitudes. 14th Report: The End of Conservative Values?* (Gower, 1997), p. 35.
9. In the field of industrial relations, Hyman in particular has argued that there has been a specific rejection of collective action among workers: see R. Hyman, 'Trade Unions and the Disaggregation of the Working Class', in M. Regini (ed.) *The Future of Labour Movements* (Sage, 1992) and 'Changing Trade Union Identities and Strategies', in R. Hyman and A. Ferner (eds) *New Frontiers in European Industrial Relations* (Blackwell, 1994).
10. H. Phelps Brown, 'The Counter-Revolution of Our Time', *Industrial Relations* 29 (1990), pp. 1–14.
11. K. Brook, 'Trade Union Membership: An Analysis of Data from the Autumn 2001 LFS', *Labour Market Trends* (July 2002), pp. 343–54.
12. A. Bryson and R. Gomez, 'Marching on Together? Recent Trends in Union Membership', in A. Park, J. Curtice, K. Thompson, L. Jarvis, and C. Bromley (eds), *British Social Attitudes: The 19th Report* (Gower, 2002), p. 57.
13. *Ibid.*, Table 3.1.

The fall in the coverage of collective bargaining since the 1970s provides further evidence of the transformation in industrial relations. One source of information is the Workplace Employee Relations Survey (WERS). It found that 70% of employees in workplaces of 25 employees or more were covered by collective bargaining on pay in 1984, but only 54% in 1990 and 41% in 1998.[14] Similarly, the 2001 Labour Force Survey (LFS) found that the pay of only 36% of employees was affected by a collective agreement, less than half the coverage of collective bargaining at its peak in the mid-1970s.

Here too, closer inspection if anything suggests a worse picture. In particular, the period since the late 1970s has seen substantial change in the levels of collective bargaining. In 1980, WERS found that multi-employer bargaining affected the pay of some or all employees in 68% of workplaces with a recognized union and 25 or more employees.[15] In 1990, the figure was 60%, but by 1998 had decreased to 34%. When the decline in recognition is taken into account, the result is a decline in multi-employer bargaining from 43% of all workplaces with 25 or more employees in 1980 to 31% in 1990 and 14% in 1998. In concrete terms, what the figures show is that multi-employer bargaining has all but disappeared from the private sector. Whereas in 1980 over a quarter of private sector workplaces with 25 or more employees were covered by such bargaining, by 1998 that had fallen to four per cent – as against 41% in the public sector.

A final piece of evidence for change concerns the process of collective bargaining: the decline in the extent of industrial action to historically low levels (see Table A2 in the Appendix). In the 20 years 1960–79, the average number of recorded strikes was 2,527 per year. This is more than ten times the average number of recorded strikes in the decade 1993–2002 (an average of 203 a year). The fall in working days lost to industrial action has been even greater. In the 20 years 1970–89, the average number of working days lost each year was slightly over 10 million (10.04 million). By contrast, in the decade 1993–2002, the average was only slightly above one-twentieth that rate (575,000 per annum).

There is, on the other hand, no evidence of a strong trend towards a narrowing in the scope of collective bargaining. In particular, the WERS series has found no more than a modest decline in the extent of collective bargaining on non-pay issues in workplaces where unions are recognized.[16] There is also a mixed picture as regards variability in terms and conditions. Case-study evidence suggests that for pay the trend is for greater individualization, with performance- or merit-related elements becoming more common, and that that is linked to the absence of recognized trade unions. For other terms and conditions, by contrast, the trend is towards greater standardization.[17]

---

14. N. Millward, J. Forth and A. Bryson, 'Changes in Employment Relations, 1980–1998', in M. Cully, S. Woodland, A. O'Reilly and G. Dix, *Britain at Work: As Depicted by the 1998 Workplace Employee Relations Survey* (Routledge, 1999), pp. 241–2 (hereafter Cully *et al.*).
15. *Ibid.*, pp. 228–9.
16. N. Millward, A. Bryson and J. Forth, *All Change at Work? British Employment Relations 1980–1998 as Portrayed by the Workplace Industrial Relations Survey Series* (Routledge, 2000), pp. 167–73.
17. W. Brown, S. Deakin, M. Hudson, C. Pratten and P. Ryan, *The Individualisation of Employment Contracts in Britain* (Department of Trade and Industry, 1998), pp. 26, 59, 61.

3. THE LEGAL FRAMEWORK OF COLLECTIVE WAGE FORMATION

3.1 Developments prior to 1997

Collective laissez-faire

The traditional approach of British labour law was characterized by Kahn-Freund in the 1950s as 'collective *laissez-faire*'.[18] That meant 'allowing free play to the collective forces of society', while 'limit[ing] the intervention of law to those marginal areas where the disparity of ... the forces of organized labour and of organized management is so great as to prevent the successful operation of ... "negotiating machinery".'[19] In Kahn-Freund's account, labour law under collective *laissez-faire* had three elements. The first was the absence both of 'regulatory' laws specifying wage levels or other terms and conditions of employment, and of an effective system for the identification and enforcement of individual contractual rights. The second element was the 'negative' character of legislation on trade unions and industrial relations – that is, it removed obstacles created by the common law, rather than articulating positive rights. The third element was the absence of legislation which had an 'auxiliary' role in relation to collective bargaining – in other words, which 'promote[d] collective bargaining [or] ... the application, observance and enforcement of concluded contracts'.[20]

Kahn-Freund's account has been questioned on the third point, however. Other writers take the view that the British state has traditionally used legal and administrative mechanisms in order to promote collective bargaining.[21] In particular, within the industrial relations system of the 1960s 'fair wages' mechanisms sought to extend the terms of collective agreements to workers and employers not covered by them.[22] Under the 1946 Fair Wages Resolution, government contractors were required to observe wages, hours and other conditions which were not less favourable than those established by collective bargaining or arbitration for that trade or industry in that district. In the absence of such a standard, the 'general level' was to be followed. The principle of the Fair Wages Resolutions was also applied to certain other sectors, including road haulage, public house-building, film-making, broadcasting, public road transport.[23] In addition, under Section 8 of the Terms and Conditions of Employment Act 1959, employers were required to respect 'recognized terms and conditions' for their trade or industry in that district.[24]

18. O. Kahn-Freund, 'Legal Framework', in A. Flanders and H. Clegg (eds), *The System of Industrial Relations in Great Britain* (Blackwell, 1954), and 'Labour Law', in M. Ginsberg (ed.), *Law and Opinion in England in the Twentieth Century* (Stevens, 1959).
19. Kahn-Freund (1959), pp. 223, 224.
20. Kahn-Freund, 'Industrial Relations and the Law – Retrospect and Prospect', *British Journal of Industrial Relations* 7 (1969), p. 303.
21. See, for example, P. Davies and M. Freedland, *Labour Legislation and Public Policy* (Clarendon, 1993), Chapter 1, and K. Ewing, 'The State and Industrial Relations: "Collective Laissez Faire" Revisited', *Historical Studies in Industrial Relations* 5 (1998), pp. 1–31.
22. See generally B. Bercusson, *Fair Wages Resolutions* (Mansell, 1978).
23. These were the remaining examples when the last Fair Wages Resolution was rescinded: see Road Haulage Wages Act 1938, Housing Act 1957, Films Act 1960, Broadcasting Act 1981 and Public Passenger Vehicles Act 1981.
24. G. Latta, 'The Legal Extension of Collective Bargaining: A Study of Section 8 of the Terms and Conditions of Employment Act 1959', *Industrial Law Journal* 3 (1974).

Attempts at reform, 1969–1974

The pressures upon the British industrial relations system led governments to seek to depart from the traditional collective *laissez-faire* model from the late 1960s onwards. The first attempt to do so was the Labour Government proposal in 1969 that the Secretary of State for Employment should have the power to intervene in inter-union disputes and to impose a 28-day pause for conciliation where industrial action was contrary to agreed procedures. However, the Government was unable to proceed with these proposals in the face of union opposition.[25] More radical reform came with the Conservative Government's Industrial Relations Act 1971. It introduced a legal code for industrial relations, including a presumption of the legal enforceability of collective agreements, a statutory recognition procedure and protection for the individual right to choose with respect to trade union membership (though subject to the possible lawfulness of closed shops). The 1971 Act also made major changes to the law on industrial action: legal protection was denied to industrial action relating to inter-union disputes, to unofficial action and to most secondary action, while the Secretary of State for Employment could in specified circumstances seek court orders for a cooling-off period and/or a ballot prior to industrial action. In practice, however, the 1971 Act was a failure, largely because of its rejection by Trades Union Congress (TUC) trade unions.[26] The unions refused to register for the sake of benefiting from the Act's protection, employers were in any case reluctant to use the law, and the imprisonment of trade unionists for breach of the rules on industrial action provided a focus for political opposition to the legislation. The general failure of the Act permitted its near-total repeal by the incoming Labour Government in 1974. For Kahn-Freund at least, the conclusion was that the Act had been 'an attempt to saddle the court and the legal profession with tasks they cannot fulfil'.[27]

The Labour Government's Employment Protection Act 1975 then introduced two mechanisms of importance to wage formation. Schedule 11 of the Act took over the policy of extending the terms of collective agreements to non-participant employers, but for the first time required employers to respect the 'general level' of terms and conditions where there were no 'recognized' terms and conditions.[28] In addition, under Sections 11 to 16 of the Act, a statutory recognition system was introduced, administered by the Advisory Conciliation and Arbitration Service (ACAS).[29] Between 1 February 1976 and 15 August 1980, ACAS received a total of 1,610 applications for a recognition recommendation. Of those, ACAS figures show that 1,362 applications had been dealt with, leading to 158 positive recommendations, and the achievement of voluntary recognition in a further 518 cases.[30] The legislative model was one which gave a great deal of discretion to ACAS in dealing with applications, but the result was to expose it to legal challenges taken by employers

25. See P. Jenkins, *The Battle of Downing Street* (Knight, 1970).
26. The classic study of the operation of the 1971 Act is B. Weekes, M. Mellish, L. Dickens and J. Lloyd, *Industrial Relations and the Limits of the Law: The Industrial Effects of the Industrial Relations Act* (Blackwell, 1975).
27. O. Kahn-Freund, 'The Industrial Relations Act 1971 – Some Retrospective Reflections', *Industrial Law Journal* 3 (1974), p. 200.
28. B. Bercusson, 'The New Fair Wages Policy: Schedule 11 to the Employment Protection Act', *Industrial Law Journal* 5 (1976), pp. 129–47.
29. The provision for statutory recognition in the Industrial Relations Act 1971 had been little used because of the boycott of that Act by TUC unions: see Weekes *et al.* (1975), pp. 130–47.
30. ACAS, *Annual Report 1980*, Tables 17–19.

or unions unhappy with its decisions.[31] After a series of defeats in the courts, which imposed obligations on ACAS which it often could not carry out, or which it considered contrary to good industrial relations practice, ACAS itself concluded in 1979 that the statutory system was unworkable.[32] That conclusion opened the door to the Conservative repeal of the procedure the following year.

The Conservative period, 1979–97

When a Conservative government came to power in 1979, it adopted a 'step-by-step' approach to legislation on collective labour law. Over the next decade and a half, six major pieces of legislation concerning collective labour law were passed: the Employment Acts 1980 and 1982, the Trade Union Act 1984, the Employment Acts of 1988 and 1990, and the Trade Union Reform and Employment Rights Act 1993. Reforms in the 1980–93 period prohibited the closed shop through protection for freedom of association for individual workers, and extensively regulated the internal affairs of trade unions. Legislation in the period also curtailed legal rights to take industrial action through the removal of legal immunity for secondary action, unofficial action and official action which did not satisfy complex requirements as regards ballots and notice.

The principal legislative supports for collective bargaining were removed in the early years of the Conservative government after 1979. The Employment Act 1980 repealed the statutory procedures for the compulsory recognition of trade unions for bargaining purposes, the mechanism for the extension of collective agreements to all employers in a trade or industry in a given district, and the 'fair wages' clause in the road haulage industry. The Fair Wages Resolution and related provisions were then rescinded in 1982, with effect from September 1983.[33] From that point on, there was no statutory system in Britain for extending the effects of collective agreements to those who did not wish to be bound by them.

In addition, Conservative legislation sought to frustrate attempts to promote recognition through trade union action. The Employment Act 1982 provided that any term of a contract to supply goods or services which required a party to the contract to use union-only labour, or to recognize, negotiate or consult with one or more trade unions, would be void. The 1982 Act also introduced statutory duties not to refuse to deal with a potential supplier of goods or services for the same reasons. Further provisions removed immunity from industrial action intended to achieve any of those outcomes.[34]

The Conservative government also saw legislation in support of 'derecognition' by employers. While there was no legal impediment to derecognition, there was uncertainty as to the legal position when, as part of a strategy to achieve it, an employer offered inducements to union members to enter into 'personal contracts' instead of being covered by collective bargaining. In 1994, the Court of Appeal in *Wilson and Palmer* held that the failure to extend a pay increase to those who wished

31. For a survey of the decisions, see B. Simpson, 'Judicial Control of ACAS' *Industrial Law Journal* 8 (1979).
32. See the letter from ACAS chairman Jim Mortimer to Secretary of State for Employment Jim Prior, 29 June 1979, reproduced in ACAS *Annual Report 1979*, pp. 108–12.
33. That step also rendered ineffective statutory provisions which referred to the Resolution.
34. These provisions are now TULRCA 1992, SPD. 145, 187, 222 and 225.

to continue with collective bargaining was 'action' aimed at 'preventing or deterring' trade union membership, contrary to Section 146 of the Trade Union and Labour Relations Consolidation Act (TULRCA) 1992.[35] In response, the Conservative government secured a legislative change – known as the 'Ullswater amendment' – which permitted employers to take action which deterred trade union membership if their purpose was to 'further a change in [their] relationship with all or any class of [their] employees'.[36] In the event, the House of Lords allowed an appeal in *Wilson and Palmer*.[37] The majority of the House of Lords concluded that the *omission* of not paying an increase to those who wished to remain subject to collective bargaining was not an *action* prohibited by the legislation protecting trade union membership. Four members of the House of Lords also endorsed the suggestion that coverage by collective bargaining did not, in any case, fall within the concept of 'trade union membership' so as to be protected by the legislation. If correct, this second proposition meant that there was no legal bar to employer discrimination against workers who wished to be covered by collective bargaining.

A final change in the law in relation to wage formation in the period of Conservative government was the abolition of the wages councils. The first steps were taken in the Wages Act 1986: it removed the power to establish new wages councils, deprived wages councils of power in relation to workers under 21, and provided that wages councils could do no more than set a basic hourly and overtime rate for an entire industry. The system of wages councils was then abolished altogether by the 1993 Act. The result was that the agriculture wages boards were the only statutory wage setting mechanism which remained. Outside agriculture, there was no state intervention to set a floor for wages for the first time since the Trade Boards Act 1909.

3.2 Post-1997 Labour governments

General orientation

The two Labour governments since 1997 have had an ambivalent approach both to the traditional system of industrial relations and to the reform of collective labour law. On the one hand, these governments have followed a policy on the economy and public services broadly similar to their Conservative predecessors, an approach which has necessarily implied pressure upon trade unionism and collective bargaining. In the field of collective labour law, moreover, the 1997 Government came to office having promised that it would not go back on key Conservative reforms. As Tony Blair put it in a newspaper article during the 1997 election campaign:

> The essential elements of the trade union legislation of the 1980s will remain. There will be no return to secondary action, flying pickets, strikes without ballots, the closed shop and all the rest. The changes that we do propose would leave British law the most restrictive on trade unions in the Western world.[38]

35. Associated Newspapers Ltd v. Wilson and Associated British Ports v. Palmer [1994] ICR 97.
36. Section 148(3) of TULRCA 1992, inserted by Trade Union Reform and Employment Rights Act 1993, s. 13.
37. Associated Newspapers v Wilson and Associated British Ports v Palmer [1995] ICR 406.
38. A. Blair, 'We Won't Look Back to the 1970s', *The Times* (31 March 1997).

Pursuant to that general orientation, Labour has left many of the principal Conservative changes in place, including the restrictions on industrial action and the prohibition on commercial contracts requiring union labour or recognition. In the particular case of the prohibition on the closed shop, the Labour period in office has seen the entrenchment of the position it inherited, through the incorporation of the ECHR by the Human Rights Act 1998. It is clear that Article 11 ECHR requires contracting states to protect the right not to join a trade union.[39] If the legislative protection for that right were removed, the 1998 Act would permit Article 11 ECHR to be invoked immediately against public employers, while the possibility would arise of a declaration in the British courts that the legislative position was incompatible with Britain's ECHR obligations.

That said, post-1997 governments have improved the legal position with respect to trade unions and wage formation in a number of respects. That was initially done by the Employment Relations Act 1999, and further changes have now been proposed in the Employment Relations Bill 2004. One significant innovation in collective labour law was the establishment of a right for individual employees to be accompanied – including by a trade union representative – in disciplinary or grievance hearings called by their employer.[40] Another was the conferral for the first time of automatic protection against dismissal arising out of official industrial action lasting at least eight weeks.[41] There have also been three significant developments in the law relating to wage formation, which are here considered separately: the minimum wage, the statutory recognition procedure, and the reform of the law on trade union membership.

The minimum wage

The first major change in the law relating to wage formation in the post-1997 period in office does not directly concern collective labour relations. This was the statutory minimum wage, introduced under the National Minimum Wage Act 1998.[42] There are two levels, one for adult workers over 21, and another 'development rate' for those between 18 and 21. The two rates are set by the government (through the Secretary of State for Trade and Industry), after recommendations from the Low Pay Commission which have usually – though not invariably – been followed. The minimum wage is enforced either through legal action taken by the workers entitled to it, or by the Inland Revenue.

The minimum wage rates have developed as follows:

The minimum wage system has been a significant innovation in the British labour market, whether by comparison with the Conservative *laissez-faire* approach, or with

38. A. Blair, 'We Won't Look Back to the 1970s', *The Times* (31 March 1997).
39. *Young, James and Webster* v. *United Kingdom*, [1982] EHRR 38 and *Sigurjonsson* v. *Iceland* [1993] 16 EHRR 422.
40. Employment Relations Act 1999, s. 10.
41. TULRCA 1992, s. 238A, inserted by Employment Relations Act 1999, Sch. 5, para 3. Protection continues beyond eight weeks where the employer has not taken 'such procedural steps as would have been reasonable for the purposes of resolving the dispute'. Previously, workers were protected only against selective dismissal, and then only for three months: see TULRCA 1992, s. 238.
42. The Agricultural Wages Boards continue to operate as before, save that they cannot now set a level of wages below the national minimum wage.

Start date	Main rate (£ per hour)	Development rate (£ per hour)
1 April 1999	3.60	3.00
1 June 2000	–	3.20
1 October 2000	3.70	–
1 October 2001	4.10	3.50
1 October 2002	4.20	3.60
1 October 2003	4.50	3.80
1 October 2004	4.85	4.10

the earlier wages councils. Nevertheless, it has been the subject of a number of criticisms. One objection has concerned the failure to provide a minimum wage for workers under 18. In response, a minimum wage of £3.00 an hour has now been announced for 16 and 17 years from 1 October 2004 – but even then, there will be no minimum wage for workers under 16, apprentices under 19, or apprentices under 26 and in the first year of an apprenticeship. The system is also open to criticism for setting a single rate for the whole of Britain, thereby denying the possibility of sectoral rates, or of allowance for the substantial regional disparities in income and living costs.

A further possible ground of criticism is that the effects of the minimum wage in its early years have been modest.[43] The Low Pay Commission estimates that 1.2 million jobs – roughly five per cent of the employed workforce – had a wage increase as a result of the introduction of the minimum wage in 1999, and that the uprating of October 2001 affected between 1.1 million and 1.5 million jobs.[44] The minimum wage is thought to have had only limited spillover effects on the wages of other workers, with the Low Pay Commission doubting that there were any effects above the 16th percentile in the years 1998–2002.[45] Similarly, no significant adverse effects of the minimum wage on employment levels have been detected.[46] The limited and concentrated effects of the minimum wage have permitted the Low Pay Commission and Government to be more ambitious in announcing upratings for 2003 and 2004 which – unlike in earlier years – are above the expected increase in average earnings. The Low Pay Commission has in addition recommended that above-average increases be considered for subsequent years.[47] It remains to be seen, however, if even those steps will lead to widespread effects on other workers.

Statutory recognition

In the field of collective labour law, the most important development of relevance to wage determination was the re-introduction of a statutory recognition procedure

43. See, generally, D. Metcalf, 'The National Minimum Wage: Coverage, Impact and Future', *Oxford Bulletin of Economics and Statistics* 64 (2002), pp. 567–82, and R. Dickens and A. Manning, 'Minimum Wage, Minimum Impact', in R. Dickens, J. Wadsworth and P. Gregg (eds), *The Labour Market under New Labour: The State of Working Britain* (Palgrave, 2003).
44. Low Pay Commission, *The National Minimum Wage: Fourth Report* (2003), paras 2.6 to 2.9.
45. *Ibid.*, paras 2.34 to 2.43.
46. *Ibid.*, paras 2.50 to 2.69.
47. *Ibid.*, para 6.39.

under the 1999 Act, with effect from June 2000.[48] Under the procedure, a union[49] may apply to the Central Arbitration Committee (CAC) to be recognized as entitled to bargain over pay, working hours and holidays – but only those subjects – with an employer of more than 20 employees. If the two sides cannot agree on the 'appropriate bargaining unit', then it is determined by CAC. The key question is then whether the union has sufficient support in that bargaining unit. Ordinarily, the union is entitled to be recognized where it can show that more than 50% of the employees in the bargaining unit are members. That test may, however, be disregarded by CAC 'in the interests of good industrial relations', or where there is reason for doubt as to the support among the union members for the union's conducting collective bargaining on their behalf. If union membership is insufficient, or is disregarded, then CAC is required to conduct a ballot. In that event, the union is entitled to recognition where a majority of those voting, and 40% of those eligible to vote, support the proposal. Once the principle of recognition has been established, the 'method' of collective bargaining is agreed by the parties or, failing that, is determined by CAC, having regard to a code of practice issued by the Secretary of State for Trade and Industry.[50] If the employer then fails to comply with the method of collective bargaining which has been agreed or determined, the remedy is the specific performance of the employer's obligations as if these were contractual provisions.[51] A final point is that, where a union application is accepted by CAC, but is unsuccessful, that union is barred for three years from making a further application for that or a similar bargaining unit.

The statutory procedure has been at least moderately successful in promoting collective bargaining. Of 232 applications which had been made and completed by 31 March 2003, statutory recognition was the outcome in 58 cases, and CAC was aware that voluntary recognition had resulted in 43 of the withdrawn applications.[52] The existence of the statutory procedure is also thought to have contributed to an increase in voluntary recognition in cases where no application was made.[53] For example, a TUC survey found 869 voluntary recognition deals in the three years from November 2000 to October 2003. By contrast, a similar survey found only 190 such deals in a near three-year period prior to the statutory recognition procedure coming into force (January 1997 to October 1999).[54] It is also significant that CAC has so far avoided being undermined by litigation, as happened to ACAS in the

48. TULRCA 1992, Sch. 1A, inserted by Employment Relations Act 1999, s. 1 and Sch. 1. For a review of the legal provisions, see B. Simpson, 'Trade Union Recognition and the Law, A New Approach – Parts I and II of Schedule A1 to the Trade Union and Labour Relations (Consolidation) Act 1992,' *Industrial Law Journal* 29 (2000), pp. 193–222.

49. More than one union can apply together, and where they do so essentially the same procedure applies as for a single union. In the multi-union case, however, the unions are required to show that they will cooperate and that they will enter into an arrangement with the employer concerning the conduct of collective bargaining: TULRCA 1992, Sch. 1A, para 37.

50. Trade Union Recognition (Method of Collective Bargaining) Order 2000, SI 2000 No. 1300.

51. This is in contrast to the model under Section 16 of the Employment Protection Act 1975, which permitted CAC to determine the terms of employment of the employees in question.

52. CAC, *Annual Report 2002/03*, pp. 18–21.

53. For this conclusion with respect to the two-year period following the coming into effect of the statutory procedure, see S. Wood, S. Moore and K. Ewing, 'The Impact of the Trade Union Recognition Procedure under the Employment Relations Act, 2000–2', in H. Gospel and S. Wood (eds), *Representing Workers: Union Recognition and Membership in Britain* (Routledge, 2003), pp. 136–40.

54. See TUC, *Focus on Recognition – Trade Union Trends Survey* 04/01 (2004).

1970s,[55] even if two successful challenges in 2003 may be a sign of greater difficulties to come.[56] The Government's 2003 review of the 1999 Act concluded that 'the procedure is, overall, working well'.[57] In line with that assessment, no significant alterations to the statutory recognition procedure have been proposed in the Employment Relations Bill 2004.

Trade union membership rights

There have also been important developments in the law giving protection to trade union membership. One change made by the 1999 Act overcame the interpretation of the notion of 'action' short of dismissal by the House of Lords in *Wilson and Palmer* by providing that *any* 'detriment' short of dismissal – i.e. an action *or* an omission – would trigger the application of the law relating to trade union membership.[58] The 1999 Act also created a power for the Secretary of State to make regulations to protect workers who were dismissed or subjected to detriment for refusing 'to enter into a contract which includes terms which differ from the terms of a collective agreement which applies'.[59] That power, however, is limited by a provision that the payment of lower wages to workers covered by collective bargaining is not to be a 'detriment' for these purposes, and in the event has never been used.

The decision of the European Court of Human Rights in *Wilson and others* v. *United Kingdom* in July 2002 has been the catalyst for further developments in this area.[60] The Court held unanimously that the pre-1997 law had breached Article 11 ECHR in permitting employers to discriminate against employees who wished to be covered by collective bargaining. Significantly, its decision was based on the proposition that 'employees should be free to instruct or permit the union to make representations to their employer or to take action in support of their interests on their behalf'. Based on that premise, the Court's conclusion was that 'it is the role of the State to ensure that trade union members are not prevented or restrained from using their union to represent them in attempts to regulate their relations with their employers'. The implication is that Article 11 ECHR requires contracting states to prohibit employer action which 'prevents or restrains' recourse to union representation, irrespective of whether that action is discriminatory.[61]

The judgment in *Wilson* has led to a series of proposals in the 2004 Bill for the reform of the law relating to trade union membership. First, important new rights are

55. By the end of March 2002, there had been two unsuccessful challenges by employers – *Fullarton Computer Industries* v. *CAC* [2001] IRLR 752 and *R (Kwik-Fit)* v. *CAC* [2002] IRLR 395. There had also by then been two unsuccessful applications by unions, taken by the British Airline Pilots' Association (arising out of a recognition dispute with Ryanair) and the British Association of Journalists (arising out of a recognition dispute with the Essex Chronicle): see CAC, *Annual Report 2001/02*, pp. 3–5.
56. *R (British Broadcasting Corporation)* v. *CAC* [2003] EWHC 1375 and *R (Gatwick Express)* v. *CAC* [2003] EWHC 2035.
57. Department of Trade and Industry, *Review of the Employment Relations Act 1999* (February 2003), p. 28.
58. This change applies to the protection with respect to union membership, participation in union activities and also non-membership of a union: see TULRCA 1992, s. 146.
59. Employment Relations Act 1999, s. 17.
60. (2002) 35 EHRR 20.
61. See K. Ewing, 'The Implications of *Wilson and Palmer*', *Industrial Law Journal* 32 (2003), pp. 1–22.

proposed with respect to employer 'inducements'.[62] Workers will have the right not to be made an 'offer' by their employer, the 'sole or main purpose' of which is to discourage them from union membership, participation in union activities or use of union services.[63] Workers will also have the right not to be made an 'offer' by their employer the 'sole or main purpose' of which is to bring about a cessation of collective bargaining over some or all of their terms of employment. Second, the existing protection against detriment or dismissal on grounds of membership of a trade union or participation in its activities is to be extended.[64] It is now proposed that protection be given where an individual uses the services of a trade union, or where they refuse one of the newly prohibited inducements. Gaps in the protection of individual rights with respect to trade union membership certainly remain under the 2004 proposals: there is no protection with respect to union activities, union services or collective bargaining at the point of hiring,[65] while the protection with respect to collective bargaining does not in terms preclude dismissal or other forms of detriment. There is also room for differences of interpretation as to what is an 'offer' for the purposes of the two rules against 'inducements'. Nevertheless, it is clear that the 2004 Bill proposes a significant advance in the legal protection given to trade union membership and collective bargaining.

4. CURRENT CHALLENGES AND REACTIONS

Industrial relations

Because Labour governments since 1997 have, on the whole, taken a more benign view of trade unionism than their Conservative predecessors, the possibility of a reversal of the decline suffered by trade unions and collective bargaining has become an important question in recent years. Some commentators are optimistic. Heery, Kelly and Waddington, for example, have written of 'union revitalization'.[66] They base their assessment in part on the continuing stability of the absolute number of trade union members in recent years (see Table A1 in the Appendix). They also point to the changes taking place within the union movement, aimed in particular at the recruitment of younger members,[67] and to the more benign state policy, as reflected above all in the statutory recognition procedure. One might add that it is also likely that trade unionism and collective bargaining have found renewed social acceptance in recent years, as part of a general reaction against neo-liberal tendencies in public policy.

Others, however, are more cautious regarding trade union prospects.[68] It is significant that trade union density and collective bargaining coverage have not yet

62. Employment Relations Bill 2004, clause 28.
63. The proposal would also apply to inducements aimed at discouraging non-membership of a union.
64. Employment Relations Bill 2004, clauses 30 and 31. The protection against dismissal is in TULRCA 1992, s. 152, and also applies to dismissal and detriment because of non-membership of a union.
65. See TULRCA 1992, s. 137.
66. E. Heery, J. Kelly and J. Waddington, 'Union Revitalization in Britain', *European Journal of Industrial Relations* 9 (2003), pp. 79–97.
67. See E. Heery, M. Simms, R. Delbridge, J. Salmon and D. Simpson, 'The TUC's Organising Academy: An Assessment', *Industrial Relations Journal* 31 (2000).
68. See, for example, D. Metcalf, 'Trade Unions', in Dickens, Wadsworth and Gregg (2003), and H. Gospel and S. Wood, 'Representing Workers in Modern Britain', in Gospel and Wood (2003).

increased to any great extent, given that both political and labour market conditions have been favourable for most of the period since 1997. As we saw in Section 2, there are in any case significant structural obstacles to a resurgence of trade unions, given in particular the weakness of trade unions and collective bargaining in the private sector, and the significantly lower rate of union membership among younger workers.[69] The most that can be said with confidence is that the position of trade unions has stabilized since 1997, and that at least many of the conditions for revitalization are in place. Whether revitalization in fact occurs is likely to depend not just on union organising efforts, but also on uncertain economic and political developments.

Labour law

We saw in Section 3 that the significant innovations in the law relating to wage determination of 1998 and 1999 have been followed by a period of stability. This is exemplified by the 2004 Bill, which, on the whole, has proposed only very modest changes to collective labour law and the minimum wage. The only significant innovations in the Bill concern the law relating to trade union membership and were necessitated by the judgment in *Wilson*.

Trade unions and other commentators continue to argue for further changes in collective labour law. Much of the recent focus has concerned the details of the statutory recognition procedure. In particular, the TUC has called for the extension of the procedure to employers of 20 employees or less, and for the addition of pensions, training and equality to the list of subjects covered by statutory recognition. It has also demanded that there be no exceptions to the rule that statutory recognition follow from 50% union membership in a bargaining unit; for removal of the requirement that 40% of those eligible to vote support recognition in a ballot; for removal of the possibility that employer recognition of a non-independent union can block an application; and for a definition of terms of employment by CAC where an employer fails to comply with the specified 'method' of collective bargaining.[70]

Other recent proposals concern trade union rights of access to actual or potential members. At present, trade unions have rights of access to a workforce only during the statutory recognition procedure. Under the 1999 Act, these rights of access arise once an employer has been notified that a recognition ballot is to take place, and the Employment Bill 2004 proposes to go further and allow access from the point at which an application for recognition is accepted by CAC.[71] What is lacking, however, is a general right to organize, independently of the statutory recognition procedure. For that reason, it has been proposed that the concept of an 'unfair labour practice' should be introduced into British law, so as to give unions a right not to be

69. The relationship between younger workers and trade unions has been a significant research question in recent years: see J. Waddington and A. Kerr, 'Unions Fit for Young Workers?', *Industrial Relations Journal* 33 (2002), pp. 298–315, and S. Machin, 'New Workplaces, New Workers: Trade Union Decline and the New Economy', in Gospel and Wood (2003).

70. See TUC, *Modern Rights for Modern Workplaces* (2002), paras 46–104, and *Review of the Employment Relations Act 1999: TUC Response* (2003), paras 1.4–1.45.

71. See TULRCA 1992, Sch 1A, para 26(3), and the Code of Practice on Access to Workers during Recognition and Derecognition Ballots, 2000. The proposal to confer a right of access from acceptance of the application is in Clause 5 of the Employment Relations Bill 2004.

obstructed in respect of access to a workforce they have organized or are seeking to organize.[72]

The legal framework governing collective bargaining has, by contrast, attracted less attention in recent years. The Institute of Employment Rights has called for the application of the statutory recognition procedure to multi-employer situations, and also for the extension of multi-employer collective agreements to non-participants.[73] Ewing has gone further and argued that, in the absence of such a mechanism, restrictions on union recognition requirements in commercial dealings and on industrial action aimed at securing such a requirement, should be repealed.[74] For the moment, however, it appears that the focus on recognition has led to a reluctance to pursue other possible legal changes which might help strengthen collective bargaining.[75]

72. For a detailed study, see K. Ewing, S. Moore and S. Wood, *Unfair Labour Practices: Trade Union Recognition and Employer Resistance* (Institute of Employment Rights, 2003). See also Institute of Employment Rights, *A Charter of Workers' Rights*, ed. K. Ewing and J. Hendy (2002), pp. 109–11.
73. Institute of Employment Rights (2002), pp. 119–20.
74. K. Ewing, 'Trade Disputes and the Law', Appendix to TUC, *Review of the Employment Relations Act 1999: TUC Response* (2003), para 10.
75. However, some optimism has been expressed regarding the potential of Council Directive No. 2002/14 establishing a framework for informing and consulting employees in the European Community, OJ 2002, L80/29. See also B. Bercusson, 'The European Social Model Comes to Britain', *Industrial Law Journal* 31 (2002), pp. 209–44.

PART II: THE GERMAN SYSTEM OF COLLECTIVE WAGE FORMATION FROM A BRITISH PERSPECTIVE

5. INTRODUCTION

This analysis of the German system of collective wage formation from a British perspective shall begin with two preliminary observations. First, while the relevance of other national systems for understanding the specific nature of the German system is an axiom of comparative research, there is also a more general European perspective. Secondly, the operation of other mechanisms of wage determination, apart from collective wage formation, should be considered in the different national contexts. Collective bargaining may be central to wage formation, but the converse is not necessarily the case: the emergence of issues other than wages in collective bargaining may have significance for the relative importance of collective wage formation to general structures of collective bargaining.

Comparative and European perspectives

Analysing the German situation from the perspective of other EU member states is a classic comparative exercise. However, further insights – and an alternative vision – may result from a *European* perspective. This addresses a different question: whether features of the German system are consistent with a system of industrial relations, or even of collective wage formation, at EU level. The relevant issues concerning the German system of collective wage formation are addressed not from a national, but from an EU perspective.

If an EU system of industrial relations or of collective wage formation is in the process of development,[76] the extent of the mutual influence between the *German* system and an *EU* system is important. How much does, or should, the EU system affect the German system, and, vice versa, how much does or should the German system affect an EU system of industrial relations or collective wage formation?

For example, there are attempts under way by the ETUC and the European Metalworkers' Federation (EMF) at transnational coordination of collective bargaining over wages.[77] This has aims going beyond purely national objectives: influencing interest rates set by the European Central Bank, and promoting a macroeconomic dialogue over the Broad Economic Policy Guidelines (BEPGs) adopted by the EU member states. In this EU context, the influence of the German system of wage formation, and its results, is particularly important.

The German system would be illuminated by combining *both* comparative perspectives: national *and* EU.[78] The German system influences and is influenced by

76. For legal obstacles see B. Ryan, 'Pay, Trade Union Rights and European Community Law', *International Journal of Comparative Labour Law and Industrial Relations* 12 (1997), pp. 305–25.
77. F. Traxler and E. Mermet, 'Coordination of Collective Bargaining: The Case of Europe', *Transfer: European Review of Labour and Research* 9 (2003), pp. 229–46, and F. Traxler, 'Coordinated Bargaining: A Stocktaking of Its Preconditions, Practices and Performance', *Industrial Relations Journal* 34 (2003), pp. 194–209.
78. This combination may be regarded as a *European* perspective, as when *European labour law* is perceived as an amalgam of EU and member state labour laws: B. Bercusson, *European Labour Law* (Butterworths, 1996).

both other member states and the EU system. There is some evidence that national systems of collective wage formation interact with each other.[79] Similarly, developments at EU level influence national systems of collective wage formation.[80]

Structural changes in collective bargaining and wage formation

Focusing on systems of collective wage formation at national and EU levels could imply that wage formation is essential to the structure of collective bargaining. Yet the centrality of *wage* formation to *collective bargaining* structures may be undermined if wage formation is the result of other mechanisms: minimum wage laws, equal pay/non-discrimination principles, job evaluation, formal indexing procedures (wages tied to inflation, interest rates), and so on. Such alternative mechanisms for pay determination reduce the scope of collective wage bargaining. As a consequence, structures of collective workers' representation (trade unions, works councils) may adopt other roles: providing information or legal advice, or monitoring compliance.[81]

Structural changes in *collective bargaining* may be determined by factors other than collective wage formation. Changes may result from a reduction in the relative importance of collective bargaining in wage formation,[82] or a transformation in the nature of the wage–work bargain.[83] Non-wage issues may create pressures for change in structures of collective bargaining which focus primarily on wage formation.[84]

6. COMPARING THE BASIC FEATURES OF THE GERMAN AND BRITISH SYSTEMS

The comparison begins with basic features of industrial relations in Germany and Britain with a view to identifying significant aspects of the German system. In what follows, an attempt is made to indicate differences and similarities between Germany and Britain as regards their industrial relations systems, their structures of collective wage formation, and the legal framework governing collective wage formation.

79. In the discussion at the project workshop of 19 November 2002, Antoine Jacobs stated that 'If the trade unions in Germany settle for a wage, the Dutch unions coordinate their efforts'. Thomas Blanke referred to the German 'system of inter-regional collective bargaining which often looks to the procedures and results of collective bargaining in Holland' (p. 8).
80. Niklas Bruun refers (Nordic draft report, pp. 10–11) to the influence on the Swedish system of collective wage formation of EU discrimination legislation on age and sex, which requires detailed scrutiny of pay structures.
81. See the contributions on the British, German and Nordic situations on pp. 15–16 of the transcript of the workshop of 19 November 2002.
82. As in the case of working time: see S. Lehndorff, 'From "Collective" to "Individual" Reductions in Working Time? Trends and Experience with Working Time in the European Union', *Transfer: European Review of Labour and Research* 4 (1998), pp. 598–620.
83. The shift from quantitative to qualitative issues.
84. One influence for change is female participation in the workforce and in trade unions, which shifts attention to issues apart from wages, such as work–life balance.

Industrial relations systems

A number of important differences between the German and British systems of industrial relations are particularly relevant to collective wage formation. First, *de-industrialization* has had an important impact on industrial relations in Britain.[85] The decline of the manufacturing sector and the increase in employment in the private services sector has been much more dramatic in the UK than in Germany. This has consequences for industrial relations in general, since organization – especially of trade unions – is much weaker in the private services sector.

Second, the extent of the *internationalization* of the economy is said to be extraordinary in the UK compared to Germany.[86] This exposes industrial relations to special pressures. For instance, it may limit the employer's ability or willingness to increase pay by reference to lower labour standards outside the country.

Third, the *sectoral* dimension of the German system (trade union and employer organization, collective bargaining) contrasts with the focus of the British system on the *workplace*, establishment or enterprise level, not the industry level. This is linked with *employer solidarity*. Employer organizations, particularly at sectoral but also at national level, remain relatively strong in Germany. They have declined in Britain and no longer play a significant role in industrial relations.[87]

Fourth, there is the geographical dimension: *east/west* in Germany and *north/south* in the UK. For example, representation through works councils, especially in medium-size firms, is considerably lower in the former East Germany compared with West Germany. In the West, about half of establishments in the private sector adhere to industry-wide collective agreements; only a quarter in the East do so.[88] Although regional differences exist in the UK (north/south), they are not so extreme as in Germany.

Finally, '*shareholder value extremism*' is a dominant feature of management culture in the UK,[89] less so in Germany. There is specific pressure on industrial relations generally (and employment and wages in particular) when the company's share price is given top priority in decisions affecting the enterprise.

85. 'By 1990, manufacturing accounted for only 23% of all employment, compared with 30% in 1980 and 38% in 1960. The rate of decline between 1960 and 1990 was more rapid than that in most industrialized countries: manufacturing's share fell by 41%, compared to 22% in France and 8% in Germany', P. Edwards *et al.*, 'Great Britain: From Partial Collectivism to Neo-liberalism to Where?', in R. Hyman *et al.* (eds), *Industrial Relations in a Changing Europe* (1998), pp. 1–54, at p. 8 (hereafter, Edwards *et al.*).
86. W. Schmidt and B. Dworschak, 'Industrial Relations in Britain and Germany Compared: Marks "Benchmarking" a New System of Employment Regulation beyond a Pure Industrial Relations System in the UK?', paper prepared for the 13th World Congress of the International Industrial Relations Association (IIRA), Berlin, September 2003, p. 10 (hereafter, Schmidt and Dworschak).
87. 'Discussion of pay determination has centred around the level of collective bargaining. The consistent picture over several decades, from surveys and case studies alike, is of decentralization. In the latter half of the 1980s, it was estimated that one million employees moved out of the coverage of industry-level agreements ... Most notable was the collapse of the national agreement between the Engineering Employers Federation and the Confederation of Shipbuilding and Engineering Unions in 1990, which had been the benchmark for many other agreements', Cully *et al.*, p. 106.
88. R. Dombois, 'Collective Bargaining and Employment Regulation in Germany – The Erosion of Industry-Wide Collective Bargaining and New Needs for Differentiated Regulation Patterns', in A. Mateo and C. Prieto (eds), *Collective Bargaining and the Social Construction of Employment* (Brussels: ETUI, 2001), pp. 131–63, at pp. 138, 150 (hereafter, Dombois).
89. Schmidt and Dworschak, p. 11.

On the other hand, there are a number of similarities between the German and the British systems of industrial relations. The first is the *absence of workplace collective bargaining*; in both Germany and the UK, collective bargaining is not conducted at workplace level. In Germany, collective bargaining is undertaken by trade unions at sectoral or regional level, not by works councils at the workplace. In the UK, the absence of collective bargaining at the workplace is due to trade union weakness at workplace level and the unwillingness of employers to engage in collective bargaining.[90] Second, *industrial action during the term of collective agreements is rare* in both countries, but for different reasons. In Germany, this is due to legally binding no-strike clauses in the agreement. In the UK, there are many legal procedural obstacles to strike action apart from the collective agreement. Third, despite legal provision for works councils in even small establishments in Germany, most do not have them.[91] To that extent, *industrial relations in small workplaces* in Britain[92] and Germany are not so different:[93] the employer dominates.

In conclusion, the *similarities between the same sector* in the UK and Germany may be greater than the differences between industrial relations or collective wage formation in general. Similarities between the same sector in the UK and Germany may also be greater than differences between different sectors *within* the UK and Germany. In other words, there is some similarity in industrial relations in the *same* sectors in both countries. Despite overall differences in industrial relations, the services or manufacturing sectors in *both* countries will be more *similar* to each other (in terms of working time, variable pay, and so on) compared to the differences *between* the services and manufacturing sectors *within* each country.[94]

90. 'In the public sector, the role of workplace management in pay setting was negligible. A much higher proportion of employees were covered by "some other form" of pay determination, most likely ... by either an indexation formula or a review body ... Only one in five private sector workplaces engaged in collective bargaining, whereas four in five had pay set by management and one in ten negotiated on an individual basis with some employees. Two-fifths of public sector workplaces did not engage in collective bargaining, more than offset by those where pay was set in some other way', Cully *et al.*, p 107.
91. 'In spite of the legal provisions, in many small and medium-sized companies no works council exists. ... [One estimate is] that only 24% of all eligible private enterprises, covering 60% of the private sector workforce, have a works council. The proportion is only 10% in the smallest establishments with 5 to 20 employees, and about 30% in plants with 20 to 50; whereas virtually every establishment with more than 300 employees has one', O. Jacobi, B. Keller and W. Muller-Jentsch, 'Germany: Facing New Challenges', in A. Ferner and R. Hyman (eds), *Changing Industrial Relations in Europe* (Blackwell, 1998), pp. 190–238, at p. 211 (hereafter, Jacobi *et al.*). Furthermore (p. 215): 'At one extreme there is a large sector of small and medium-sized establishments with rather informal labour relations. Many are sweat-shops, but the more dynamic establishments work on the basis of an implicit reciprocity and a kind of "tacit participation" by the workforce, mostly without an elected works council.'
92. 'Almost ... half of workplaces had no union members. Nearly a tenth of workplaces had some union members, but no [108] recognized unions. Two-thirds of workplaces had no worker representatives. Nearly half of workplaces had no joint consultative committee, either at the workplace or at a higher level in the organization. Taken together, 32% of workplaces met all of the above conditions – in these workplaces there was an absence of any formal structure representing employees' interests. These workplaces were mostly small and mostly stand-alone sites. They were disproportionately found in certain industries, including construction, hotels and restaurants and other business services', Cully *et al.*, pp. 107–8.
93. Dombois, pp. 140–1: 'In small firms, whether in the industrial or craft sectors, not only is there less scope internally for flexible manpower development but works councils, in so far as they exist at all, have little bargaining power.'
94. 'The differences between the sectors are partly more distinct than those between the countries', Schmidt and Dworschak, p. 5.

Collective wage formation

These general differences between the German and British industrial relations systems reveal themselves in differences specific to collective wage formation. The first is fundamental: the prominence of *collective* vs *individual wage determination*. Wage formation in Germany is primarily a subject for collective bargaining. In the UK it has become primarily individualized and is not a bargaining process; in most cases, management unilaterally determines wages and the employee agrees.[95]

Instead, the phenomenon of *benchmarking* prevails. Individual wage formation in the relatively tight labour markets of the UK requires employers to adhere to the 'going rate' needed to obtain labour. These 'benchmark' wage levels are made available through surveys carried out increasingly by specialized commercial services.[96] This has implications for the *role of trade unions*. Collective bargaining gives a central role to trade unions in wage formation in Germany. In the UK, individualization of wage formation implies a different role for trade unions. Instead of negotiating, trade unions' role is to *monitor compliance* with pay structures and *represent* their members in individual disputes.[97]

These structural differences have implications for *income inequalities/wage dispersion*. Income inequalities in Britain are among the highest in the EU. This is linked to general industrial relations features: in particular, individualization of pay bargaining in an expanding and relatively non-unionized service sector.[98] Trade

---

95. 'The coverage of collective bargaining can be broken down into 15% of employees covered by multi-employer collective bargaining, 7% of employees covered by workplace bargaining, and the remaining 13% covered by single-employer bargaining at some level of the organization higher than the workplace. Collective bargaining covered 61% of public, but only 24% of private sector employment. In the private sector, multi-employer bargaining remains a significant institution in construction only. In manufacturing, where twenty years ago workplace bargaining was so dominant, it now accounts for the pay of less than 20% of employees. Individual negotiation of pay is confined to a very small percentage, mostly in managerial grades. For half of all employees and for two-thirds of employees in the private sector, pay is set unilaterally by management within the enterprise', W. Brown, S. Deakin, D. Nash and S. Oxenbridge, 'The Employment Contract: From Collective Procedures to Individual Rights', *British Journal of Industrial Relations* 38 (2000), pp. 611–29, at pp. 615–16 (hereafter, Brown *et al.*).
96. Schmidt and Dworschak, pp. 13–14. Examples are Incomes Data Services (IDS) and Industrial Relations Services (IRS), the Labour Research Department and, of course, some trade unions and employers' associations: 'there is less fragmentation in determining pay and conditions in Britain than a focus on multi-employer bargaining would indicate'.
97. 'Union representatives may also be viewed as "voice mechanisms", operating as a channel for communication between local membership and management, and assisting in the resolution of disputes and grievances ... WERS98 provides evidence that worker representatives are increasingly conforming to this role, attaching greater importance to "dealing with problems raised by the treatment of employees by management, and to resolving disputes" ... rather than the more "traditional" activities of maintaining wages and benefits', A. Bryson and D. Wilkinson, *Collective Bargaining and Workplace Performance: An Investigation Using the Workplace Employee Relations Survey 1998*, DTI, Employment Relations Research Series No. 12 (2001), p. 9.
98. 'A notable trend in many countries from about 1980 was a widening gap between the top and bottom of the pay distribution. In Britain in 1979 a male manual worker at the highest decile of the income distribution earned 2.4 times as much as a worker in the lowest decile; by 1993 the figure was 3.5 ... the increase in inequality was, compared to other OECD countries, particularly sharp in Britain and the US ... The most likely explanation lies in the structure of collective bargaining ... [B]argaining coverage has declined, and the sole statutory means to regulate wages, the Wages Councils, were weakened in 1986 and abolished in 1993 ... widening the gap between the low-paid under the scope of the Councils and average wages ... Thus inequality was the result, not of inexorable market forces, but of changes in the pattern of bargaining, reflecting employer choices and changes in the legal framework of pay determination', Edwards *et al.*, p. 9.

union organization is a critical factor in wage dispersion.[99] Again, there are important differences between the UK and Germany in the use of *variable pay systems*. The proportion of total pay accounted for by incentive payments is said to be around three per cent on average in the UK (for male workers, manual and non-manual). In Germany, it is said to be 15% for manual workers; almost seven per cent for non-manuals (retail: nine per cent).[100]

Despite these structural differences in collective wage formation in Britain and Germany, one important similarity is the degree of *standardization*. Standardization of pay structures is achieved in Germany by collective bargaining. Standardization is also possible in the UK despite individualization of wage formation.[101] Standardization of pay structures is achieved in the UK by employers' practice of formalising standard individual contracts, and by 'benchmarking'. 'Mimetic' wage-setting in the UK replaces collective bargaining and achieves the equivalent result to formal sectoral bargaining rounds in Germany.[102]

Legal framework

Comparison of the legal framework of collective wage formation in Britain and in Germany reveals differences and similarities. There are important differences in the *level of legalization*. There has been significant legalization of the *individual* employment relationship in the UK.[103] This contrasts with the juridification of *collective* labour relations in Germany, for example, in terms of workplace and company board representation. Again, in Germany, *collective agreements*, including

99. 'Workers in the organized sector have much lower pay dispersion than those in the unorganized sector', and 'unions narrow the wage differentials between women and men, blacks and whites, those with health problems and those without, and between manual and non-manual workers', Schmidt and Dworschak, pp. 14–15.

100. Schmidt and Dworschak, p. 3. However, there is some dispute over the data. Variable pay is said to be under-recorded in the UK.

101. 'We conclude that there is a high degree of standardization of employment contracts within British workplaces, so far as both pay and non-pay entitlements are concerned. This is irrespective of trade union presence. Factors related to transaction costs and to internal equity and motivation within organizations would appear to limit how far the individualization of contracts can be taken, even in situations where union influence over the setting of pay and conditions has been effectively removed ... Although in past decades the standardization of employment contracts was brought about primarily through the mechanism of collective bargaining, its survival in a period of union weakness suggests that standardization may have substantial benefits for employers', Brown *et al.*, p. 620.

102. In the UK: "Regular pay rounds contribute to both transparency and reasonable expectations about temporary wage stability ... Regular pay rounds are a survival of collective bargaining, i.e. a relic of traditional industrial relations' (Schmidt and Dworschak, p. 12). This is said to be a key factor in mimetic wages, which replaces collective bargaining in wage determination, but is said to be contingent on a pre-existing collective bargaining system (p. 13). In Germany, formal sectoral bargaining rounds achieve the same result. But cf. Dombois, p. 156, who highlights the dilemma of industry-wide bargaining allowing ever more flexibility, thus undermining its standardising function.

103. '[I]n the 1960s ... the enactment of statutory employment protection rights began to revive the individual contract of employment as a focus for and instrument of employment regulation. As collective bargaining entered a period of crisis and erosion in the 1980s and 1990s, legal governance of the employment relationship increased in importance, rather than withering away. From this perspective, the significance of individualization lies not so much in the reduction of regulatory influence on employment, but rather in a shift in the mode of regulation from the collective towards the individual level', Brown *et al.*, p. 627.

no-strike clauses, are legally binding. In the UK, collective agreements are rarely, if ever, legally binding. Although strike action is closely regulated by law, no-strike clauses in collective agreements are irrelevant to the legal regulation of industrial action.

Specific to legal regulation of wages in Britain is the issue of *overtime*. In Britain, individual employees can agree to work any number of hours, and payments for overtime working are central to the earnings of British manual workers. This contrasts with Germany, where the pay bargaining agenda focuses on basic rates rather than overtime. The UK position would be changed if the Working Time Directive's maximum 48-hour working came into force: 'In contrast to Germany with its statutory works councils, Britain has no institution that is interested in restricting overtime hours.'[104]

A final difference of major significance has been the UK government policy of *privatization and contracting out*. Trade unions in public services are strong in both countries, but German public sector industrial relations have been less affected than the British by the policy of privatization and contracting out of public services to private employers. This has weakened public sector trade unions and collective industrial relations. Collective wage formation in the public sector affected by privatization and contracting out has declined as a result of this change in the legal structure of public service provision.

There are some parallel developments in the legal framework of collective wage formation in Germany and the UK. For example, as regards the *role of workplace representatives,* industry-wide agreements in Germany are challenged by demands for more flexibility: 'the industry-wide collective bargaining system is undergoing a gradual change of function: it is relinquishing much of its normative power and is becoming an instrument of procedural control and management'.[105] This parallels the shift of British trade unions from the role of collective bargaining to monitoring compliance with legal requirements regarding pay. In Germany, the monitoring function is supposed to devolve to works councils. Again, *industrial action* by trade unions in the UK has been subjected to extremely detailed and complex legal regulation since 1980. This parallels what is said to be the juridification of the law of industrial conflict in Germany.

Conclusion

It may be that the general context of industrial relations needs to be distinguished from the specific issue of collective wage formation: 'the comparison of industrial relations in [Germany and the UK] shows more divergence than convergence ... it seems as if institutional developments in the field of industrial relations are more distinct than the developments of pay and working time'.[106] In other words, there are *differences* in institutional developments (relatively stable coverage of collective agreements in Germany vs decline in the UK, stability of German works councils vs decline of plant bargaining/representation in the UK), but *similarities* in pay formation in both countries.

104. Schmidt and Dworschak, p. 14.
105. Dombois, p. 156.
106. Schmidt and Dworschak, p. 6.

On the other hand, other key industrial relations indicators, such as union density and militancy, are *similar* in the UK and Germany, but do not adequately explain *divergences* in pay formation:[107] the extent of variable pay, wage inequalities/dispersion, relatively high increases in non-manual wages, the labour share of productivity increases, and so on.

It might be useful to correlate (i) differences in industrial relations and collective wage formation in each country; (ii) similarities in industrial relations and collective wage formation in each country; (iii) differences in industrial relations with similarities in wage formation in each country; and (iv) similarities in industrial relations with differences in wage formation in each country.

The analytical comparative matrix is as follows:

Two parallels:

Differences in industrial relations – differences in wage formation
Similarities in industrial relations – similarities in wage formation

Two deviations:

Differences in industrial relations – similarities in wage formation
Similarities in industrial relations – differences in wage formation

7. VULNERABILITIES AND STRENGTHS OF THE GERMAN SYSTEM FROM A BRITISH PERSPECTIVE

Vulnerability: Collective wage formation in the 'modern economy'

Union membership in Germany has shifted from industry to the service sector, from blue-collar to white-collar work.[108] However, unionization of white-collar (and female) employees has not reflected the growth of that sector of the labour force.[109] This is not so different from the position in the UK. What is different in Germany is the exceptional importance of the industrial manufacturing sector. This is reflected in both the concentration of union membership and the centrality of wage negotiations in that sector.[110]

The exceptional centrality of the industrial manufacturing sector to the German system of collective wage formation may become a *vulnerability* with the growth of the services sector and competition from industrialising low-wage competitor

107. Cf. 'As long as union membership and industrial action can be seen as indicators of trade unions' strength and working class power, the influence of employees on determining pay should be as strong in Germany as in Britain at best', Schmidt and Dworschak, p. 7.

108. Jacobi *et al.*, p. 203: 'Between 1950 and 1995 the percentage of blue-collar workers in DGB unions fell from 83 to 63, while that of white-collar staff rose from 11 to 29 and of *Beamte* from 6 to 8.'

109. *Ibid.*: 'Nearly half of all blue-collar workers (43.6%) are members of a DGB union, but only 16.5% of *Angestellte* and 30.9% of *Beamte*. Male workers are 36.5% organized in DGB unions, women only 21.8%. Thus membership composition is more in line with the labour force of 1950 than that of today. The very low density rate among younger workers (17%) is particularly worrying.'

110. *Ibid*, p. 216: 'pilot agreements reached in key areas of the engineering industry (usually Baden-Wurttemberg) are the model for the rest of this sector and exert influence on all other industries. This creates a specific German form of "pattern bargaining" with IG Metall as pace-setter: other wage agreements are generally within a narrow margin of the engineering settlement.'

economies in the Third World and in the new EU member states. This may be reflected in the tendency referred to as 'wildcat cooperation': 'the explicit or tacit agreement on lower wage rates and higher working hours than the industry-wide collective agreement stipulates in response to a crisis of competitiveness'.[111]

Instability: European integration

European integration has potential destabilising effects on collective wage formation in Germany. Unlike Britain, in Germany, at the macroeconomic level, there seems to have been an informal but important exchange of signals between the central bank (Bundesbank) and the trade unions over wage and interest rate policy. Economic and Monetary Union has removed this source of relative stability.[112]

European integration initiatives may also threaten the system of collective wage formation at enterprise level, and specific features of the German system. For example, German employers were successful in defeating a Commission proposal on mergers and take-overs, which would have exposed management to hostile take-overs with potentially destabilising effects. Similarly, German trade unions were able to influence the new European Company Statute so as to protect the German system of company supervisory board representation. Both EU initiatives could have undermined structural features underpinning the stability of the system.

Strength: legal framework

Legal qualities of the German system of collective wage formation may be a strength contributing to its ability to survive, and contrast particularly with the British system.

A heavily *juridified system* of collective wage formation can be changed only through changes in the legal framework. The obstacles to legal change promote the stability, even the survival of the juridified system of collective wage formation.[113] It is arguable that the British collective bargaining system's self-concept as 'voluntarist', with 'legal abstentionism' on the part of the state, provided less

111. *Ibid*, p. 221: 'Decentralization is inevitable; the question is whether it will involve the displacement of state and institutional control by market forces, or whether new regulatory structures will emerge that are compatible with the increased autonomy at lower levels of the system.'
112. *Ibid*, p. 230: 'Unlike the employers, the trade unions were slow to recognize the new dynamic of European integration … Two concerns have, however, forced them to take European integration seriously. First, the likely introduction on schedule of the single currency has caused intense discussion of the unions' response to the powerful European Central Bank and the need to develop a European employment strategy. Second, the erosion of national capacities to regulate wages and working conditions has raised the question of compensatory EU regulations.'
113. Jacobi *et al.*, p. 200: 'Up to the 1970s, it was common to criticize the high degree of juridification of Germany industrial relations (Erd, 1978, 1979); but the positive effects have since become more evident. Legalization now appears not so much as a restriction on collective action as a relatively effective institutional buffer against attempts to change the system drastically. It places a brake on aggressive moves by employers when capital has the upper hand; and on major changes by conservative or liberal governments … All these rules create a legal institutionalized framework for the voluntary interaction of the actors at different levels. Individual and collective actions, and their consequences can be predicted by the other side, leading to an iterated fame of mutual interdependence, cooperation and compromise'.

protection when its survival was threatened by economic and political changes in the Thatcherite 1980s.[114]

Labour relations is a central government competence in the German *federal system of government*, which also, however, reserves important competences for the *Länder*. By making changes dependent on more than one tier of government, constitutional federalism promotes survival of the existing system. It is argued, for example, that this constitutional structure means that a radical privatization policy, such as that adopted by the British government in the 1980s and 1990s, could not have been imposed in Germany.[115]

Finally, the existence of a mechanism for the *extension of collective agreements* is at least a potentially valuable resource, though its practical importance is not so evident. The number of extended agreements rose from 534 on 1 January 2001 to 542 on 1 January 2002, covering a total of 0.9 million workers. However, of these, 0.6 million work for employers already covered by collective agreements due to their affiliation to employers' organizations, so only 0.3 million employers are covered by virtue of extension alone.[116] There were only 59 newly extended agreements during 2001, the lowest since records began in 1975.[117]

8. CHALLENGES TO THE GERMAN SYSTEM

8.1 Employers 'outside collective agreements'

In Germany, the problem of employers 'outside collective agreements', if it is a problem, differs depending on whether it is characterized as:

1. *decentralization*: employers not bound by sectoral agreements, but instead by company level agreements;
2. *variation*: employers negotiating pay below the collective agreement;
3. *informal compliance*: employers applying collective agreements although not bound by them;
4. *evasion*: employers covered by collective agreements, but paying wages in violation of the agreement), with or without the consent of the works council or workers concerned;

114. Employers too may support survival of the legal framework of the system of collective wage formation. For example, the National Labor Relations Act (NLRA) in the United States: 'The NLRA remains attractive to employers because it (1) preempts the states from enacting labor laws more favorable to employees; (2) bans the secondary boycott, a union tactic that would exert real pressure on employers to make concessions; (3) diffuses momentum for the legislation of minimum terms and conditions of employment by proffering a means through which employees can (however illusorily) pursue their own preferences; and (4) creates an image of nuanced balancing of employer and employee interests that stifles public sentiment for a stronger collective bargaining law', M.H. Gottesman and M.R. Seidl, 'A Tale of Two Discourses: William Gould's Journey from the Academy to the World of Politics', *Stanford Law Review* 47 (1995).
115. Jacobi *et al.*, p. 228: 'Privatization has been on the political agenda since the 1970s ... Why did the German governments give privatization such low priority? ... the federal constitution gives considerable autonomy to the *Länder*, many of which are controlled by the SPD. In contrast to Britain, it is impossible for central government to impose a general policy of privatization.'
116. The Project *Information Source*, p. 6, gives figures for 1997 of 700,000 employees bound merely by extension of the agreement, about 2.5% of all employees.
117. 'Germany: Collective Bargaining in 2002', *European Industrial Relations Review* 351 (April 2003), pp. 21–5, at p. 22.

5. *avoidance*: no collective agreements at all and employers not informally complying with collectively agreed standards.

1. Decentralization

Decentralization means employers will not be bound by sectoral agreements. This loses some advantages of centralized bargaining, such as lower transaction costs and removing wages from plant level conflict. Bargaining at plant level leads to more days lost in strike action.[118] There are said to be about 5,000 companies which bargain independently about wages and conditions, and usually do not belong to an employers' association. The number has almost doubled since 1990. However, empirical evidence is that in 1995 only eight per cent of establishments and 11% of employees were covered by company agreements, whereas 63% of establishments and 72% of employees were covered by industry-wide collective agreements.[119]

2. Variation

Collective agreements may include opening clauses allowing employers to pay less than the agreed rates. These clauses are of different kinds.[120] It is estimated that 21.7% of sectoral collective agreements have made use of an opening clause.[121]

3. Informal compliance

It seems that legally only union members are eligible to be paid wages negotiated by their union in the collective agreement. However, employers pay all employees, regardless of union membership, by way of a 'reference clause' (*Bezugnahme-klausel*) included in individual employment contracts.[122] Some 15% (western Germany and 24% (eastern Germany) of employees work at firms that are not bound by collective bargaining, but use the terms of collective agreements in any case. This may be because the employer is bound by the individual employment contract to apply the terms of the collective agreement. This is less of a constraint than where the employer is bound to the collective agreement by virtue of membership of the employer's organization.[123]

---

118. C. Schnabel, 'The Reform of Collective Bargaining in Germany: Corporatist Stability vs. Firm Flexibility', in R. Hoffmann *et al.*, *The German Model of Industrial Relations between Adaptation and Erosion*, Dusseldorf (1998), pp. 83–95, at p. 87 (hereafter, Schnabel): 'Relatively centralized collective bargaining between encompassing trade unions and employers' associations can lower transaction costs and internalize external effects of wage-setting. Through negotiations at the branch level the relationship between management and works councils usually is only marginally affected by conflicts about wages and working conditions. The centralization of collective bargaining thus is a peace-keeping element, which improves social partnership at the plant level.'
119. *Ibid.*, p. 88. For similar figures, see Project: *Information Source*, p. 4: 'The share of employees working in companies covered by company agreements is almost stable in the west of Germany (about 8%). It is higher in the area of the former GDR, but decreasing there from 12% (1998) to 10% (2000).'
120. *Ibid.*, pp. 90–93. For a longer and more varied list of the types of opening clauses currently in force, see 'Germany: Collective Bargaining in 2002', *European Industrial Relations Review* 351 (April 2003), pp. 21–25, at pp. 23–24.
121. T. Schulten, 'Variable Pay in Germany', EIRO (April 2001), p. 6 (hereafter, Schulten): http://www.eiro.eurofound.ie/2001/04/word/de0011294s.doc.
122. Project: *Information Source*, p. 5.
123. Project: *Information Source*, pp. 5–6.

4. Evasion

The payment of wages in violation of a binding collective agreement is said to be a growing problem, to the extent that only 60% of east German enterprises (with about 83% of all employees) pay the contractually prescribed rates.[124]

5. Avoidance

It is stated that the proportion of employees whose terms of employment are regulated by collective agreements (sectoral and company level) in Germany (west) has fallen from about 82% in 1995 to 70% (2000).[125] Another estimate by the German Economics and Labour Ministry is that out of a total of 27.8 million employees subject to social insurance, around 25 million are covered by a collective agreement at either sectoral or company level. This equates to a coverage rate of 90%.[126] The discrepancy may be due to the inclusion in the Ministry's figures of employees whose terms of employment reflect the collective agreement, though their employers are not formally bound by it.[127]

Conclusion

There appear to be a number of problems. They differ in character, but may be linked so that their solutions operate together in practice.

The challenges presented by *decentralization* and *variation* are structural. Their solution depends, first, on policy decisions about the nature of the industrial relations and collective wage formation systems. How much decentralization and how much

124. Jacobi *et al.*, p. 220: 'One problem of growing importance, formerly almost unknown in the west, is that an increasing number of companies (particularly small and medium sized enterprises and unorganized firms) do not pay the collectively agreed wages ... Frequently underpayment reflects an attempt to save jobs and involves not only a tacit agreement between management and the works council, but also with the union. Thus collective agreements no longer "take wages out of competition"'. As Schnabel puts it, p. 86: 'Therefore, many small and medium-sized companies pay less than the collectively agreed wage, mostly through informal agreement with their workforce ... In the case of companies which are bound by collective agreements this is a violation of the law, but the collective bargaining parties tacitly put up with it.'
125. Project: *Information Source*, p. 3.
126. 'Germany: Collective Bargaining in 2002', *European Industrial Relations Review* 351 (April 2003), pp. 21–25. at p. 21. This figure is reported alongside other data for 2001 which state that in the west 63.1% of employees work in establishments covered by a sectoral accord and 7.6% in establishments covered by a company accord. This compares with figures of 62.8% and 7.3% respectively in 2000. In the east, 44.4% of employees worked in establishments covered by a sectoral agreement and 11.8% in establishments covered by a company-level agreement. This compares with figures of 45.5% and 9.9%, respectively, in 2000. Overall, 70.7% of employees in the west and 56.2% of employees in the east work in establishments that are covered by a collective agreement. The figure for the whole of Germany is estimated at around 69%. These figures are slightly higher than the overall figures for 2000 (an overall rate of 68% in the whole of Germany, 70.1% in the west and 55.4% in the east).
127. Overall, the Ministry calculates that in 2001, for the whole of Germany, 69% of employees worked in establishments covered by a collective agreement, slightly higher than the overall rate in 2000 of 68% for the whole of Germany. However, the Ministry also calculates that another 15% of establishments in the west and 24% of establishments in the east that are not covered by collective agreements orient their terms and conditions to the relevant collective agreement. On this basis it is estimated that collective agreements set the terms and conditions one way or another for some 85% of all employees in Germany. The figure for 2000 was 84%.

variation is desired? Thereafter, technical solutions, including legal techniques, may be used to achieve the desired policy result.

The challenges presented by *informal compliance* and *avoidance* are also structural, but could be resolved by extension of collective agreements.

The challenge presented by *evasion* is less structural to the industrial relations system, and more a problem for legal enforcement.

However, policy choices with respect to decentralization and variation (for example, severe restraints or relaxation) may also go towards resolving challenges of evasion and avoidance. Evasion and avoidance may be more difficult if effective legal restraints are adopted to prevent decentralization and variation. Similarly, evasion and avoidance may be less needed if relaxation allows for decentralization and variation.

8.2 Wage flexibility: problem or solution?

What is flexibility?

Whether more flexibility (more wage flexibility, more regulatory flexibility) is needed today than 20 years ago is a question exhaustively discussed in the professional and academic literature of economics and industrial relations, as well as law. In Britain, the debate was summed up in the title of a book on the subject, *Farewell to Flexibility?*[128] In short, 'flexibility' is a euphemism for unfettered management decision-making. The question of whether more flexibility is needed is basically that of whether more unfettered management decision-making is needed.

The answer to this question can be economic, political and/or legal. In terms of *economic* efficiency, it may be that managements in general, in specific industries, in companies or establishments are – or are not – best left unfettered in their decision-making. If their flexibility should be limited to maximize efficiency, then the question is 'How?' In *political* terms, the question is mainly one of democratic decision-making in the enterprise and workplace (leaving aside the civil liberties of individual employees and the interests of shareholders or other lenders of capital). In *legal* terms, to some extent the answer is provided by EU directives which require information and consultation of worker representatives in certain situations (transfers of undertakings,[129] collective dismissals[130]), with respect to certain aspects of work (health and safety[131]) and, with the implementation of the new EC framework Directive 2002/14 on information and consultation,[132] general issues affecting the workforce.

128. A. Pollert (ed.), *Farewell to Flexibility?* (Oxford: Blackwell, 1991).

129. Council Directive 77/187 of 14 February 1977 on the approximation of the laws of the member states relating to the safeguarding of employees' rights in the event of transfers of undertakings, businesses or parts of businesses, OJ L 61/26, as amended by Directive 98/50/EC of 29 June 1998, OJ L 201/88 of 17.7.98. Consolidated in Directive 2001/23 of 12 March 2001, OJ L/82/16.

130. Council Directive 75/129 of 17 February 1975 on the approximation of the laws of the member states relating to collective dismissals, OJ L 48/29, as amended by Directive 92/56 of 24 June 1992, OJ L 245/92. Consolidated in Council Directive 98/59/EC of 20 July 1998, OJ L 225/16.

131. Council Directive 89/391/EEC of 12 June 1989 on the introduction of measures to encourage improvements in the safety and health of workers at work. OJ L 183/1.

132. Council Directive No. 2002/14 establishing a framework for informing and consulting employees in the European Community. OJ 2002, L80/29.

Flexibility and wages

The debate on flexibility in Britain is less concerned with wages, not to mention collective wage formation through sectoral agreements.[133] Rather it is seen as a problem of work organization, qualifications and skills, technology, management techniques, and so on. Flexibility retains its primary significance: should management have unilateral decision-making power? From a British perspective, therefore, it seems that flexibility relates to different areas in Germany and Britain: while in Germany flexibility is demanded in relation to wages – and that is why sectoral agreements are relevant – in Britain wage flexibility is less of an issue and sectoral agreements are absent: flexibility is said to be needed, but in other spheres.

Flexibility and sectoral agreements

In the German context, the question of whether more flexibility is needed should be distinguished from the question of whether sectoral collective agreements are an obstacle to flexibility. If the answer to the first question is negative, then sectoral agreements, even if inflexible, are irrelevant. If the answer is positive, however, the question still has to be addressed: Are sectoral agreements an obstacle to more flexibility? If sectoral agreements are *not* an obstacle to flexibility (as may be evident through opening clauses, avoidance or even evasion), then they are irrelevant.

However, *if* more flexibility is needed, and sectoral agreements *are* an obstacle to flexibility, how can the latter be achieved? In the German context, the question as regards sectoral wage agreements is one of *constraints* on (wage) flexibility imposed specifically at *sectoral* level. This question is meaningless in the British context. By explaining why, however, some light may be cast on the German situation.

A British perspective

In Britain, sectoral agreements were prevalent at different stages of industrial relations history, beginning with the end of the nineteenth century. Their influence has been determined more by shifts in the balance of industrial power. When unemployment was low and unions were strong (1950s–1960s), employers promoted sectoral agreements to stabilize wage rates, but wage drift meant sectoral agreements were often exceeded in workplace bargaining. When unemployment was high and employers were strong (1920s–1930s), unions promoted sectoral agreements to prevent undercutting, but employers sought to eliminate them or were frequently able to evade them.

At present, unemployment (said to be low in comparison with other countries, but high in comparison with earlier periods) and union weakness contribute to a situation in which sectoral agreements have mostly disappeared from the private sector and are under great pressure in the public sector. As already mentioned, flexibility is still an issue in Britain, but sectoral wage agreements are not seen as the problem.[134]

133. This is largely because wage flexibility has already been achieved through the demolition of collective bargaining arrangements, almost completely at centralized level and largely at enterprise and workplace level.

Flexibility and collectivism

If the objective of flexibility is to maximize unilateral management decision-making, and this is accepted from the point of view of economics, politics and law, then it is a question of developing the appropriate industrial relations structure and legal framework.

Flexibility may be constrained in different ways. There may be collectively negotiated flexibility or individually negotiated flexibility within a collective framework, at sectoral or at some other collective level. It may seem that a collective dimension limits flexibility. Traditionally, the preference for sectoral collective agreements in Germany has been justified by the need to protect wages against lower-cost competition. This reflects the fundamental axiom of labour law that individual flexibility is equivalent to unilateral management decision-making.

Yet, as already indicated, there are powerful pressures limiting flexibility and imposing standardization of wages and conditions even within systems of strongly individualized wage formation, as in Britain.

'Traditional' political vs 'modern' economic arguments

Protection against lower-cost competition is invoked as a political/social justification for sectoral collective agreements. In Britain, this justification has been subordinated to arguments of 'economic efficiency' based on labour markets. Wage levels are judged in terms of what is necessary to attract and retain workers, not 'fair' wages or other labour standards. In the British context, reducing lower-cost competition as regards labour is an argument *against* sectoral collective agreements. The economic objective is not to protect wages against lower-cost competition, but to *promote* wage competition. This is seen as desirable to combat 'rigidity in pay structures' and increase 'wage flexibility'. 'Economic efficiency' does not exclude wage competition – on the contrary, it supports it.

Of course, there have traditionally been *political* arguments in Britain for protection against low pay. The *economic* arguments for protecting wages against lower-cost competition have mainly concerned the fact that wage competition is inefficient, not the protection of wages. Instead, the argument is, for example, that wage competition is economically inefficient because it encourages employers to compete through low labour costs rather than more efficient capital investment, new technology or improved work organization, or that in tight labour markets, wage competition can lead to an inflationary pay spiral.

In sum, in Britain protecting wages through sectoral agreements is a 'traditional' *political* argument, sometimes based on 'modern' economics. 'New' Labour (and other 'conservatives') oppose sectoral agreements, preferring 'modern' political arguments based on 'traditional' economics.[135]

---

134. However, even now there are continuing efforts by the New Labour government to eliminate what remains of centralized bargaining in parts of the public sector. For a detailed argument for the re-instatement of sectoral agreements in Britain, see K. Ewing (ed.), *Working Life: A New Perspective on Labour Law* (Lawrence and Wishart/The Institute of Employment Rights, London, 1996), Chapter 3 (hereafter, Ewing).

135. Again, for traditional arguments for protecting wages through sectoral agreements see Ewing (ed.), Chapter 3.

9. RESPONSES TO THE CHALLENGE

9.1 State intervention

Contemporary conventional wisdom in Britain views structural labour market reforms as necessary to compete in a global economy (vocational training, information technology and other skills, mobility, flexibility, and so on). State intervention is acceptable to achieve these structural reforms. The collective bargaining system is perceived as marginal, if not antipathetic insofar as it is an obstacle to these structural reforms. However, where the collective bargaining system cannot be circumvented, or where it could even contribute to achieving these structural reforms, state intervention might be envisaged. Again, the objective is not to stabilize the collective bargaining system *per se*, but only insofar as this promotes the desired structural reforms.

The implications for Germany are that if the collective bargaining system can be used to achieve structural reforms, it can be so exploited. One comparison of collective wage formation in Germany (sectoral agreements) and Britain ('benchmarking') points to the potential of the sectoral agreement system in Germany and argues that the British system requires state intervention to achieve policy goals:[136]

> the benchmarking system is not even capable of changing norms purposefully. Generally speaking, when compared with the sectoral agreement model, the benchmarking system lacks the capability of control ... neither employees and trade unions nor employers can articulate and [enforce] their collective class interests ... the British benchmarking system ... does not allow for consciously controlled changes without state intervention.

A concrete example is given:[137]

> In order to avoid problems of social cohesion, state intervention seems to be more necessary under the conditions of the British than ... of the German system. Thus, the state is a necessary co-actor of this system in order to limit social inequality via the national Minimum Wage legislation. The European working time directive will probably eliminate another weak point of the British system.

In the British context, intervention to promote structural reforms through the legal system could have the (unintended?) effect of further weakening the marginalized collective bargaining system. It could also expose the legal system to unsustainable burdens and costs (for example, the high transaction costs of individualized legal claims and dispute resolution mechanisms; the risks of administrative and bureaucratic failure) so that state intervention was ineffective.

In contrast, if the German collective bargaining system was exploited as an instrument for achieving structural reforms, it could operate to stabilize the system. On the other hand, that system runs the risk of alienating the membership (of both trade unions and employers' organizations) if it is adversely affected by the structural reforms their organizations are implementing.

136. Schmidt and Dworschak, p. 14.
137. Schmidt and Dworschak, p. 15.

The weakened British system of collective bargaining has much less to lose. This partially explains the 'partnership' strategy of the Trades Union Congress (TUC), which aims to persuade the government – so far unsuccessfully – that the collective bargaining system can function to achieve structural reforms, and thereby help promote collective bargaining.

9.2 A statutory minimum wage

In Britain, minimum rates of pay in specific low-wage sectors were established on a tripartite basis in Wages Councils from 1909 until they were abolished in 1993. The tripartite structure was intended to provide a platform for the development of collective bargaining in sectors where it was absent. However, wages councils did not succeed in establishing collective bargaining in those sectors and some argue that they were an obstacle. Other methods of minimum wage protection included procedures for the extension of collective agreements to enterprises where wages fell below the collectively agreed standard. These gave trade unions a role in seeking the extension of their collective agreements.

It is said of the British National Minimum Wage Act 1998 (NMWA) that '[i]ts most significant drawback [with regard to enforcement] is the lack of a formal role accorded to trade unions ... It remains problematic ... to consider the NMWA as representative of regulation in labour law given this exclusion of trade unions.'[138]

A statutory minimum wage policy can have different objectives: reducing poverty, relieving pressure on the social security system, preventing low wage competition among employers, and so on.

Assuming the concern in Germany is the diminishing use of collective agreements, the objective of the statutory minimum wage is presumed to be to reinforce the collective bargaining system. If so, the British experience suggests two specific factors in considering whether it is appropriate. First, are collective agreements relevant in establishing the minimum wage standard? Second, are trade unions engaged in the enforcement process?

9.3 Equal pay for men and women

Pay for men and women workers in Britain

Full-time women workers in Britain earn an average 81% of the gross wages earned by full-time male workers. Part-time women workers (about half of all women workers) earn about 60% of the hourly rate earned by full-time men. In the case of full-time workers, women's earnings have increased substantially relative to men over the last quarter century. The position of part-time women workers has barely changed. In 1990 British women had the lowest wages, relative to men, of all women in the European Community. By 1995, there had been only a small improvement in

138. Paul Skidmore, 'Thinking about Enforcement: The Minimum Wage in Practice', in H. Collins *et al.*, (eds), *Legal Regulation of the Employment Relation* (Kluwer, 2000), pp. 346–69, at p. 350 (hereafter Collins *et al.*). Skidmore concludes: 'It would be contrary to the tradition of over a century of labour law to seek to develop it further without them ... To incorporate trade unions must be one of the key challenges for regulatory theory in its future application to labour law' (p. 369).

this relative position, with British women still occupying the lower half of the EU scale in terms of the gender pay gap.[139]

The role of individual equal pay law

One assessment of the role of individual equal pay law is as follows:[140]

> What is of particular interest about the relative position of British women is the apparent lack of relationship between equal pay/equal value legislation and the size of the gender pay gap. The Equal Pay Act 1970 has entitled women in Britain to equal pay for equal work since 1975, and to 'equal pay for work of equal value' since 1984. The Act has generated a large volume of litigation. By contrast, the European Commission reported, in 1994, that there had been no equal pay litigation in Luxembourg, France or Italy or Greece; that '[i]n other Member States there has been little litigation in which different jobs have actually been compared' ... Of those Member States whose legislation was singled out for favourable comment by the European Commission in its *Memorandum on Equal Pay* [1994] – three (Ireland, the Netherlands and the United Kingdom) are in the bottom half of Member States in terms of women's relative wages, while France and (the former West) Germany just scrape into the top half.

The author concludes:[141]

> It appears that there is no direct relationship between the existence of comprehensive equal pay legislation and that of a relatively small gender-pay gap. The reasons for this are not difficult to fathom in the UK context ... [a number of factors are indicated] ... Finally, the model adopted by the [Equal Pay] Act is an individual one, potential applicants having to discover the existence of pay disparities, to select comparators who may or may not be regarded as appropriate by an employment tribunal, and to run the risk of victimization.

Alternatives to individualized equal pay law

The approach advocated by the British Equal Opportunities Commission[142] is the imposition on employers of an obligation to monitor the pay of men and women and to eradicate sex-based discrimination. Having set out this 'currently fashionable approach to equal pay reform', McColgan states:[143]

> It is perhaps time for those concerned with the gender-wage gap to consider the possibilities associated with a movement towards increased centralization

139. Aileen McColgan, 'Regulating Pay Discrimination', in Collins *et al.*, pp. 203–23, at pp. 203–8.
140. McColgan, p. 209.
141. McColgan, p. 210.
142. And, in 1995, by the European Parliament in its Resolution on the memorandum on equal pay for work of equal value, [1996] OJ C065/43.
143. McColgan, pp. 222–3.

> of pay determination ... some of those energies currently directed towards amendment of the existing equal pay and equal opportunities legislation could, perhaps, more effectively be directed towards extending union recognition and, in particular, the coverage of collective agreements.

The role of collective bargaining should not be ignored. One Anglo-German comparative study refers to the role of trade unions as follows:[144]

> workers in the organized sector have much lower pay dispersion than those in the unorganized sector ... unions narrow the wage differentials between women and men, blacks and whites, those with health problems and those without, and between manual and non-manual workers.

Individual equal pay complaints to tribunals, if successful, could threaten to disrupt established grading scales and differentials in pay structures. This can stimulate trade unions and employers to undertake negotiations to eliminate sex discrimination in pay rates. The threat of such individual equal pay claims was the driving force behind a major exercise involving over one million local authority workers in the United Kingdom.[145]

9.4 Variable pay

In Britain, the use of variable pay systems was encouraged by Conservative governments from the early 1980s to motivate individual employees. However, as one text states:[146]

> a negative feature of both performance-related and profit-related pay is the degree of wage insecurity which they may induce. Linking all or part of pay to individual performance is nothing new, as the long tradition of piece-work contracting in many industries indicates. Where the measurement of performance is not straightforward, however, the possibility of abuse of such payment systems arises. In the past this has been addressed by collective bargaining and through shop-floor custom and practice, as well as by legislation in some exceptional instances. Few of these regulatory constraints now remain in place.

The power of the employer to withhold payment of wages was traditionally governed by the Truck Act 1896 which aimed to prevent employers withholding wages as a form of enforcing discipline at work. This was replaced by the Wages Act 1986 which provided a statutory remedy of compensation for 'a deduction from wages'. This is said to have:

144. Schmidt and Dworschak, pp. 14–15. See, generally, P. Almond and J. Rubery, 'The Gender Impact of Recent European Trends in Wage Determination' *Work, Employment and Society* 4 (1998), pp. 675–93.
145. See B. Bercusson, *European Labour Law* (London: Butterworths, 1996), Chapter 14: 'EC Equality Law in Context: Collective Bargaining', pp. 199–203.
146. S. Deakin and G. Morris, *Labour Law*, 3rd ed. (London: Butterworths, 2001), p. 303.

> increasingly become the standard method by which employees claim any money owing from the employer, thereby avoiding claims in the ordinary courts for breach of contract. This result has been achieved by a combination of the broad definition of wages contained in the statute and the wide definition given to the concept of a 'deduction' from wages by the courts.[147]

The key was the removal of the concept of the unfairness of a deduction related to disciplinary matters:[148]

> Thus, as a practical matter, most workers are likely to use this jurisdiction in any dispute with an employer over wages, whether it be related to unauthorized disciplinary penalties, failure to pay a sum owed, or a deliberate unilateral reduction in pay by the employer.

In sum, variable pay opens the door to a multitude of disputes over pay. In the absence of collectively agreed dispute resolution mechanisms, the burden falls on the state system of employment tribunals.

10. COLLECTIVE WAGE FORMATION AND WAGE FLEXIBILITY

Flexibility downwards

The basic question is whether flexibility is downwards (reduction of labour standards, perhaps due to wage competition), or also upwards (improvement of labour standards, perhaps due to tight labour markets).

In the case of downward flexibility, safeguards are needed against substandard conditions. If flexibility is upwards, there may be issues of competitiveness or discrimination.

Insofar as it engages existing agreements, achieving flexibility should be firstly in the hands of the parties to the agreement, not subject to state intervention. There should be minimum procedural and substantive rules. *Procedural* rules would require negotiation over flexibility, with perhaps arbitration if no agreement is reached. *Substantive* rules would require minimum labour standards as safeguards for wages (temporary not permanent reduction), hours of work (minimum and/or maximum hours), holidays (minimum paid annual leave), and so on.

For example, one proposal for re-establishing sectoral agreements in Britain recognizes the importance of dealing with the flexibility issue.[149] It proposes that sectoral agreements impose a non-derogatable minimum – though improved benefits would be allowed – on conditions of non-discrimination and that improvement overall should not leave some workers below the prescribed minimum. If so, a procedure should be allowed for claims to raise those left behind. As to variations in sectoral agreements leading to less favourable terms, including those negotiated at local level, this was acceptable provided certain safeguards were met. In particular, that they be permitted only by a collective agreement with an independent trade union in accordance with a prescribed procedure.

147. H. Collins, K.D. Ewing and A. McColgan, *Labour Law: Text and Materials* (Oxford: Hart, 2001), p. 79.
148. *Ibid.*
149. Ewing (ed.), Chapter 3, pp. 78–79.

Flexibility upwards

The British lesson is summarized in one comparative study as follows:[150]

> Generally speaking, when compared with the sectoral agreement model, the [British] benchmarking system lacks the capability of control ... As a result, in a situation of weak union power, low wage increases are more likely to occur in Germany than in Britain. In return, German trade unions can achieve a 'solidarity wage policy. [...]
>
> [I]f the erosion of the sectoral agreement model in Germany will continue, it seems improbable that this would lead to a determination of pay and conditions by the market but by mechanisms similar to the described benchmarking system. 'Mimetic wages' and uncontrolled isomorphism would most likely be a consequence, and growing incomes inequality between employees could be another. When assisted by the state, both inequality and pay rises could be restricted, but the latter seems unlikely in the foreseeable future. In particular for employers, a dismantling of the sectoral agreement model therefore would hold serious risks.

11. COLLECTIVE WAGE FORMATION AND SOCIETAL CONTROL

The conclusion from the British experience appears to be that abandoning collective wage formation threatens a degree of loss of control over the process and outcomes of wage formation. This can lead to sub-standard wages, with consequent inequality, poverty and their social discontents, variable pay with considerable scope for individual disputes, consequent discontent and burdens on the state's dispute resolution machinery, and, last but not least, a long-term loss of the socialized discipline of solidarity which collective organization can exert in the pursuit of societal goals.

150. Schmidt and Dworschak, pp. 14–16.

APPENDIX

Table A1: Trade Union Membership and Density

Year	CO Members (UK, '000)	CO Density (GB)	LFS Members (GB, '000)	LFS Density (GB)
1965	10 181	40.5	–	–
1966	10 259	40.5	–	–
1967	10 188	41.0	–	–
1968	10 191	41.4	–	–
1969	10 470	42.6	–	–
1970	11 187	45.8	–	–
1971	11 135	46.3	–	–
1972	11 359	47.2	–	–
1973	11 456	46.4	–	–
1974	11 764	47.4	–	–
1975	12 026	49.1	–	–
1976	12 386	50.6	–	–
1977	12 846	52.3	–	–
1978	13 112	53.0	–	–
1979	13 289	52.9	–	–
1980	12 947	51.9	–	–
1981	12 106	51.0	–	–
1982	11 593	49.9	–	–
1983	11 236	49.2	–	–
1984	10 994	47.7	–	–
1985	10 821	46.0	–	–
1986	10 539	45.3	–	–
1987	10 475	44.1	–	–
1988	10 376	43.2	–	–
1989	10 158	41.2	8 939	39.0
1990	9 947	40.0	8 835	38.1
1991	9 585	39.1	8 602	37.5
1992	9 048	37.8	7 956	35.8
1993	8 700	36.7	7 767	35.1
1994	8 278	34.8	7 530	33.6
1995	8 089	33.6	7 309	32.1
1996	7 935	32.4	7 244	31.2
1997	7 795	31.3	7 154	30.2
1998	7 807	30.8	7 155	29.6
1999	7 898	30.4	7 277	29.5
2000	7 779	29.4	7 351	29.4
2001	7 751	29.0	7 295	28.8
2002	–	–	7 302	28.7
2003	–	–	7 353	28.9

Certification Officer figures are for *all members of United Kingdom* unions. Union density estimates are for *employees in Great Britain*. These are based upon the approach taken by R. Bailey and J. Kelly, 'An Index Measure of British Trade Union Density', *British Journal of Industrial Relations* 28 (1990), which was to subtract 10% of the total to allow for union members who were not employees or who were outside Great Britain. The Bailey and Kelly estimates are used for 1967 to 1987. The approach is then continued to estimate union density for subsequent years, using Labour Force Survey data for total employees for the spring of the year in question.

Labour Force Survey figures and estimates of union density for employees in Great Britain are from 'Trends in Union Membership; Labour Force Survey; Great Britain, 1989–2003', available at http://www.dti.gov.uk/er/emar/trade_data03.pdf

Table 2A: Strikes: Number and Days Lost

Year	Number of strikes	Days lost ('000)	Year	Number of strikes	Days lost ('000)
1960	2 832	3 024	1981	1 344	4 266
1961	2 686	3 046	1982	1 538	5 313
1962	2 449	5 798	1983	1 364	3 754
1963	2 068	1 755	1984	1 221	27 135
1964	2 524	2 277	1985	903	6 402
1965	2 354	2 925	1986	1 074	1 920
1966	1 937	2 398	1987	1 016	3 546
1967	2 116	2 787	1988	781	3 702
1968	2 378	4 690	1989	701	4 128
1969	3 116	6 846	1990	630	1 903
1970	3 906	10 980	1991	369	761
1971	2 228	13 551	1992	253	528
1972	2 497	23 909	1993	211	649
1973	2 873	7 197	1994	205	278
1974	2 922	14 750	1995	235	415
1975	2 282	6 012	1996	244	1 303
1976	2 016	3 284	1997	216	235
1977	2 737	10 142	1998	166	282
1978	2 498	9 405	1999	205	242
1979	2 125	29 474	2000	212	499
1980	1 348	11 964	2001	194	525
			2002	146	1 323
Averages					
1960–69	2 446	3 555			
1970–79	2 608	12 870			
1980–89	1 129	7 213			
1990–97	295	759			
1998–2002	185	574			

Sources: Figures for 1960–1976 are taken from C. Smith, R. Clifton, P. Makeham, S. Creigh and R. Burn, *Strikes in Britain* (HMSO, 1978): Table 1; for 1977–1995, from K. Sweeney and J. Davies, 'Labour Disputes in 1995' *Labour Market Trends* (June 1996), p. 272; for 1996–2002, from J. Monger, 'Labour Disputes in 2002' *Labour Market Trends* (June 2003), p. 285.

The 'number of strikes' for 1960–76 refers to strikes beginning in the given year. All other figures refer to strikes in progress in the year.

4. The Netherlands: In the tradition of intersectoral pacts

Antoine T.J.M. Jacobs

1. INTRODUCTION

The current system of industrial relations in the Netherlands – the buzz-word for it is the '*poldermodel*' – is characterized by a great readiness on the part of all participants to engage in bargaining, using a mixture of formal and informal processes, and by an atmosphere of harmony.

The Dutch system of collective wage formation went through a deep crisis as early as the 1970s. After the Second World War it was a very centralized system with strong interference from the public authorities and not – as in Germany – characterized by the principle of '*Tarifautonomie*' (collective bargaining autonomy).

After a crisis that lasted about 20 years (1965–1983) the Netherlands, like Germany, adopted a system of collective wage formation based on the principle of 'Tarifautonomie' with only indirect influence from government.

The current system is a mixture of centralized and decentralized arrangements, sometimes with more emphasis on centralized activity and at other times on decentralized activity.

In section 2 we describe the Dutch system of industrial relations and collective wage formation, followed by the legal framework (section 3) and the current challenges (sections 4 and 5) facing the Dutch system of wage determination. We shall then examine the differences and similarities between the Dutch and the German systems of collective wage formation (section 6), and finally the strengths and weaknesses, as well as the decentralization and growing flexibility, of the German system will be considered from a Dutch perspective (sections 7 and 8).

2. THE DUTCH SYSTEM OF INDUSTRIAL RELATIONS AND COLLECTIVE WAGE FORMATION

2.1 The social partners

Employers

In the Netherlands there are employers' associations in every sector of the economy. Almost all of them are affiliated to one of the three umbrella organizations:

- VNO-NCW, representing large and medium-sized enterprises in industry, commerce, banking, insurance and other services;
- MKB-Nederland, medium-sized and small enterprises (not agriculture);
- LTO-Nederland, representing agricultural enterprises.

The employers' organization rate is high – almost 100% among large enterprises.

Trade unions

There are hundreds of trade unions in the Netherlands, with memberships varying from a few hundred to close to 500,000.

The most important Dutch trade unions are at present grouped together in three rival confederations:

- FNV, the result of a merger (1982) of the Catholic Trade Union Confederation and the Social Democratic Trade Union Confederation; now the most powerful confederation in the Netherlands (about 1.2 million members);
- CNV, comprising mostly Protestant unions (300,000 members);
- Unie MHP, a confederation of white-collar unions founded in 1972 (around 175,000 members).

In addition to those affiliated to these confederations there are a number of independent unions for specific occupational categories – such as KLM cabin crew – and a number of radical left-wing and autonomous unions. Sometimes they are influential in an important sector of the economy, such as the ports, the railways or air travel.

The Netherlands is one of the least unionized countries in the EU: only some 22% of Dutch employees belong to unions affiliated to FNV, CNV or Unie MHP, with a further two per cent affiliated to other unions. Rates of unionization vary considerably from one sector to another.

In the Netherlands there is no specific law on trade unions and employers' associations, unlike in many other countries. Both enjoy a general freedom of association which is recognized and guaranteed in Article 8 of the Dutch Constitution. Both are subject to the law governing associations elaborated in Book 2 of the Dutch Civil Code which applies to all associations. Trade union rights are almost entirely based on voluntary arrangements, with only a few aspects regulated by statute or quasi-statute (see section 3).

2.2 Works councils

In the Netherlands there is not a single strand of workers' representation, as in the UK and Scandinavia, but, like most continental European countries, two: trade unions and works councils.

Legally, all Dutch enterprises with more than 50 employees must have a works council. Its composition, powers and facilities are regulated in detail (see section 3.3). This law reflects the Dutch love of consensus, making managerial decisions subject to extensive information and consultation of workers' representatives.

2.3 The pattern of collective wage formation

Dutch industrial relations are characterized by continuous negotiation between the social partners. Most collective bargaining is done at sectoral level: these industry-wide agreements cover some 70% of all employees. Around 10% of workers are covered by collective agreements concluded at enterprise level: Dutch trade unions sign such company-level, in-house collective agreements with companies which are not members of an employers' federation. Although the absolute number of valid company-level agreements is relatively high (900 in contrast to 300 sectoral agreements) they are still of comparatively modest significance in macroeconomic terms. However, their importance can vary considerably from sector to sector: in industries dominated by a small number of companies – such as the mineral oil industry, the chemical industry and banking – in-house collective agreements are the most important type of agreement.

In the Netherlands, collective bargaining is done at either industry or enterprise level. In the past it was seldom done at both levels, as was the case, for instance, in Italy and France.

It should be noted, however, that supplementary bargaining at enterprise level is gaining ground, although this trend has more to do with works councils than with the unions. From a strictly formal point of view, the works council does not 'bargain' with the employer, but only gives its 'advice' or 'consent'.

One of the most fertile areas of bargaining is the organization of working time, as both the Working Time Act and collective agreements contain numerous opening clauses which give works councils the legal possibility to make arrangements with the employer on working time, deviating from the standards set in the Act and in the collective agreement.

As a result, works councils are increasingly involved in bargaining: on the one hand, they are often required to give flesh to vague provisions in collective agreements; on the other hand, in enterprises which are not covered by collective agreements dealings with works councils may lead to quasi collective agreements. The former practice is accepted by the unions, the latter not.

Collective bargaining is a regular event every year or two years in the 80% of the Dutch labour market that is covered by collective agreements.

Collective agreements traditionally cover the working conditions of blue-collar employees; since the Second World War they have covered white-collar employees as well. Workers with incomes above 75,000 euros are normally outside the collective bargaining system. A number of collective agreements have also regulated some of the working conditions of higher-paid employees, but not pay.

The hard core of the legal framework concerning collective wage formation in the Netherlands is to be found in the Act on collective agreements of 1927, which provides for a legalized system of collective agreements, as well as in the Act on the extension of the provisions of collective agreements of 1937 which ensures wide coverage for this system (see section 3.2). In addition, the Wage Determination Act, notably in Article 10, recognizes freedom of collective bargaining, which is not open to government interference, unless there are urgent external reasons (see section 2.5). Finally, mention should be made of Article 27 (3) of the Works Councils Act which guarantees the priority of the collective agreement over agreements between employers and works councils, which is comparable with §§ 77(3) and 87(1) of the German Works Constitution Act (see section 3.3).

2.4 Strikes

In the Netherlands a climate of industrial peace predominates. Compared to other countries, Dutch employees and their unions rarely resort to strike action. The number of working days lost over the years because of strikes is one of the lowest in the Western world (see section 6). Major or long-term disputes are rare.

In large parts of the Dutch economy, especially in private manufacturing and retail, the trade unions are too weak to organize strikes, venturing to take such action only if the employers make extreme demands. In a number of other sectors, however – such as construction, railways, ports, air travel, hospitals, and lower level civil servants – the Dutch unions are still strong enough to organize strikes more easily. Such strikes can seriously disrupt the country.

The industrial disputes that take place nowadays are generally of short duration. They serve to indicate the precise state of socio-economic and political power relations, which is continually changing. Neither of the social partners attempt to 'conquer' the other. When the various parties have established the 'lie of the land' a compromise is reached and life continues until there are further doubts about the current constellation of power relations.

Notwithstanding the low incidence of collective conflicts, the Netherlands has experienced most types of industrial action. The most common form nowadays is a selective strike disrupting (parts of) a sector or enterprise, organized by the major unions in order to achieve an improvement or to prevent a deterioration in working conditions when collective agreements come up for renewal. Sometimes strikes have been called in protest against particular government interventions in social affairs. Thus, most strikes arise from genuine disputes of interest. Strikes originating in disputes of rights are rare, as unions and employers prefer the judicial means of resolving them. Strikes are sometimes accompanied by picketing, but this is much less violent than has been known in the UK, for instance. Over the last fifty years employers have never resorted to lock outs

There is no statutory regulation of strikes in the Netherlands. All strike law is produced by the courts (see section 3.4).

Arbitration is seldom used as a means of resolving industrial disputes. Mediation and conciliation may occur on an occasional basis if industrial conflict lasts for a long time. However, all this takes place on a strictly voluntary basis. There is no law in this field except in relation to the civil service (see section 3.4).

2.5 The system of intersectoral regulation and concertation

After 1945 the Netherlands had a stringent system of centralized wage bargaining under strict government control on the basis of the Extraordinary Decree on Labour Relations. After around 1960 this system was gradually relaxed to leave increasing room for free collective bargaining, but initially the time was not ripe for complete freedom. The wage provisions of the Extraordinary Decree on Labour Relations were replaced by the Wage Determination Act of 1970 which established free collective bargaining as a principle but gave the government ample powers to intervene. During the 1970s and 1980s all government interventions in collective bargaining were highly contested: politically, in the courts and also before the ILO. Finally, in 1983 for the private sector and in 1994 for the semi-public sector (health care, social services, and so on) the government recognized freedom of collective bargaining as an overriding principle, only to be abandoned in extreme circumstances. This new deal was reflected in an amendment of Article 10 of the Wage Determination Act, which since 1986 has read: 'Our Minister can take general measures concerning wages and other conditions of employment if such measures are, according to his judgment, required in suddenly arising emergency situations, caused by one or more external factors.'

Recent years have seen mounting criticism of the annual pay rises of top managers. A recent act of parliament obliges companies listed on the stock market to disclose the salaries of their managers.

The public authorities have continued to intervene directly in the area of civil service wages, since in this area they are the employer. This involves (including education employees) around 15% of the working population. The determination of working conditions and terms of employment in the public sector now increasingly resembles the private sector collective bargaining system.

In contrast to the situation in other countries such as France and Italy, the Netherlands does not have an incomes policy conducted explicitly by the state through state enterprises, since such enterprises are very rare in the Netherlands (and employ less than two per cent of the total working population).

Due to the long history of centralized wage policy, the practice of institutionalized consultation and cooperation of the social partners is well developed at national, intersectoral level.

The best known institutions at national level are the bipartite Labour Foundation and the tripartite Social and Economic Council.

The Labour Foundation (*Stichting van de Arbeid*) was established in 1945 under private law on a bipartite basis, composed of representatives of the main trade union confederations and employers' organizations. Within its framework, all-industry collective negotiations between employers and trade unions take place occasionally. Sometimes this results in the issue of recommendations to the social partners at the sectoral/enterprise level. These recommendations have no formal legal status but may substantially influence collective bargaining at sectoral or enterprise level.

The Labour Foundation is also frequently consulted by the government on labour law and social security matters.

The membership of the Social and Economic Council (Sociaal-Economische Raad, SER) is broken down as follows: one third of the members represent the employers' confederations; one third represent the trade union confederations; and one third are independent experts, appointed by – but not accountable to – the government. The Council was set up in 1950 under the Business Organization Act to play a number of roles, but it has proved most successful in its advisory capacity. The Council has an impressive secretariat at its disposal and is financed by contributions from business.

The Stichting van de Arbeid and the Sociaal-Economische Raad have their headquarters in the same buildings (belonging to the SER) in The Hague. Most of the leading personalities serve on both bodies.

It is quite common that the representatives of the trade union confederations and the employers' organizations in the Labour Foundation and the Social and Economic Council engage in lengthy negotiations in order to issue their advice unanimously. They know that unanimous advice cannot be ignored by the government and parliament.

Good examples of the influence of the Labour Foundation and the Social and Economic Council on socio-economic policy-making in the Netherlands include the following:

- In 1982, amidst the worst post-war economic recession, the so-called Wassenaar Agreement was concluded within the framework of the Labour Foundation relating to a reduction in working hours; the agreement was obtained in exchange for the moderation of pay rises.

- In 1993, on the eve of the realization of the single market in the EU, the Social and Economic Council issued a unanimous advice on the economic aims and strategies which should be pursued.

It is usual for the government and the intersectoral social partners to meet twice a year, spring and autumn, to exchange views on the development of the economy and any required measures.

Normally these meetings take the form of a meeting of a number of cabinet ministers (prime minister, finance minister, social affairs minister) with the leaders of the Labour Foundation (Stichting van de Arbeid).

Sometimes these meetings are talks with no strings attached, but sometimes, especially if the economic situation is deteriorating, there is a lot of pressure on the parties to reach some sort of understanding.

There is no statutory possibility for the government to force the social partners to conclude any kind of social pact. However, the government may present a large package of measures to entice or threaten the social partners into bargaining agreements: tax concessions, parliamentary bills to improve or to reduce certain aspects of the welfare state, and so on.

These intersectoral meetings may have a wide range of outcomes. The spring meetings often have a merely consultative character, however, and often there is insufficient pressure to persuade the intersectoral social partners and the meetings may not produce any result. Sometimes the social partners reach bilateral agreements; sometimes tripartite agreements are concluded.

Still, the most binding agreements are never binding in court. All agreements are merely political: if one party fails to keep to the agreement the sanctions can only be political (the other party considers itself released from any obligation).

Likewise, these agreements have no formal binding force in relation to the intersectoral social partners, individual employers or employees or sectoral organizations of employers and employees.

Here again the binding force of intersectoral agreements is merely political. It is assumed that the intersectoral social partners have so much sway over their members – and will exercise it – that the material contents of the intersectoral deals will be translated into the material contents of formal collective and individual agreements. In Dutch practice this is usually the case; deviations tend to be treated indulgently by the major players at intersectoral level. One should never overlook the fact that intersectoral bargaining has many symbolic aspects.

I may illustrate this with the intersectoral agreements of 2002 and 2003.

In autumn 2002 the dark prospects for the Dutch economy in 2003 led the government to confer with the Labour Foundation and to reach an agreement with the social partners on a maximum wage increase in 2003 of 2.5%. This 'recommendation' by the Labour Foundation was passed on to employers and unions in all sectors of the Dutch economy and indeed almost all new collective agreements were concluded close to this 2.5% increase.

Such situations do not present themselves every year, particularly not when there is a booming economy. However, they occur frequently under gloomy economic circumstances because there is much pressure from politicians, economists and the media to reach this type of agreement.

On 14 October 2003 the Dutch social partners agreed on a social pact for 2004 and

2005. In exchange for a two-year wage freeze[1] the government launched some positive social measures[2] and was prepared to withdraw some of its earlier announced plans to tackle certain aspects of social security legislation.[3]

The government stated at the time that if no agreement could be reached on early retirement by April 2004, it would reintroduce its proposals to withdraw the fiscal incentives applying to early retirement arrangements. However, by the end of May 2004 the talks on this issue between the intersectoral social partners were still in deadlock. The government therefore announced that it would move forward with its plans to withdraw the tax incentives on early retirement schemes. The unions stated that they no longer felt bound to honour the wage freeze for 2005. The government responded in turn that it would consider refraining from extension erga omnes of collective agreements which did not respect the wage freeze deal for 2005.

There are a number of other institutions in the Netherlands in which representatives of trade unions and employers' organizations meet frequently:

- consultative bodies in the area of social security and personnel policy;
- the administrative boards of pension funds;
- joint industry committees and industrial boards.

Given the multitude of organizations in the Netherlands it is clear that not every trade unions and employers' association can be invited to sit in all the aforementioned institutions. The selection of trade unions and employers' associations which are entitled to have seats in those institutions is largely based on criteria of representativeness drawn up by the Social and Economic Council.

3. THE LEGAL FRAMEWORK OF COLLECTIVE WAGE FORMATION

3.1 Trade union law

In the Netherlands there is no specific law on trade unions and employers' associations, in contrast to many other countries. Both enjoy general freedom of association which is recognized and guaranteed in Article 8 of the Dutch Constitution. Both are subject to the law governing associations elaborated in Book 2 of the Dutch Civil Code, which applies to all associations.

In recent years, the Netherlands has signed a number of international documents recognising trade union freedom whose regulations will probably be directly binding on all employers and employees, and enforceable before the courts.

The rights of trade unions are almost entirely based on voluntary arrangements. Only a few aspects have been regulated by statute or quasi-statute. Dutch unions have a right to information and consultation in the case of collective dismissals under

1. A zero wage increase for 2004 and an 'approaching zero' increase for 2005; scope for negotiating one-off payments in sectors and companies which were performing well; for details see EIRR (2003), pp. 16–17.
2. New initiatives to promote youth employment; conversion of subsidized jobs into proper jobs; and additional money to be made available to people living on the social minimum for more than three years; sickness insurance premiums to be reduced by 24.5 euros in 2004.
3. Postponement of the plan to repeal tax breaks for pre-pension and early retirement schemes until 2006; dropping of the plan to deduct redundancy payments from unemployment benefits; scrapping of the plan to take partner's earnings into consideration in the award of labour disability benefits.

the Notification of Collective Dismissals Act and in the case of a planned merger or takeover (under the so-called Merger Code, a document issued by the Social and Economic Council). Many unions have obtained additional rights on information and consultation by way of the collective agreements negotiated with the employers.

3.2 Statutes on the collective agreement

Collective bargaining is supported by two acts of parliament which clarify the priority of the collective agreement over individual employment contracts, and lay down formal criteria for the parties to the collective agreement.

- The Collective Agreements Act of 1927 recognizes the binding force of collective agreements in relation to individual employment contracts. It establishes that any stipulation agreed by an employer and employee contrary to a relevant collective agreement is null and void. Any such stipulation is automatically superseded by the provisions of the collective agreement. In addition, the provisions of the collective agreement supplement the contents of individual contracts of employment.
- The Extension of Collective Agreements Act of 1937 gives the government the power to extend the binding force of a collective agreement to the personnel of *all* enterprises in a certain branch of industry. If the minister uses this power, outsider employers and all their workers are mandatorily bound to the collective agreement.

The democratic imperative has led the legislators to limit the minister in exercising this power: he may only extend the collective agreement at the request of the social partners involved and if the agreement (without extension) already applies to a significant majority of those employed in a certain branch of industry (see section 6.2).

The mechanism of extension is frequently used. Each year the majority of industry-wide collective agreements are declared generally binding by Ministerial Order.

Some years ago the mechanism of extension came under sharp attack from economists as it in fact creates 'wage cartels'. Around 1990 some ministers considered doing away with it, but a few years later the government of the day decided to maintain the instrument as it contributes to peaceful relations on the labour market.

Every trade union and employers' association is entitled to conclude a collective agreement as soon as it complies with some minor formal requirements. As opposed to Germany and France no conditions relating to the size, independence or representativeness of the parties to the collective agreement are laid down in law or case law.

A collective agreement is normally signed by all the unions active in the economic sector or enterprise concerned, or by none of them. Until recently, cases in which collective bargaining gives rise to disagreement between the unions concerned were not as frequent as, for instance, in France, although they did occur. The overall picture was that multi-unionism was not a problem in the Netherlands as employers did not systematically attempt – as they do in the UK – to deal with a single union at the negotiating table. Such a premeditated strategy would be incompatible with traditional Dutch pluralism. In recent years, however, Dutch industrial relations have experienced increasing problems in this field.

Unlike France, there is no general legal obligation on employers to bargain with the unions. Collective bargaining is a question of power relations. Only in a few specific cases – such as collective redundancies, mergers and takeovers – is there something similar to an obligation to bargain (see section 3.1) and in isolated cases a court may force an employer to bargain with the unions.

The absence of a legal obligation to bargain is immaterial for 80% of Dutch businesses in which regular collective negotiations are self-evident and application of the collective agreement is widespread. The great majority of the employers do not dislike collective agreements, which for them are the key to orderly, stable and predictable labour relations.

The employers and employees bound by a collective agreement must respect it. In the case of collective agreements made generally binding by a Ministerial Order both unionized and non-unionized employees may take legal action to claim the rights contained in the substantive part of the agreement (‘*normatives Teil*’).

In the case of a collective agreement which is not made generally binding by a Ministerial Order only the unionized employees of an employer bound to the collective agreement have a clear legal right to enforcement of its provisions. Other employees may, however, successfully secure implementation of a collective agreement before the courts if this has been expressly agreed in the individual contract of employment or if it can be construed from notions of civil law, such as custom and practice.

Moreover, signatory organizations of the collective agreement are entitled, because of this status, to sue in their own name members of other signatory organizations who have not respected the collective agreement.

In some branches of industry and in major enterprises, the collective agreement nominates specific bodies before which infractions of the collective agreement may be brought. This is not, however, a very common practice.

In the Netherlands the observance of collective agreements is never subject to penal sanctions.

Disputes relating to the contractual part of the collective agreement (‘*obligatorisches Teil*’) may be brought before the ordinary law courts but only by the signatory parties to the agreement. However, these parties are normally reluctant to bring their differences to court. They may also try to resolve them by way of a strike, but this would enable the court to give an opinion on the matter if he is asked for an injunction. In some cases the social partners bring the matter before a board of mediation/arbitration but usually they put the problem on the backburner until the next round of collective bargaining.

3.3 Industrial democracy

Since 1971 the Works Councils Act (Wet op de ondernemingsraden) has regulated the composition, election and powers of works councils in detail and also sets out possibilities for settling any disputes which might arise.

Large enterprises maintain an entire network of works councils: works councils at local (plant) level; a works council for all plants with interrelated products (‘division’); and a central works council for the group at national level. Following an EU directive and the Dutch statute implementing it, those enterprises which meet the requirements of the Directive must also have a European Works Council.

The Works Councils Act obliges all types of work organization with over 50 employees to set up a works council. Special arrangements apply for the organization of workers' representation in firms with more than 10 but fewer than 50 employees.

The Works Councils Act covers profit-making businesses and non-profit-organizations alike, including the civil service and even religious organizations like the Salvation Army.

The law prohibits any detrimental treatment of employees as a consequence of their candidature for or membership of the works council or its committees. Members, former members and candidate-members of the works council can be dismissed only with prior judicial consent.

The law obliges the employer and the works council to meet whenever either side requests it.

The Works Councils Act gives the works council a wide variety of general competences and powers, for example, concerning operating costs, the invitation of experts, training of its members and the use of certain facilities belonging to the enterprise, such as somewhere to meet. The Act empowers the works councils to promote the implementation of all relevant provisions governing terms and conditions of employment, employees' health and safety, work progress discussions, decentralization, the distribution of tasks within the enterprise and the employment of handicapped workers. It must ensure that no discriminatory measures are taken and, in particular, encourage equal treatment of men and women. Other provisions include the following:

- The works council is entitled to appoint at least half the administrators of company institutions dealing with employee welfare and must be consulted on the appointment of the managing director.
- The works council is entitled to raise any issue it considers appropriate with the employer and to receive information on such issues.
- Works councils have certain participation rights under the Health and Safety at Work Act and – in large enterprises – a say in the composition of the Supervisory Board.
- The works council must be informed and consulted on any major economic decision – including mergers, relocations, closures and lay-offs, financial changes and large investments, changes to work organization, use of new technology, and so on – that the employer is planning. Its advice must be requested in sufficient time for it to have an appreciable impact on the management decision. If the decision subsequently taken is contrary to the works council's advice, the works council may appeal to the Court of Appeal of Amsterdam (Enterprise Bench). This court may quash the employer's decision if it establishes that the employer could not in all fairness have taken the decision had they considered all the relevant interests. A further appeal to the Supreme Court is also possible.
- The employer is required to seek the approval of the works council on all policy decisions (not decisions on individual matters) in the social field. This includes recruitment, training, promotion, work schedules, wage systems and redundancies.

However, the last cited power of the works council cannot be exercised if the issue is conclusively dealt with in a collective agreement with a trade union: the collective agreement takes precedence over other (that is, company or individual) provisions.

If the works council does not approve, then the employer cannot take the planned decision. In that case the employer may request the mediation of the Joint Industrial Committee. Joint Industrial Committees have been established on a standing basis in all sectors of the Dutch economy. Their composition and powers and the appointment of their members are regulated by the Works Councils Act.

If the mediation of the Joint Industrial Committee is unsuccessful, the employer can then go to the District Court (*sector kanton*) to seek its approval of the planned decision, which supersedes the consent of the works council. Appeals against the decision of the District Court may be brought before the Court of Appeal, with a further appeal to the Supreme Court.

The statutory provisions on the powers of the works council are helpful in persuading the employer to adopt transparency of decision-making and to reach agreement with workforce representatives, notably on the social consequences of his or her decisions.

If conflicts emerge and the matter is taken to court, judges are normally keen to oblige employers to stick to the procedural rules which compel them to inform, consult and sometimes even seek the approval of workers' representatives.

However, the courts are very reluctant to challenge the economic rationale of managerial decisions. At the end of the day management in the Netherlands is still free to take what economic decisions it pleases, provided these decisions are taken according to the procedures for information and consultation laid down by statute and the social consequences are duly taken into account.

In Dutch enterprises there is no workers' representation on the supervisory board of large companies, as there is in Germany. As an alternative to the German system, in the Netherlands a system was devised in 1971 in which works councils in major companies were given the power to short-list and provisionally to veto candidates for all seats on the supervisory board. This system will be replaced next year by a system comparable to the German model of codetermination as embodied in the Works Constitution Act of 1952.

3.4 The law on strikes

In the Netherlands the right to strike is not mentioned in the Constitution or in statutory law. All strike law is the result of case law and therefore somewhat inconsistent.

The right to strike was fundamentally recognized by the Dutch Supreme Court in 1986 on the basis of Article 6, paragraph 4 of the European Social Charter, ratified by the Netherlands in 1980.

Although the right to strike is secured by case law it is not an absolute right. The Supreme Court has imposed two sorts of conditions.

First, major procedural rules must be observed. This condition enables judges to prohibit strikes called before negotiations have broken down or which violate the so-called 'peace obligation'.

According to the Supreme Court a strike can be justified only if this weapon is used as a last resort.

Second, the Supreme Court requires that the strike be not 'unreasonable'. This condition enables judges to prohibit strikes on the grounds that the damages will be excessive in proportion to the interests at stake. To the Supreme Court this means that a strike can be justified only if it does not disproportionately encroach on the rights of others.

Although there are few strikes in the Netherlands, the general public is seldom very sympathetic.

If the trade unions choose to refrain from strike action, the workers will usually follow their example. Although the legality of wildcat strikes is measured against the same criteria as that of official strikes, wildcat strikes are few. This is because the individual employee's legal position is weak without trade union support. Employees participating in a strike forfeit their right to wages and are not entitled to social security benefits; only in union-supported strikes will they be provided with strike pay from union strike funds.

Prevailing legal doctrine considers the strike as a suspension of the contract of employment. Consequently, strikers do not run the risk of disciplinary action (such as dismissal) by their employer. No action for compensation can be taken against strikers. However, from the moment the court has ruled that the strike is illegal, employers may take disciplinary action against individuals who continue to strike, provided the disciplinary action is not disproportionate.

In the Netherlands most collective agreements contain no-strike clauses, but even if such a clause is omitted a peace obligation will be assumed. However, the peace obligation is not absolute. Certain strikes may be in conformity with this obligation, but it is not always easy to determine which ones. The binding force of this obligation on individual employees is also obscure.

Many more aspects of the law on strikes are uncertain. There is no case law on lockouts at all. Uncertainty also exists with regard to strikes by civil servants. The courts have been prepared to accept the legality of public servant strikes, but civil servants such as policemen and prison guards will certainly not be allowed to strike for a substantial period. However, it remains difficult to determine what is allowed and to whom?

There is no legislation promoting conciliation, mediation and arbitration in labour disputes, except in relation to the civil service.

Collective agreements in some cases contain provisions relating to the procedures to be followed in the event of an industrial dispute, but these provisions are very rarely used.

Industrial disputes of longer duration are sometimes handled on an ad hoc basis by a mediator who must be a person of some standing.

3.5 The concepts of the 'just wage' and the minimum wage

There is no generally applicable legal concept of a 'just wage' in Dutch labour law, but there is a concept of a minimum wage, which must be applied universally. The Act on Minimum Wages and Minimum Holiday Allowances of 1968 fixes the minimum wage in the Netherlands at around 1,200 euros a month gross in the case of an employment relationship based on the standard working week. This applies to all employees aged between 23 and 65 years in all sectors of the economy, without exception or differentiation. Part-timers are entitled to a proportionate minimum wage and young people are entitled to a minimum youth wage, a percentage of the full minimum wage, varying from 30% at 15 years to 85% at 22 years.

The statutory minimum wage has strong legal force, although in the Netherlands there are no penal sanctions on infringements of payment of the statutory minimum wage, as there are in France. Effective enforcement must be achieved by means of civil procedure. All pay agreements – in both collective and individual agreements – which are below the level of the statutory minimum wage are null and void. On the pay slip – which is obligatory under statutory law – the employer must state the relevant statutory minimum pay so that the employee can easily compare it with his salary. If the employer is in arrears with payment of the minimum wage he has to pay an additional amount by way of punitive damages. In principle, the employee must himself go to court to enforce payment of the statutory minimum wage, though if the statutory minimum wage is asserted in the collective agreement (which is often the case) then the trade unions can take the employer to the court, too. The Labour Inspectorate regularly monitors payment of the statutory minimum wage, and its reports show that the law is applied in more than 95% of cases. In cases in which the law is not applied the Labour Inspectorate informs both the offending employers and the affected employees of its findings. Scholars in the Netherlands are in no doubt of the effective observation of the Dutch statutory minimum wage.

The procedure for fixing the minimum wage is very simple and depoliticized. Every six months the Dutch Public Office of Statistics works out the average level of pay rises in the collective agreements of Dutch workers and the Minister subsequently adjusts the minimum wage by the same percentage by Royal Decree. There is never any political debate on this point. No Minister would dare to tamper with this procedure. Only if the economy has run into big trouble may government and parliament, after an open debate, adopt exceptional legislation to skip automatic adaptation of minimum wages for a year or so. This was done several times between 1983 and 1995. As a result, the level (measured in terms of purchasing power) of the statutory minimum wage has been effectively reduced if one compares its current level with that of the 1970s.

The Dutch statutory minimum wage is very much supported as a 'red line' for all low incomes in the Netherlands because all minimum social security benefits are linked to the statutory minimum wage. In principle every two-person household is entitled to minimum benefits at the level of one minimum wage, be it by way of old age pension, survivors' benefit, sickness pay, unemployment benefit, disability benefit, and so on. Nobody is obliged – in order to receive such payments – to perform work below the level of the statutory minimum wage.

At the beginning of the 1990s it was discovered that the effective minimum wage was often 10% to 30% above the statutory minimum wage because in collective agreements the lowest wage scales (just above the minimum wage) were removed or not used. Economists blamed this as one of the reasons for much of the long-term unemployment in the Netherlands, although the economy was booming again.

In the 1990s the Dutch government tried to remedy this by a number of measures.

In the first place the government refused to lower the statutory minimum wage but it introduced large reductions in taxes and social security contributions for workers paid at or near the minimum wage level.

Second, the government pressed the social partners to engage workers at the statutory minimum wage level by threatening to refuse to extend collective agreements to outsiders if the social partners did not reintroduce into their collective agreement the lowest wage scales or scales just above the statutory minimum wage.

Obviously, the statutory minimum wage has an indirect effect on higher wages as it effectively (not formally) forces employers to increase all wages above the minimum wage by at least the same percentage as the rise in the minimum wage. However, the rise in the minimum wage is the retroactive expression of average pay rises, so the minimum wage cannot be blamed as the cause of this chain of events.

It may strike foreign observers that the level of the Dutch minimum wage is very high.

This impression may be corrected with reference to the statutory minimum wage for young people (under 23), which is far from high. France, for example, does not have a special minimum wage for youngsters. Therefore many Dutch enterprises make use of the cheap labour of teenagers doing part-time jobs while still at school.

However, to the extent that the impression that the Dutch minimum wage is high is correct, it should be attributed to political and cultural factors. Just as the Dutch landscape is very level, so is Dutch political/cultural philosophy. The Dutch do not like extremes in any direction. They abhor extremely high incomes and dislike poverty and poor social conditions for the lower-income sections of the population. Notably during the 1960s and 1970s there was a strong drive for 'social justice' and 'solidarity pay'. Upgrading the minimum wage was an aim of most political parties. Some political parties even wanted the maximum wage to be maintained at a level no higher than four or five times the minimum wage! When during the 1980s recession hit the Netherlands and the standard of living fell, Dutch politicians tried frantically not to touch the lower-income sections of the population. The Netherlands remained one of the countries in which differences in income levels were smallest. By the end of the 1980s and the 1990s economic prosperity returned to the Netherlands and differences in income levels grew substantially. However, this occurred not so much as a result of lowering the incomes of the low paid as by allowing the incomes of the middle class and above to rise more substantially. The described policy of moderate wage increases was pursued to stabilize standard (collectively agreed) pay levels (not to lower pay levels) and it left room for all sorts of extra pay rises, which were agreed individually.

3.6 Equal pay

In addition, there is legislation on equal pay for men and women. The principle of equal pay for equal work by men and women is laid down in the Act on Equal Treatment of Men and Women. Workers can sue their employer if they think that this principle has not been respected. Before going to court, however, workers may put the dispute before a commission of experts, the Equal Treatment Commission, which will then make a recommendation in writing. The Courts are free to use or ignore the Commission's recommendation. The Supreme Court has held, however, that these recommendations are of particular value in subsequent legal proceedings, and so courts therefore have to argue why they have not followed such recommendations.

Equal pay for men and women is now generally accepted, but major differences still persist. Most collective agreements have been purged of clauses leading to the unequal treatment of men and women and, apart from incidental cases, no problems have surfaced in recent years. The persistence of unequal pay is mainly due to the women's lower levels of education and availability, on average, on the labour market.

Other statutory provisions have extended the concept to equal pay on other grounds, such as between part-time and full-time workers.

4. CURRENT CHALLENGES TO DUTCH COLLECTIVE WAGE DETERMINATION

Many challenges concerning social or economic developments and political disputes as they affect the system of collective wage formation in the Netherlands have been debated in recent years.

For instance, from a legal-academic point of view, in 1999 the late Max Rood – Professor in Labour Law at Leyden – sketched four challenges to labour law in general, which certainly apply to the system of collective wage formation in the Netherlands: (i) the current dominance of neo-classical economic theories; (ii) the rise of individualism in Dutch society; (iii) the enormous diversification of jobs on the labour market; and (iv) diminishing trust in the regulatory power of the nation state.

Applied in concreto to the system of wage formation in the Netherlands the main challenge concerned how a free system of wage formation could be combined by the social partners with:

a. the need to prevent labour costs from rising too much in order not to jeopardize the competitiveness of the Netherlands;
b. the desirability of maintaining a balance between wage development in the private sector and that in the (semi-)public sector and social security benefits.

Both these challenges require a certain amount of centralization of collective bargaining, and this in a period in which industry is urging decentralization. That is the third challenge.

The fourth challenge is: who – on the employees' side – should participate in the decentralization of wage formation, the trade unions or the works council? And, if the trade unions, which ones?

One of the urgent legal challenges of the Dutch system of collective wage formation is as follows. The Dutch Minister in his policy of extending sectoral collective agreements (see section 3.2) often exempts from extension companies which have their own in-house company collective agreement. In the past this exception was invoked for bona fide cases like Philips, which is exempt from the collective agreement for the Dutch engineering industry because it has its own company collective agreement, concluded with the major unions. However, in recent years some employers have concluded in-house collective agreements with so-called "yellow unions", enabling them to avoid extension of the sectoral collective agreement to their company.

As Dutch industrial relations have not seen yellow unions for a very long time there is much uncertainty about the proper legal instruments to deal with them.

5. REACTIONS: STATE, SOCIAL PARTNERS AND ENTERPRISES

The principal change made to the system in reaction to the various challenges was already in operation in the 1980s and at the beginning of the 1990s: the near-total abolition of all instruments of state control on wage formation (see section 2.5). Only auxiliary forms of state intervention, such as the statutes on collective agreements, minimum wages and equal pay remained on the statute book.

A major change was made in 1996 concerning the law on individual wage formation on the issue of the 'reglement' (English: 'company handbook', French 'règlement intérieur', art. L122–33 French Code du Travail). Some 15 years ago the Dutch Supreme Court created confusion regarding the binding force of the 'reglement'. The Dutch parliament reacted by completely deleting this source of labour law from the statute book (as is the situation in Germany). As an alternative a provision was inserted in the Dutch Civil Code which states that even if the contract of employment or an applicable company manual contains a written provision pursuant to which the employer is empowered to modify unilaterally the working conditions set out in the contract of employment, the employer may invoke such a provision only if he has such a strong interest in the modification that, according to the standards of reasonableness and fairness, the interest of the employee who would be harmed by the modification must be overridden.

Recently in Germany the statutory rules on so-called '*Allgemeine Geschäftsbedingungen*' (general business conditions) were declared applicable to contracts of employment. In the Netherlands this example has not yet been followed. Both contracts of employment and collective agreements are still explicitly exempt from the Dutch rules on '*Allgemeine Geschäftsbedingungen*'.

The major change in collective bargaining as regards procedure and organization is in the sphere of decentralization.

As already mentioned, both employers and employees are increasingly interested in decentralising collective bargaining. There is nowadays a strong tendency to give collective agreements – and certainly those at sectoral level – more or less of a framework character. Details should be settled at enterprise level in agreements with either trade unions or works councils.

Usually, details are settled in agreements with works councils because the trade unions seldom have bargaining agents at enterprise level.

However, there are a number of legal problems in this field which have not yet been solved. One problem is the binding force in relation to individual employment contracts of agreements with works councils to concretize sectoral collective agreements. In the Netherlands this binding force is not – unlike in Germany, with the *Betriebsvereinbarung* or works agreement – established by law. It is dependent on auxiliary legal constructions (such as incorporation clauses in individual employment contracts).

Another problem is the question of whether the Minister may or should extend erga omnes such decentralization clauses in sectoral collective agreements. The Minister is not prepared to do so with open-ended decentralization clauses.

All these legal problems and uncertainties have delayed rapid development of this decentralization trend. The trade unions are reluctant to agree to glib solutions to these problems because they fear that this would open the floodgates for employers who would prefer to completely circumvent the trade unions and to negotiate only with the works councils (or even with yellow unions). The trade unions in the Netherlands favour controlled decentralization in which the conditions and the content of company-level bargaining are stipulated by the bargaining parties at sectoral level through instruments such as opening clauses or delegation clauses. They reject uncontrolled decentralization characterized by a de facto undermining of the existing collectively agreed standards.

So far, it seems that the social partners at sectoral level in the Netherlands have been successful in checking this internal erosion of sectoral collective bargaining.[4]

4. F. Tros, *Decentralisatie van arbeidsverhoudingen* (Utrecht, 2000).

Nor have there been many reports of companies covered by collective agreements actually violating the legally binding norms of a valid collective agreement. Compliance with collective agreements is still the norm in all sectors of the Dutch economy, although there are always minor exceptions.

A major change in the contents of collective bargaining is that collective agreements are tending to expand into new areas of regulation, such as the financing of kindergartens and personal arrangements for training. They increasingly contain flexible aspects, such as flexible working hours, variable pay forms, and so on.

Company wage policies have also changed as regards the flexibility (or standardization) of wages (for example, variable pay forms, equal pay) and the internationalization of companies. For many years additional payments above those laid down in collective agreements have been part and parcel of pay practice at company level and have offered companies a wide range of options for a more flexible pay policy relative to the minimum standards laid down in sectoral collective agreements.

Variable pay forms such as performance-related pay and profit-related pay are increasingly applied, but there is still much opposition from the unions to particular forms of variable pay and therefore development is not rapid in quantitative terms. Variable pay probably does not exceed 10% of the entire wage bill in the Netherlands.

The internationalization of companies is having a creeping impact on company wage policies. Employers are nowadays less inspired by merely social, national or even patriotic considerations in the formation of their wage policies. They are now primarily driven by shareholder value, with an increasingly global dimension.

In the end, decentralization may well come to play only a modest role in collective bargaining in the Netherlands. The sectoral level is still dominant, and even the all-industry level is making itself felt. Wage bargaining at company level is still very secondary. The prevailing situation is that everybody follows trends set by particular wage leaders. If wages are tending to rise two per cent, they will rise two per cent on average everywhere. If some employees are compensated with bonuses, similar employees will be compensated by bonuses everywhere. All this, of course, subject to variation according to the economic performance and character of companies.

Again, this outcome is very much the result of the political culture of the Netherlands: the Dutch love of 'equal treatment', for no deviations from general trends, and the fact that 16 million people are living in an open and tolerant society in a very small territory – all this means that trends are followed and that the possibilities for employers to deviate from these trends are limited.

The prolongation of the working week is a case in point.

Before 2004 no employer in the Netherlands would have dared to propose to their staff a prolongation of the working week. The trend for a number of years has been to shorten the working week, which has fallen from about 40 hours to an average of 37 hours a week (with a number of variations according to the character of the company).

However, not many months ago the trend in Germany and in France of discussion of prolongation of the working week reached the Netherlands. Some government ministers have called for prolongation of the working week, along with some leading employers and economists. At the same time, as might be expected, some trade unionists and left-wing academics and politicians have argued against it. However, in the first half of 2004 this was merely under discussion and nothing had been done about it. Then, in July 2004 a small subsidiary of a foreign multinational company in the north of the Netherlands was the first to reintroduce a 40-hour week for the same pay as the 36-hour week! This act of decentralization at the company level immediately gave the debate new momentum.

This example may illustrate the pluralistic character of wage determination in the Netherlands: while most developments are predominantly centralized, everybody is following general trends in a decentralized way. However, new trends may emerge, even at a decentralized level. They will be allowed to flourish only if they are accepted at centralized levels; otherwise, after a certain time they will perish.

6. THE NETHERLANDS AND GERMANY: DIFFERENCES AND SIMILARITIES IN THE SYSTEMS OF COLLECTIVE WAGE FORMATION

Comparison of the basic features of industrial relations – and also the legal framework of collective wage formation – in Germany with those of the Netherlands shows that both countries have several features in common, but also quite a few differences.

6.1 Similarities

1) Both countries have an orderly and legalized system of collective agreements, mostly at the sectoral level, but occasionally at the enterprise level.

One superficial difference is that German sectoral collective agreements are often concluded at *Land* level, while Dutch collective agreements almost always have national scope. However, this is not a significant difference because the Netherlands is about the size of the largest German *Länder*.

In both countries collective agreements mostly set minimum standards, allowing enterprises to offer more favourable conditions of employment. Also in both countries collective agreements are usually renewed, mostly on a regular basis (every one or two years).

In both countries collective agreements are legally binding between the parties and contain mandatory rules for individual contracts of employment, which are bound to the collective agreement. Therefore, in both countries they are not merely 'gentlemen's agreements' as they are in the UK.

In both countries non-extended collective agreements in principle are only binding on employment relationships in respect of which both employer and employee are members of parties to the collective agreement or are themselves party to the collective agreement. Outsiders are in principle not affected.

However, in both countries some exceptions are made. In Germany, for example, exceptions are made for '*betriebliche und betriebsverfassungsrechtliche*' standards, which are binding for the entire workforce of a bound employer (§ 3(2) TVG). In the Netherlands the bound employer is obliged to apply the collective agreement provisions on working conditions to the entire workforce, but the non-unionized employees are not entitled to take legal action in case of non-application.

Both countries have on the statute book an instrument for the extension of collective agreements, but extension practice varies considerably.

2) Both Germany and the Netherlands have a dual system of workers' representation (unions and works councils), as opposed to one-tier systems in the UK and Scandinavia and triple systems in France and Italy.

In both countries the trade union avenue is largely unregulated by the law, whereas the works council avenue is highly regulated.

The unions in both Germany and the Netherlands are overwhelmingly organized as 'industrial unions' rather than 'craft unions'.

Otherwise, however, there are a number of differences (see section 6.2).

The elaborate statutory rules on works councils in Germany are quite similar to those in the Netherlands, but the differences should not be ignored (see section 6.2).

3) Both countries have good strike records and interventionist control of strikes by the courts. In 2002 President of IG Metall Klaus Zwicker observed that in the Netherlands there were too few strikes. 'The longer a model of cooperation like that of the Netherlands remains in existence, the more people think that everything is OK.' In his experience it is better to bargain with companies in which there has been successful industrial action.

Table 1: Days lost because of strikes ('000 workers)

	FR	**GER**	IT	**NL**	UK	USA
1950–1959	315.5	**47.5**	301.5	**19.4**	135.9	550.2
1960–1969	138.5	**12.0**	730.5	**16.7**	145.7	382.3
1970–1979	167.8	**44.7**	1041.0	**35.7**	521.6	457.1
1980–1989	61.7	**22.9**	433.3	**12.8**	292.8	132.0
1990–1999	31.2	**10.5**	110.6	**19.3**	25.0	37.0

The German law on strikes certainly deviates in a number of details from the Dutch law on strikes, notably on wildcat strikes and civil servant strikes. Nevertheless, the German law on strikes is much closer to its Dutch equivalent than to those of France or the UK.

There are no explicit guarantees of the right to strike in the German and Dutch Constitutions. German and Dutch law on strikes is almost entirely judge-made law. In both countries the courts are actively involved in regulating strikes, as opposed to, for example, Belgium where the courts are kept out of it.

In both Germany and the Netherlands the courts adhere to a number of principles to control strike behaviour, such as the peace obligation, the ultima ratio doctrine, and the proportionality rule, which substantially limit the freedom to strike.

On the other hand, in both countries the courts have upheld other principles, like the principle of suspension of contractual obligations, which created the room for legal strike action.

This strong and effective judicial control of industrial action in both countries has been conducive to a low strike record and an orderly system of wage formation through collective bargaining.

6.2 Differences

There are some significant differences between the industrial relations systems and laws of Germany and the Netherlands.

1. One particularly striking difference between the German and the Dutch systems of industrial relations is on the trade union side. German unions are much stronger than their Dutch counterparts. One reason for this is the domination of DGB which most

of the time presides over an almost unitary trade union movement. In the Netherlands, although FNV is by far the largest trade union confederation, the other components of the trade union movement are not to be neglected. They are always present with their own agenda on bargaining round tables and in consultative bodies. This creates a pluralist trade union situation. And even if this pluralism does not diminish trade union strength as it does in France, it certainly gives the Dutch trade unions a weaker position than in Germany. The second reason for the relative weakness of the Dutch trade union movement is the rate of unionization: only around 24% of workers are unionized in the Netherlands. This rate of unionization has substantially lagged behind that of Germany for many years – only in recent years has the German rate also fallen dramatically. Because of their weakness Dutch unions started to merge much earlier than in Germany where the process took off late in the 1990s with the formation of the Verdi union. From a financial point of view the union mergers in the Netherlands were a disaster. This, together with losses made by the Dutch unions on the stock market, left them in dire financial straits. They now even rely heavily on sponsorship by the employers' associations, which cannot be good for their independence. Because of these weaknesses the Dutch unions are more moderate and prepared to compromise than in Germany. This is not to say that the Dutch unions are powerless and completely under the influence of the employers. As long as the unions behave reasonably they maintain a high standing in public opinion and in the political arena. That is their main power base. Dutch employers are more union-friendly and inclined to compromise than their German counterparts. The phenomenon of falling membership of employers' organizations in Germany is not matched in the Netherlands. Although there are no official statistics the members of employers' organizations employ 80–90% of the Dutch labour force. Therefore the percentage of employers covered by a sectoral collective agreement remains quite constant at about 70% of the labour force, about the same as 10, 20, even 30 years ago. In the Netherlands the grey areas without collective agreements are not expanding as they are in Germany, and the influence of collectively agreed norms and provisions at sectoral level is not receding as it is in Germany. If in the Netherlands the employers one day started to desert the employers' organizations in the same numbers as they apparently are in Germany this would put a bomb under the Dutch system of industrial relations, given the importance of the extension mechanism and its legal aspects in the Netherlands. However, so far Dutch employers seem disinclined to sabotage the existing system of industrial relations which guarantees them a quiet labour market. Such an approach would strongly be rejected by Dutch public opinion and in the political arena.

2. German unions refused to assume the status of 'eingetragene Vereine' (registered associations), whereas the Dutch unions are all officially registered associations according to the general statutory rules on associations. In Germany the existence and activities of the social partners are recognized as a fundamental right in the Constitution; in the Netherlands no specific constitutional guarantee applies to the social partners.

Since the establishment of the German Federal Republic German industrial relations law has been dominated by the principle of bargaining autonomy (*Tarifautonomie*), which the German judiciary has given constitutional status based on Article 9.3 of the German Constitution.

In the Netherlands the absence of a constitutional principle of bargaining autonomy has allowed the state to develop a tradition of intervention in the process of collective bargaining.

3. In Germany, collective bargaining at national, intersectoral level is much weaker than in the Netherlands. The Dutch system of collective bargaining has always been characterized by a highly complicated combination of intersectoral- and sectoral-level regulations.

In the Netherlands the social partners and the state have a tradition of intersectoral collective bargaining going back more than 50 years. There are a number of important institutions at which bargaining takes place as a continuing process, including the Labour Foundation and the Social and Economic Council.

Although collective bargaining is now free, the Dutch continue to hold egalitarian views on annual pay rises. The trade unions strive towards solidarity-based income development, transgressing the boundaries between sectors and between workers and non-workers.

During the 1960s and the 1970s a close link was established between the statutory minimum wage, the level of social security benefits and the wages of civil servants, as well as wage growth in the private sector. Although some of these linkages have formally been broken since the 1980s, harmonious development of all incomes remains a much-valued characteristic of the Dutch social model, which is a strong motive for the government and the social partners to seek agreement on wages and economic developments at intersectoral level.

Therefore strong political pressure is put on the private sector unions to moderate their annual pay claims. Sometimes the aforementioned linkages are more or less openly used as bargaining chips, a practice which is of course the more contested the more openly it happens. But the pressure is always there.

The present government recently introduced a new form of pressure, announcing that it would continue to extend collective agreements only if they developed along moderate lines.

Unions and employers in the private sector react differently to these pressures, depending on the current circumstances. Sometimes, notably when the Dutch economy is in trouble, they are prepared to bow to pressure by concluding a central agreement which is then followed in all sectors.

Sometimes, notably in periods of economic boom, unions and employers refuse to conclude central agreements and leave wage formation to the actors in the various sectors of the economy.

Even in that case the major employer and trade union confederations try to harmonize their strategies in the various sectors: the employers clearly from a desire not to be played off against one another; the trade unions because their members include many public sector employees and others who are dependent on social security benefits, giving them grounds to fear what would happen if the various linkages were jeopardized by excessive pay rises in the private sector.

This system of collective bargaining at intersectoral level – leaving formal collective bargaining to the social partners in the various sectors – to my knowledge does not exist in Germany and constitutes one of the main differences between the systems of collective bargaining in the two countries.

All this makes sectoral and company collective bargaining freer in Germany than in the Netherlands, where the idea of '*Tarifautonomie*' is much less developed than in Germany; Dutch politicians and lawyers are not so reluctant to intervene in the process of collective bargaining as in Germany.

4. As already mentioned, formal collective bargaining at sectoral level is very much the same in Germany and in the Netherlands. There may be some differences in terms of wage leadership. While in Germany the metal industry sector plays a crucial role in determining overall wage levels, in the Netherlands wage leadership is much more diffuse (Philips, the docks, construction, and so on).

The main difference, however, lies in the extension of collective agreements.

In the Netherlands this instrument is applied frequently, while in Germany its use seems rather limited. The first reason for this is that Dutch employers apparently favour it more than German employers. They request that the Minister apply this instrument together with the unions, although a request by one of the signatory parties suffices.

Most Dutch employers see extension as a positive instrument which averts excessive competition and therefore excessive labour market unrest. They believe that individual or enterprise-level wage setting creates more conflict than collective wage setting. The government favours extension because a wide range of extended collective agreements gives it a good excuse to avoid legislating and to leave standard setting to the social partners.

In Germany the employers are perhaps less sympathetic to extension because they want to compete on labour costs as well.

The legal requirements constitute a second possible reason why extension is more widespread in the Netherlands than in Germany: in both Germany and the Netherlands the law requires that extension is possible only if the employers bound to a collective agreement employ at least 50% of the employees in the sector. However, in Germany two additional conditions apply to extension: the extension must be in the public interest and employers may veto it. Both conditions are lacking in the Netherlands. The quantitative requirement (the employers bound to the collective agreement employ at least 50% of the employees covered by the collective agreement) is independent of the unionization rate, but entirely dependent on the employers' organization rate. Therefore, extension would decline dramatically also in the Netherlands if the employers withdrew from employers' associations, as they are doing in Germany. However, as already mentioned, this is not the case.

5. A further difference between the wage formation systems of the Netherlands and Germany lies in the law and practice of collective bargaining at enterprise level. Collective bargaining at enterprise level is more developed in Germany than in the Netherlands. One historical reason for this is that the old centralized policy of wage control in the Netherlands did not leave room for collective wage formation at the enterprise level.

As a result the Dutch unions did not develop their presence within enterprises, putting the emphasis on bargaining at intersectoral and sectoral levels.

Finally, a number of specific differences in the law and practice of works councils may be important in this respect. The German DGB has a firm grip on many works councils. The overwhelming majority of German works councils see their activities within the context of the overall objectives formulated by the trade unions. For a variety of reasons the Dutch trade unions have much less influence on works councils. Consequently, DGB has accepted a clear negotiating role for works councils in Germany in the conclusion of 'Betriebsvereinbarungen' or works agreements of a mandatory character. In the Netherlands the trade unions have always been reluctant to agree to a clear bargaining role for the works councils, which indeed is lacking in the law. Company pacts on employment and competitiveness (Bündnis für Arbeit) and in-house bargaining in which the employees make certain concessions in terms of working time or pay in return for some form of employment guarantee of the kind found in Germany are almost completely unknown in the Netherlands.

German works councils are also involved in individual personnel matters (such as hiring and firing), while Dutch works councils are not. In the Netherlands there is no direct representation of the workers on the supervisory boards of large enterprises as there is in Germany. By way of compensation Dutch works councils have a somewhat stronger influence on economic decision-making: for example, they may temporarily halt economic decisions by appealing to a specialized court. Codetermination is also a major difference between the German and Dutch industrial relations law, but it is uncertain whether this difference is important for wage determination.

6. A final major difference in the legal framework of collective wage formation is the absence in Germany of any effective statutory minimum wage (the relevant Act is not applied). In the Netherlands there has been a minimum wage since the 1950s (see section 3.5). A statutory minimum wage may be considered as a safety net for the weakest categories of workers (poorly qualified workers, casual workers, immigrants, and so on).

7. STRENGTHS AND VULNERABILITIES OF THE GERMAN SYSTEM FROM A DUTCH POINT OF VIEW.

1. From a Dutch point of view the German system of collective wage formation with its strong support (both popular and legal) for the decentralized formation of working conditions ('*Tarifautonomie*') undoubtedly represents a strength. In principle labour-law protection based on legally binding collective agreements is much more flexible and adaptable to circumstances than a system of labour-law protection predominantly based on statutory law.

However, the German system of collective wage formation may be vulnerable to the extent that German unions and employers are arguably less creative in finding solutions to mitigate high labour costs while maintaining a high level of social protection than unions and employers in the Netherlands. The reasons for this weakness do not lie in the character and principles of the German system of collective labour relations, but are rather cultural and structural. The Netherlands has always been much more a nation of merchants than Germany, which is traditionally rather a nation of manufacturers. Merchants are typically more inclined to compromise, to be pragmatic and to promote win–win situations than manufacturers are. Also, the fact that the Netherlands is a much smaller country makes the Dutch more aware than the Germans of the fact that they have to adapt to new international realities if they are to survive economically.

Finally, the weak position of the trade unions in the Netherlands makes them eager to compromise with employers who also know that neither Dutch public opinion nor political parties would support extreme positions. I have the impression that in Germany both unions and employers are less eager to compromise because they feel strong enough to stubbornly defend their position, even against public opinion and political parties.

2. Significant wage differences between men and women are apparently another vulnerable aspect of the German industrial relations system. Trade unions try to reduce wage discrimination by collective bargaining, but this means that outside the scope of collective agreements equal pay law as it applies to individuals is ineffective; indeed, it is questionable whether equal pay can be guaranteed to individuals solely by law.

One cause of this problem in Germany may be that women who are discriminated against rarely sue the company individually in German courts and alternatives for implementing equal pay legislation seem to be lacking in German law.

In the Netherlands a Commission on Equal Treatment – which is easily accessible – has been operating successfully for 20 years.

The Commission receives hundreds of submissions each year regarding pay differentials. In general, writing a letter to the Commission suffices for it to start its inquiries and to give an opinion. This opinion is not legally binding, but most employers follow it because if the employee should subsequently take the case to court, failure to have done so will count strongly against them. The trade unions do not generally play a role in these complaints, although they may incidentally support a complaint or even lodge complaints themselves. Often trade union–friendly lawyers are nominated as members of the Commission. Provisions in collective agreements have sometimes been identified as causes of unjustified pay inequalities. This has forced the social partners to revise the relevant provisions in subsequent wage rounds.

In 1997 Andreas Mittmann in his dissertation 'Gleichbehandlung von Frauen und Männern im niederländischen und deutschen Arbeitsleben' [Equal treatment of men and women in Dutch and German working life] (Sinzheim: Pro Universitate Verlag, p. 240), suggested the creation in Germany of an agency like the Dutch Commission on Equal Treatment.

3. The most significant vulnerability of the German system of wage formation has emerged as a result of employers' defection from employers' associations, which has considerably reduced the number of collective agreements in Germany. The fact that Germany also lacks a legal minimum wage is leaving an ever greater number of workers without adequate protection against low wages. In the Netherlands, on the other hand, even if the employers withdrew from collective bargaining they would still be bound to a statutory minimum wage.

In the Netherlands a statutory minimum wage has coexisted with an extensive system of collective bargaining for almost half a century. Its function has not been to prevent the small part of the Dutch economy in which no collective agreements exist to undermine wages in the rest of the economy, but rather to ensure that all working people in the Netherlands have a decent (minimum) share in prosperity.

The existence of a statutory minimum wage may weaken the pressure on workers to unionize. One might ask whether the low unionization rate – around 24% – in the Netherlands has something to do with the existence of a statutory minimum wage and the generous practice of erga omnes extension of collective agreements.

In any case, the vulnerability of the German situation can be seen in the international dimension of the labour market. Since there is neither a statutory minimum wage nor erga omnes extension of collective agreements, German employers may engage foreign workers under very poor working conditions, notably by the legal construction of posting workers (Arbeitnehmerüberlassung). Under the European Convention on the Law applicable to contractual obligations of 1980 member states may apply mandatory national laws to employment contracts governed by a foreign legal system. However, with its lack of mandatory wage provisions Germany has few instruments available to stop the import of low-wage workers from abroad, so that it is not by chance that Germany is the country hardest hit by the open international labour market. It therefore pushed hard to get the so-called Posted Workers Directive adopted by the European Commission. The very existence of this Directive and of the German statute to implement it are proofs of the vulnerability of the German system.

8. DECENTRALIZATION AND THE GROWING FLEXIBILITY OF THE GERMAN SYSTEM FROM A DUTCH POINT OF VIEW

Panel data indicate that the number of German employers bound by sectoral collective agreements has shrunk constantly since 1995. A growing number of smaller employers do not apply any union contract at all.

Many German employers (and political parties) have criticized inflexible wage regulations in sectoral collective agreements, asserting that companies need more wage flexibility and more flexible regulations today than 20 years ago. However, the desire for less rigidity and more flexibility on the employers' side must have been felt by employers at all times, although in closed economic systems employers can put up with rigidities when all their competitors are equally bound by them. Now that economies are becoming increasingly open, rigidities are more difficult to endure than in the past.

Traditionally, the preference for sectoral collective agreements in Germany has been justified by the need to protect wages against lower-cost competition. The sectoral collective agreement is a major instrument by which wages and working conditions are taken 'out of competition'. The Dutch still believe very strongly in the ideal that employers should compete on the quality of their products and not on wage costs. Dutch employers are still inclined to prefer the rigidities of collective agreements to the social unrest that could result from a breakdown of the system of sectoral collective bargaining.

The fact that without collectively negotiated wage norms at sectoral level each company has to create its own remuneration system, and that this may produce increasing wage conflicts in each company, is one of the main reasons why Dutch employers still prefer sectoral collective agreements, even in sectors in which such agreements are rigid and could be avoided because of trade union weakness.

Besides collective bargaining one might imagine alternative wage formation procedures. US industrial relations show us that unilateral wage formation is a real possibility. Such wage structures can be laid down in company handbooks, which can obtain legally binding force by a clause in the individual contract of employment. In the USA this method is nowadays found more frequently than collective bargaining, although that has not disappeared altogether and flourishes in a number of industries. Wage levels set in collective agreements often serve as reference points for wages in companies in which wage setting occurs in unilateral fashion.

American and Japanese companies have already imported this system to the Netherlands. There has been little research on this phenomenon nor is there much case law. Most of these firms have wage structures on which they have consulted – in one way or another – the works council. They derive their legally binding force from clauses in individual employment contracts.

It is possible that this American model may spread in Europe in the near future. In the Netherlands this development would not be welcomed because it would lead to confusion in terms of working conditions and hinder solidarity. It is therefore likely that in the Netherlands, apparently more than in Germany, the social partners will still struggle to keep alive the many sectoral collective agreements and to attain more flexibility by other means.

A first instrument – used in both Germany and the Netherlands – is variable pay systems, such as payment by results, performance-related pay and financial participation. Notably in 1999–2000 there was a drive in the Netherlands for more flexible wage forms. The unions accepted some and rejected others. The employers themselves are divided on the issue: some dislike flexible wage structures because they are too cumbersome, requiring detailed assessment of their employees.

The 'promise' of such pay systems, of course, is that they may result in higher labour productivity. The downside is that they can often leave employees with too little money in their pockets. Another risk is that employees become excessively money-driven by such systems to the detriment of their health and/or the quality of their work.

In my view, statutory law should put a cap on such wage forms. In the Netherlands no such legal restrictions exist, but the opposition of the unions has been sufficient to put a brake on this development.

A second instrument involves giving sectoral collective agreements more or less of a framework character, with details being settled at enterprise level in agreements with either trade unions or works councils (see section 5).

A third instrument is company-level deals under which employees give up some of the rights acquired in the sectoral collective agreement. Such deals seem to be somewhat more feasible in Germany (Bündnis für Arbeit) than in the Netherlands.

As already mentioned, the Dutch Government has urged the parties to collective agreements to make it possible for employers to obtain permission to deviate from sectoral agreements. Such procedures have in fact been created but there has been little research on the recent application of such opening clauses. One may assume that they are incidentally but not widely applied. In a recent case an employee contested the binding force of a simple contract between an employer and a single union which authorized the employer on an ad hoc basis, not via the official opening clauses, to deviate *in peius* from the sectoral collective agreement. The Supreme Court rejected the binding force of this agreement and confirmed the rights of the worker under the collective agreement.

This example shows that deviations from collective agreements are regarded by the courts with suspicion. Such deviations must be based on explicit opening clauses in the collective agreement.

In my view the use of clauses to deviate from collective agreements should never be left unchecked nor should deviations be left to the consent of works councils or individual workers, if this deviation is to the detriment of such workers. In such cases it should require the consent of the unions.

A final instrument by means of which to retain sectoral collective agreements and their extension on the one hand and to make wage formation more flexible on the other, might be reform of erga omnes extension. I once proposed that statutory law should allow enterprises to deviate by a maximum of 10% below the wage level in the extended sectoral collective agreement. This would create some flexibility for the employers without depriving the workers of protection. Moreover, it would provide the social partners with an indication of the market conformity of the wage level.

In the course of this debate no Constitutional questions have been raised on the issue of whether reform of erga omnes extension is legally possible. As already mentioned, the notion of 'free collective bargaining' is not as strongly developed in the Netherlands as in Germany.

9. CONCLUSIONS

In the Netherlands the traditional system of collective wage formation – involving a significant level of government intervention – was fundamentally changed in the 1980s and the beginning of the 1990s. Since then a new system of free collective bargaining has emerged in which centralization and decentralization are at odds and must somehow be combined by way of a compromise. This struggle to strike a balance has so far been unsuccessful. The struggle will continue in the years to come and we must await the outcome.

Several developments concerning the German system of collective wage formation have been reported recently (for example, shrinking number of employers bound by collective bargaining, increasing adoption of opening clauses in collective agreements). It is difficult to determine whether these developments indicate a fundamental change in the German system. Mention of this phenomenon in debates in the Netherlands tends to give rise to expressions of amazement: apparently the fundamental character of these developments has not yet been perceived abroad.

Although the technicalities differ, collective agreement systems in most European countries are encountering the same problems. Everywhere there is pressure from employers to reduce wage costs because otherwise their products and services can no longer be marketed. Similar economic challenges are likely to transform wage formation systems and produce different solutions. In the Netherlands opening clauses in collective agreements have so far not been exploited to the full, but a decrease in the number of employers bound by collective agreements is not noticeable. Collective bargaining at national, intersectoral level is still an important feature of wage formation in the Netherlands.

No further convergence of collective wage formation in Germany and in the Netherlands – which have numerous common features – is likely in the foreseeable future.

In Germany some scholars are questioning whether the state should intervene to stabilize the collective bargaining system. In my view the state should do so, a view confirmed by a recent (February 2003) World Bank study which indicates that countries with a mature system of trade unions and collective bargaining perform better than other countries. However, there are the usual exceptions: the USA and the UK are performing well with lame-duck systems of trade unions and collective bargaining.

No easy conclusion may be drawn. However, in countries with a mature system of collective bargaining and trade unions there is more coherence in the development of wages and benefits than in other countries, which may, in the long run, better guarantee a stable, decent and prosperous society, even if in the short term the rigidities of such systems may seem a disadvantage in comparison with more free-market-oriented economies.

5. Sweden: Transition through collective bargaining

Kerstin Ahlberg and Niklas Bruun

1. INTRODUCTION

A basic feature of Swedish industrial relations, which partly explains why the system looks the way it does and without which it would not work, is the very high rate of unionization. In spite of a decline in union membership during the last decade, trade union density is still over 80%. This is true also for university graduates and public employees, who started to form their own trade unions in the 1930s. Today, trade union density is higher in the public sector than in the private sector.

Another characteristic of Swedish industrial relations is that the employers have accepted collective bargaining and collective agreements as instruments for the regulation of working life since the first decades of the twentieth century. In fact, until the 1970s, terms and conditions of employment for employees in the private sector were regulated almost exclusively through collective agreements. From 1974 onwards the legislator introduced a number of laws, and the balance between agreements and legislation was altered. Nevertheless, collective agreements are still the predominant source of norms influencing the contents of individual employment contracts. Furthermore, apart from individual contracts, they are the only instrument for regulating pay. There is no minimum wage legislation in Sweden; both trade unions and employers have always been strongly opposed to the idea that the state should take responsibility for pay determination.

A third characteristic is that the system of industrial relations and collective bargaining encompasses all wage-earners, whether white-collar or blue-collar workers or employed by public or private employers. With few exceptions, they are all covered by uniform labour legislation. Unlike in many other countries, no specific statutory rules apply to white-collar workers in contrast to blue-collar workers. Civil servants are subject to some specific legislation, but the main principles follow the general labour law pattern.

A fourth characteristic – one which may contribute to an understanding of the recent development of collective bargaining practices as described below – is the climate of cooperation on the labour market. In Sweden, trade unions and employers' associations in general recognize each other's interests: for example, the trade unions have always had a positive attitude to technological change and other measures that could increase productivity.

Finally, in spite of some remarkable recent exceptions, industrial relations in Sweden are generally characterized by a high degree of collective autonomy and non-intervention on the part of the state. When the trade unions and the employers agree to regulate matters themselves, normally the government does not venture to intervene.

Two deviations from this tradition occurred during the 1990s. In 1993 the Conservative Government forced through an amendment to the Employment Protection Act which nullified certain collectively agreed restrictions on fixed-term contracts. In 2001 the Social Democrats modified the same act with the effect that provisions in collective agreements that obliged employees to retire before the age of 67 were invalidated. In both cases, Sweden was criticized by the ILO committee on freedom of association.

2. INDUSTRIAL RELATIONS IN SWEDEN

There are three major confederations on the trade union side: one for blue-collar workers (Swedish Trade Union Confederation, LO), one for white-collar workers (Swedish Confederation of Professional Employees, TCO) and one for professional/graduate employees (Swedish Confederation of Professional Associations, Saco). The confederations are made up of national trade unions, organizing workers in a specific industry or occupation. These trade unions, in turn, consist of regional and/or local trade unions, the latter often tied to a particular company. Usually, there are three local trade unions with their own collective agreements present at each workplace – one for each confederation. As they have different membership criteria, they normally work in peaceful co-existence, although there are cases in which they compete to organize the same workers, for example in sectors in which the distinction between blue-collar and white-collar work is becoming less and less discernible.

Among the confederations, only LO concludes collective agreements. TCO and Saco have never had that role. Instead, trade unions affiliated to TCO and Saco have joined forces in cartels established specifically for collective bargaining. Examples of such cartels are the Federation of Salaried Employees in Industry and Services (PTK) and the Public Employees' Negotiation Council (OFR/SPO).

There are some small unions outside the confederations, and some of them conclude their own collective agreements. In practice, however, they cannot compete with the dominant unions.

The vast majority of private employers are affiliated to the Confederation of Swedish Enterprise (Svenskt Näringsliv, former SAF). It consists of sectoral associations (*förbund*) organizing employers within a specific branch of the economy.

For public employers there are three large organizations: the Swedish Agency for Government Employers (Arbetsgivarverket), the Swedish Association of Local Authorities (Kommunförbundet) and the Federation of County Councils (Landstingsförbundet). Since local authorities and county councils to a large extent employ the same categories of employees, such as nurses, doctors, and so on, the Association of Local Authorities and the Federation of County Councils have regularly negotiated jointly. As from 2005 they will merge and establish one joint organization.

The Swedish collective bargaining system is often described as highly centralized. However, that is only partly true.

Collective bargaining takes place at three levels:

1. National, intersectoral agreements are concluded by confederations on both sides or, on the trade union side, by a bargaining cartel. However, as a general rule,

confederations and cartels do not have a mandate to conclude directly binding agreements. Thus, these agreements do not enter into force until the competent bodies of the individual affiliates have adopted them.

From 1956 to the early 1980s, centrally coordinated negotiations at this level led to the conclusion of wage agreements for the whole private-sector labour market. Even after they had entered into force, they were not immediately applicable to individual employment contracts, but formed a framework for negotiations at sectoral level, where more specific implementing provisions and other terms and conditions than pay were agreed. However, in 1983, the Engineering Employers' Association and the Swedish Metalworkers' Union broke out of the coordinated negotiations and concluded a separate wage agreement. In the following bargaining rounds attempts were made to revive the centrally coordinated negotiations, but in 1990, the Swedish Employers' Confederation finally decided not to negotiate on wages and general terms of employment any more. Thus today, few issues, primarily labour market insurance, are negotiated at this level. A fresh example is the agreement on redundancy support between Svenskt Näringsliv and LO. It provides for a number of instruments that can be used to help blue-collar workers to find new jobs and to support them financially in case of redundancy.

2. National sectoral agreements are negotiated by national trade unions representing workers in a certain sector or a specific occupation and by sectoral associations on the employers' side. This is where agreements on wages and other terms of employment are concluded today. Such 'central' agreements exist for all sectors of the economy. Thus it is estimated that 94% of Swedish employees are covered by collective agreements.

3. 'Local' collective agreements are negotiated between the individual employer and the 'local' trade union, that is, the company trade union branch or the regional trade union body. These agreements run parallel with, and complement, the 'central' sectoral agreements. For example, sectoral agreements normally presuppose that the wage rises agreed at sectoral level are to be distributed to individual employees through negotiations at local level. However, the local trade unions also have the capacity to conclude legally binding collective agreements on any other issue that concerns the relation between employer and employee, as long as they act within the boundaries drawn up by law, superordinate collective agreements and the sectoral trade union's rulebook.

Accordingly, as we have seen, wage negotiations take place both at central and at local level, and that was true even in the days of centrally coordinated wage negotiations. Thus, while the system was extremely centralized in one sense, local trade unions regularly negotiated with the employers and often managed to get a substantial extra rise for their members in addition to the centrally agreed increases.

This relative strength at both levels is another feature that is significant for the functioning of the Swedish system. The position of the local trade unions is consolidated by the Workplace Union Representatives Act of 1974, which grants local trade union representatives time off for trade union activities – without deduction from their wages insofar as these activities concern the employer's own business.

Collective bargaining with a view to reaching a new collective agreement on wages (and other terms and conditions of employment) is classified as negotiation on *issues of interest.* However, local and central negotiations also play a very important role in the resolution of *disputes of rights*, that is, when the trade union questions the employer's interpretation of an existing collective agreement or a statutory provision. For example, if a worker has been dismissed and the trade union thinks that the dismissal is contrary to the Employment Protection Act, the case cannot be brought before the Labour Court until the trade union and the employer have tried to settle the dispute through negotiation. Normally, such negotiations must take place at both local level and, if the local negotiations fail, central level. In fact, most disputes of rights are settled through this mechanism. The settlement is often a compromise, where, for example, the employer pays substantial damages to the worker on condition that he or she accepts the dismissal, even though it may have been unjust.

3. LEGAL FRAMEWORK OF COLLECTIVE WAGE FORMATION

3.1 Private law approach

Although the right and freedom for trade unions and employers to take industrial action is guaranteed in the Swedish constitution, collective bargaining rights are not.

The legal framework concerning collective wage formation is based consistently on private (contract) law principles. The rules on collective bargaining are enshrined in Medbestämmandelagen, MBL ('the Codetermination Act').

It is easy to form a trade union and acquire collective bargaining rights. There are no formal registration or recognition requirements. Any association of employees that, according to its rulebook, has as its objective to safeguard the interests of employees in relation to the employer is a trade union in the legal sense. As such, it has a right to bargain with a view to reaching a collective agreement. Employers have a corresponding duty to enter into negotiations, although they are not obliged to compromise or conclude agreements.

There are still comparably few statutory restrictions on the bargaining parties, although the provisions on mediation were made somewhat more stringent in 2000: for example, there are no rules on ballots on the results of collective bargaining or before a decision to take industrial action.

As long as the 'old' collective agreement remains in force, the parties bargain under a peace obligation. If either party plans to take industrial action after the collective agreement has expired, it must give seven workdays' notice, both to its opposite party and to the National Mediation Office. Trade unions and employers' organizations for the private sector are entirely responsible for the scale of industrial action. In other words, no principle of proportionality applies. Since 1965, public employees have had the right to bargain collectively and conclude collective agreements on roughly the same footing as private employees. A few special provisions on industrial action exist, but even government officials have the right to strike for better pay. There is no legislation restricting strikes in essential services. However, both in the public and in the private sector, trade unions and employers' organizations have concluded basic collective agreements (of an indefinite duration) that complement the statutory rules, and in which they undertake not to resort to industrial action that threatens the public interest.

If trade unions and employers have difficulty reaching agreement, they can ask the National Mediation Office to appoint mediators to help them resolve the dispute. Before 2000, this was entirely the parties' own decision. Today, the Mediation Office can appoint mediators without the consent of the parties when it considers that there is a risk of industrial action, and summon them to a 'mild' form of compulsory mediation. In addition, it can impose a cooling-off period of 14 days when either party has announced that it intends to take industrial action. In the end, however, the parties decide for themselves whether they will accept any settlement that the mediators propose.

3.2 Concept of 'just wages'

According to Article 4.1 of the European Social Charter (ratified by Sweden), member states undertake to ensure workers' right to 'fair remuneration'. The expression 'fair remuneration' or 'just wages' can be understood in two ways: (i) in terms of the concept that it is not decent to pay a worker below a certain limit, or (ii) in terms of a concept relating to wage structures, to the factors that determine who is to be paid less and who is to be paid more.

Since pay is exclusively a contractual issue in Sweden, the concept of 'fair' or 'just' pay is not defined in legislation. However, the fact that collective agreements are generally accepted as instruments for wage setting can in itself be seen to indicate that there is a concept of 'just wages', even if it is not explicit. The content of that concept depends on the values underlying the collective agreement. This means that it may differ from time to time and from one collective agreement to another. One principle that has been consistently upheld, however, is that irrespective of an enterprise's economic situation, it must pay the minimum wage stipulated in the applicable collective agreement.[1] A fundamental idea underlying the solidaristic wage policy pursued by LO for decades was that companies that could not afford to pay the collectively agreed minimum wage should be closed down. The courts also use the collective agreement for the sector concerned as a standard in cases where workers not covered by a collective agreement call for judicial adjustment of unreasonable conditions in their employment contracts.

One could also say that a concept of what is 'fair' or 'just' indirectly emerges from collective agreements to the extent that they lay down what factors shall be considered when individual wages are set. Another way of putting it is that pay differences must be justified on objective grounds if they are to be 'just'.

3.3 Legal effect of collective agreements

According to MBL, a collective agreement is binding on the signatories and their members. In other words, the employer (as party to the agreement or as a member of the signatory employers' organization) and the members of the signatory trade union are bound in relation to each other. However, the employer is not bound in relation to workers who are not members of the trade union, and there is no general non-

1. Some examples: the Agreement between the Swedish Metalworkers' Union and the Swedish Association of Engineering Employers for 2004–2007 stipulates that the minimum wage for workers who have reached the age of 18 is SEK 13,500 (EUR 1,471) per month. According to the collective agreement between the Municipal Workers' Union and the Swedish Association of Local Authorities for 2003–2004, workers who have reached the age of 19 must be paid at least SEK 13,000 (EUR 1,417) per month. According to the collective agreement between the Union of White Collar Workers in Industry and the Swedish Industrial and Chemical Employers' Association for 2004–2007 a full-time employed worker shall have at least SEK 12,970 per month as from 1 April 2004, SEK 13,260 as from 1 April 2005 and SEK 13,600 as from 1 April 2006.

discrimination principle which guarantees non-organized workers the same terms and conditions of employment as trade union members.

This does not mean that the collective agreement does not affect the conditions of non-unionized workers. First of all, the employer is obliged to apply at least its *minimum* conditions to non-unionized workers. This does not follow from legislation, but it is an obligation towards the trade union, implied in the collective agreement itself and with the purpose of preventing low-wage competition. Secondly, unless otherwise agreed in the individual employment contract, all *general* provisions in the collective agreement have normative effect for the non-unionized workers. This follows from case law and applies irrespective of whether these provisions are favourable or unfavourable for the workers.[2] A special case is where legislation – for example on employment protection – allows for derogations from statutory provisions in collective agreements. In these cases, employers are normally entitled to apply such agreements to trade union members and outsiders alike.

Accordingly, if the employer is bound by a collective agreement, outside workers have to submit to its general terms and conditions even if they disapprove of them. On the other hand, they are also entitled to all benefits that follow from the general provisions of the collective agreement. However, a non-unionized worker cannot claim every advantage that follows from trade union membership. As we will show later in this chapter, Swedish collective agreements today contain few *general* rules on wages: collective agreements that decide wages for different types of work or specific categories of employee hardly exist any more. To an increasing extent, the sectoral agreements simply establish a framework for negotiations at local level, at which only a small proportion of wage increases are defined in general terms – for example, as a minimum guarantee for every worker – while the rest is distributed on the basis of *individual* factors. In these cases, workers who are not members of the trade union are entitled only to the minimum guaranteed amount.

In consistency with the Swedish private law approach, there is no mechanism for extending the binding force of collective agreements and giving them *erga omnes* effect. The issue was brought to the fore during the 1990s, for example when the EC Directive (96/71) on the posting of workers within the framework of the provision of services was implemented. However, neither the trade unions nor the employers are in favour of such an extension mechanism. This means that there is no statutory guarantee that foreign employers who post workers in Sweden have to pay their employees according to Swedish standards, not even in the building sector. Instead, the trade unions use their traditional means – industrial action if needed – to force these employers to sign Swedish collective agreements for their posted workers.

Once a collective agreement is concluded, its normative provisions are automatically incorporated in the employment contracts. These normative provisions are mandatory: employers and employees bound by a collective agreement cannot make individual agreements that conflict with it. This follows from statutory law. Since most collective agreements set a minimum standard, conditions that are more favourable for the worker are normally in accord with the collective agreement. However, should an employer and a worker agree on inferior terms and conditions, the agreement is void.

2. Jonas Malmberg, 'The collective agreement as an instrument for regulation of wages and employment conditions', in Peter Wahlgren (ed.), *Stability and Change in Nordic Labour Law*, Scandinavian Studies in Law 43, Stockholm Institute for Scandinavian Law (Stockholm, 2002), p. 205.

In the case of employers bound by collective agreements, workers' participation and information and consultation rights are channelled through the trade unions. Thus, apart from European works councils in international groups, there are no parallel structures for workers' representation at the workplace, which means that competence conflicts like those between trade unions and works councils in Germany do not occur.

3.4 Enforcement of collective agreements

Finally, some rules have particular significance for the enforcement of collective agreements. If a trade union thinks that an employer is not applying the wage provisions of a collective agreement correctly, the MBL gives the trade union a priority right of interpretation. This means that the employer is obliged to comply with the trade union's interpretation and to pay the workers accordingly, at least until the dispute has been settled. In other words, it is for the employer to bring the case to the Labour Court if it does not accept the trade union's interpretation. A similar provision gives the trade union a priority right of interpretation if there is a dispute about the purport of the employees' duty to work according to the collective agreement. Also, trade unions have the authority to act on behalf of their members before the Labour Court. Thus, disputes concerning the rights of individual trade union members that cannot be settled through local and central negotiations are tried in court, without the worker having to take any financial risk.

Another mechanism that indirectly promotes adherence to collective agreements is the trade union right of veto when the employer plans to engage an outside contractor to carry out certain work instead of letting its own employees do it. If it is reasonable to assume that the contracting out will contravene legislation, a collective agreement applying to the employer or the contractor, or generally accepted practice in the industry concerned, the trade union can exercize its right of veto. As a consequence, the employer is prevented from realizing its plan, provided that the veto is not unjustified.

4. CURRENT CHALLENGES

During the last decades of the twentieth century, wage costs in Sweden increased more than in other western European countries. According to leading economists, collective agreements were inflationary: for example, many of them contained 'catch-up guarantees' which ensured the employees pay rises corresponding to increases in other sectors in which there had been wage-drift while the previous agreement was still in force. Other clauses guaranteed an extra wage rise if the retail price index increased above a given limit. As a result, real wages in fact fell, although nominal wages rose considerably. In the general debate, this was explained by malfunctions in the system of collective bargaining. Part of the criticism was directed at the provisions on industrial action. It was too easy – and too cheap – to go on strike, it was argued: trade unions were able to cause much harm at low cost to themselves by bringing only a small number of members in key positions out on strike.

During the same period, unemployment rates increased beyond anything experienced in Sweden during the post-war period. Also, it was perfectly clear that

Sweden would have to bring inflation down as it prepared to join the European Union: according to prevailing economic theories, it would not be possible to reduce unemployment unless wages were kept at a 'European' level.

In parallel with this the employers, notably SAF (and its successor Svenskt Näringsliv), pursued the decentralization of collective bargaining and deregulation with neo-liberal overtones. SAF's decision on 2 February 1990 to finally opt out of the centrally coordinated wage negotiations had been in the pipeline for several years. In ICT and other 'new' sectors there was a tendency for employers to break with Swedish traditions and not apply collective agreements at all. One employers' organization even introduced a new form of membership which made it possible to be a member without being bound by the collective agreements that the organization concluded. However, apart from attacks on the right to strike, which of course is an indispensable building block in the collective bargaining system, SAF/Svenskt Näringsliv never seriously called into question the legislative framework as such. It concentrated on achieving change within the collective agreement system.

The aim of efforts towards decentralization of collective bargaining on pay has been twofold: (i) to limit total wage costs and (ii) to change wage structures.

Withdrawal from centrally coordinated negotiations was a first step that would serve to reduce total wage costs, since the employers always have to pay something at each bargaining level, SAF argued. Thus, bargaining at three levels inevitably raised costs. However, it is not enough to move from bargaining at national inter-sectoral to sectoral level. Wages determined at sectoral level do not take sufficient account of the individual company's economic situation. Therefore, ideally, wages should be set at company level.

With regard to the wage structure, the employers pointed to the fact that work in modern companies is organized in a way that gives the individual employee wider scope of action than in traditional manufacturing industry. To a greater extent than before, employees can decide for themselves how to perform their tasks as more and more businesses practice management by objectives. Consequently, the character of work varies with the worker and his or her competence and results. This, the employers argued, called for a new wage policy. Catch-up clauses and clauses that lay down pay minima, guarantee a certain rise for everyone or afford extra money for low-wage earners are simply no longer relevant. Collective agreements must provide room for individual wages that stimulate workers to develop their competences and improve their results. Wages should not be seen simply as remuneration for work, but as a productive factor.[3]

These challenges would have threatened the collective bargaining system if it had not reacted adequately. The Government demonstrated a firm resolve to take control, if necessary by legislative measures, should wages continue to increase above what was seen as responsible in relation to society as a whole. However, it would not be Sweden if the labour market parties had not in the end averted the threat of legislation by voluntarily imposing restrictions on themselves, even if it was 'a conversion on the way to the gallows'. This has happened repeatedly in the history of Swedish industrial relations, and, as we shall see below, this is what happened this time too.

This adaptation to new realities also led to a significant change in the contents of collective agreements, in response to the employers' calls for decentralization and individualization of wages.

3. Göran Trogen, 'Löneavtalen – norm för kostnadsbegränsningar eller grund för lokal och individuell lönebildning?', in *Tretton perspektiv på lönebildningen* (National Mediation Office, 2003).

5. REACTIONS OF THE STATE, SOCIAL PARTNERS AND ENTERPRISES

5.1 State intervention

Since the 1980s, both social democratic and conservative governments had demonstrated increasing discontent with the outcome of wage negotiations. In the early 1990s, the government started to deviate from the traditional attitude that the state should not interfere with the pay determination process. Its most dramatic move came on 8 February 1990, six days after SAF had decided to withdraw from the central coordinated negotiations once and for all, and in the middle of mediation in the negotiations for the whole municipal sector, a lockout of all employees in the banking sector and wild-cat strikes among employees at social insurance offices. The Social Democrat Government presented a parliamentary bill in which it proposed a two-year general wage-freeze, a two-year moratorium on industrial action for the labour market as a whole and a considerable increase in the damages to be paid by individual employees who violated the peace obligation. The prohibition on industrial action would enter into force after one week. However, the bill was rejected by Parliament and the government had to resign.

In the subsequent bargaining round, the new government tried to influence the actual contents of wage agreements by appointing a group of experts – the so-called Rehnberg group – to 'assist' labour market organizations in negotiations.[4] In the 1993 bargaining round, the same experts were appointed as mediators, and they continued to pursue the so-called policy of stabilization.

5.2 Changes in the organization and procedure of bargaining

Governments were not alone in worrying about the outcome of the bargaining rounds of the 1980s and the first half of the 1990s. Both employers and trade unions were increasingly aware of the fact that wage agreements were part of the problem in the Swedish economy. Among other things, a number of attempts were made to establish a new, common 'norm', a formula for defining what wage-cost increases the economy could stand.[5] However, it is difficult for a trade union leader to convince his or her members that they should seek only moderate wage increases, unless he or she is sure that other unions will impose the same restraints on themselves. Thus, from a trade union perspective the solution lies in centralization and coordination of bargaining. However, as already mentioned, the employers' strategy went in the opposite direction. It may have been the recurrent government attempts to intervene in the bargaining process and the 'threat' of legislation, combined with a severe setback for the employers' strategy in the bargaining round of 1995, that finally brought a number of private employers' associations to accept a return to coordinated collective bargaining, albeit in a completely new form.

Among SAF's affiliates, the most ardent advocate of decentralization of collective bargaining, even down to company level, was the Engineering Employers'

4. Nils Elvander and Bertil Holmlund, *The Swedish Bargaining System in the Melting Pot. Institutions, Norms and Outcomes in the 1990s* (Arbetslivsinstitutet, 1997), pp. 17ff.
5. On the Swedish debate on wage norms, see Nils Elvander and Bertil Holmlund, *The Swedish Bargaining System in the Melting Pot. Institutions, Norms and Outcomes in the 1990s* (Arbetslivsinstitutet, 1997), pp. 52ff.

Association. Its bargaining offer to the Metalworkers' Union in the 1995 bargaining round was a bold move: the central agreement should lay down a peace obligation and terms and conditions of employment other than pay, but nothing else. Thus wages, including the size of the minimum wage, should be left entirely to negotiations between the individual employer and the local trade union branch – under a peace obligation. In addition, none of the provisions in the central agreement should be mandatory, but subject to adaptations at company level. The employers also wanted to negotiate on deviations from the provisions of the Employment Protection Act. The Metalworkers' Union responded with an overtime ban. However, in the middle of this dispute, another of SAF's affiliates, the Employers' Federation of Swedish Forest Industries, concluded a collective agreement with the Paper Workers' Union, which guaranteed at least 3.8% in both 1995 and 1996. To cut a long story short, this made it impossible for the engineering employers to achieve an agreement that gave the metalworkers less. However, while the agreement was well within the limits of what the forest industries could afford, it was too expensive for the engineering industry. A public quarrel between the two employers' associations broke out. The engineering employers accused the forest industries of breaking employer solidarity. The latter responded that they had acted in accordance with the policy of non-coordination advocated by the engineering employers.

Several other sectors were also bargaining in 1995, and the year was characterized by strikes and lockouts. At the beginning of 1996, the Government invited the confederations on both sides to propose reforms of the system of collective bargaining and wage formation, if possible jointly, before the end of March 1997. The engineering employers' offensive had triggered off a new spirit of cooperation on the trade union side. For the first time, blue-collar and white-collar unions in the metal industry joined forces to defend national sectoral agreements. Now, they involved the other trade unions in the industry and invited their counterparts on the employers' side to talks. On 18 March 1997, eight trade unions representing all three confederations and 12 employers' associations affiliated to SAF announced that they had concluded a 'Cooperation Agreement on Industrial Development and Pay Determination'.[6]

The agreement – also known as the Industry Agreement – covers the whole of Swedish manufacturing industry and carries on the Swedish tradition of cooperation and mutual understanding between trade unions and employers. In the preamble, the parties state that there is a long tradition of bipartite cooperation in the different industries at both industry and company level, and that they wish to build on this foundation and establish practises for stronger, trust-based joint endeavours in the

6. Parties to the agreement on the trade union side are the Industrial Union, the Swedish Food Workers' Union, the Swedish Metalworkers' Union, the Swedish Paper Workers' Union, the Swedish Forest Workers Union, the Swedish Wood Industry Workers' Union (all affiliated to LO), the Swedish Trade Union for White-Collar Workers in Industry (TCO) and the Swedish Association of Graduate Engineers (Saco), and on the employers' side the Almega Industrial and Chemical Association, the Employers' Association of Swedish Building Material Manufacturers, the Employers' Association of Swedish Mine Owners, the Employers' Association of the Swedish Food Industry, the Federation of Swedish Forestry and Agricultural Employers, the Employers' Association of the Upholstery Industry, the Employers' Association of the Swedish Steel and Metal Industry, the Employers' Federation of the Swedish Forest Industries, the Swedish Engineering Employers' Association, the Swedish Employers' Federation of Welding Engineering, the Employers' Association of the Swedish Wood Products Industry and the Swedish Textile and Clothing Industries Association.

future. Thus the object of the agreement is to promote 'industrial development, profitability and competitiveness', which will 'provide the necessary conditions for reducing unemployment as well as the foundation for a healthy wage development, and good conditions for employees in other respects'.

The agreement consists of two parts. In the first, and most substantial, part the parties to the agreement describe the conditions under which Swedish industry is working and express a number of common views on what is needed to maintain a strong competitive position. Among other things, the parties note that economic policy has changed and price stability has been given a higher political priority. This makes it possible to give employees higher real wages, although nominal wage increases are lower than in the past. Consequently, improvements in real wages can be brought about without adverse effects in terms of high interest rates and erosion of competitiveness. The parties also conclude that the competitive strength of Swedish industry is based on a high level of competence among its employees and on production processes and products that are among the very best in their fields. Here, the determination and drive of its employees to tackle new tasks and to develop their competence are key factors. Apart from the factors under the control of the parties themselves, the agreement also brings up a number of issues that are in the hands of the government, such as the need to safeguard the supply of electricity at competitive prices (as Swedish industry is highly dependent on electricity) and the funding of research and development that meets the needs of industry.

In order to realize the agreement's objectives, the parties established a committee – the Industry Committee – consisting of leading representatives of the organizations concerned, and an Economic Council comprising four independent economists. The task of the Industry Committee is to monitor and promote the application of the agreement and otherwise to address issues with a view to creating stable conditions for Swedish industry and its employees. It also has specific functions during actual collective bargaining rounds, which will be described later. The task of the Economic Council is to make comments and recommendations on economic issues, when asked by negotiating parties, the person acting as an impartial chair during negotiations or the Industry Committee. The Industry Committee itself does not meet very often, but has set up a number of working groups at which the parties meet regularly. Here they discuss issues of mutual interest such as energy supply, research and development, education, the organization of production, and so on, and try to reach common positions in order to influence government policy.

The second part of the agreement deals with actual wage negotiations. As before, collective bargaining on wages and other terms and conditions of employment takes place at sectoral level. Thus each trade union still concludes its own collective agreement. However, the agreement lays down a completely new procedure for collective bargaining, promoting constructive negotiations with a balanced outcome, without either party having to resort to industrial action.

The underlying principle is that new collective agreements on wages and other terms and conditions of employment shall be reached before current agreements have expired, which means that there will be no room for industrial action: as already mentioned, the parties bargain under a peace obligation as long as the current agreement is in force. Thus, the Industry Agreement contains a number of mechanisms intended to force the parties to start negotiations earlier than before and to continue them assiduously. Another novelty in Swedish industrial relations is that the parties have agreed to ask outsiders – impartial chairs – to assist them.

The new bargaining procedure means that negotiations shall begin at least three months before the current agreement runs out, with the parties putting forward their demands. After that, additional demands may be presented only if it had not been possible to present them earlier. If no new agreement has been reached one month before the current agreement runs out, an impartial chair appointed by the Industry Committee shall enter into the negotiations on his or her own initiative and, within the limits of the agreement, do what he or she deems necessary to conclude the negotiations in due time. The role of the impartial chair under the Industry Agreement differs from that of a traditional mediator. First of all, whereas a traditional mediator is appointed to a specific dispute when negotiations have already broken down, the new impartial chairs have an ongoing mission, which means that they are informed of and follow the negotiations 'from a distance' from the moment the parties present their demands. Thus, they are already well versed in the controverted issues if the bargaining parties turn to them for help. Secondly, the task of an impartial chair is to help the parties reach not just any agreement, but an agreement in which due consideration is given to its effects on the national economy and employment, and which serves to maintain or improve the industry's competitiveness and increase workers' real wages. In order to achieve that, the impartial chair can ask the Economic Council for its opinion and set out his or her own proposals. He or she can also postpone industrial action for 14 days. If, nevertheless, industrial action cannot be avoided, all retroactive demands become void. In addition, the Industry Committee can prescribe that the action be temporarily suspended if the negotiations would thereby benefit.

The parties also agreed that these procedural provisions would apply instead of the statutory provisions on mediation, which, at that time, were entirely voluntary. In fact, the Industry Agreement gives the Industry Committee and the impartial chairs more far-reaching powers than those of the state mediators. However, it is the negotiating parties' own system.

It is no exaggeration to say that the Industry Agreement created a sensation. Some commentators greeted it as a modern counterpart of the historic Saltsjöbaden Agreement. Furthermore, in light of the private employers' call for decentralization of collective bargaining, the Industry Agreement implied a retreat. However, it was far from a step backwards to the old type of centrally coordinated negotiations in which agreements were concluded at cross-sectoral level. Under the Industry Agreement collective bargaining on wages and other terms and conditions of employment takes place at sectoral level, and ultimately each trade union and employers' association is sovereign. At the same time, negotiations are coordinated voluntarily, in the sense that the total cost is about the same for agreements for different sectors. This coordination is facilitated by the assessments of economic realities provided by the Economic Council and by the impartial chairs.

The Government too greeted the conclusion of the Industry Agreement with satisfaction. Less than a month later, it decided to set up an official committee with the task of proposing measures to improve the functioning of the pay determination process. More specifically, it was to consider whether the legal provisions on mediation and industrial action were well balanced. However, the competent Minister declared that the Government would do nothing that would disturb the working of the Industry Agreement. The committee was the fourth (!) set up to consider these issues since the beginning of the 1980s. No previous committee had led to any legislative changes.

The new committee presented its report in November 1998. It proposed some particularly controversial amendments. A new mediation authority, with a different role and enhanced powers, would replace the National Conciliators' Office. Unlike the latter, which was restricted to helping disputing parties reach an agreement irrespective of its content, the new authority would also contribute to setting wage standards. Furthermore, it would have the power to appoint a mediator without the consent of the bargaining parties, to summon them to negotiations and to postpone notified industrial action by 14 days. The committee also felt that a shift in the balance between trade unions and employers was necessary, and proposed a couple of rather far-reaching new restrictions on industrial action.

The subsequent Government bill and the amendments finally adopted by Parliament in 2000 were rather modest. With one minor exception, the right to strike was left unaffected. As regards mediation, the new authority, the National Mediation Office, has as one of its tasks to promote 'well-functioning wage formation', but this does not mean that it will impose a state incomes policy. Instead, it is to advise and assist the labour market parties with expert information on the national economy, wage statistics, and so on. Responsibility for the actual contents of collective agreements remains with the bargaining parties. However, in order to avoid industrial action as far as possible, the authority can appoint a mediator without their consent, and the mediator can summon them to negotiations. They are under no obligation to compromise, however. Furthermore, the Mediation Office can impose a cooling-off period of 14 days before industrial action can take place, and propose (but not insist) that the dispute be referred to settlement through arbitration.

Last, but by no means least, the act contains an exception to these rules. Parties that are bound by a procedural collective agreement, whereby they have created a private system of mediation that meets certain standards, cannot be subject to compulsory mediation. This provision is explicitly designed to fit the Industry Agreement. A number of similar procedural agreements have later been concluded for other sectors.

The effectiveness of the Industry Agreement has now been put to the test in three bargaining rounds. The general judgement is that it has served its purpose well. With one exception, the parties managed to reach collective agreements, even without the threat of industrial action: previously, industrial action or at least notification of industrial action had been the rule. Also, wage increases in all industry sectors have been more – although still not quite – in step with the European average, according to statistics from the National Mediation Office. At the same time, Swedish industry's competitiveness has been reinforced due to increased productivity.

The Industry Agreement might not have been so great a success had it not been the result of a genuine and far-reaching concord between employers' associations and trade unions. A number of other agreements inspired by the Industry Agreement seem to have emerged primarily as a means of avoiding interference by the National Mediation Office. One example, mentioned in the Mediation Office's annual report for 2003, is the Negotiating Agreement for the municipal sector, in which large-scale industrial action broke out in 2003. Like the Industry Agreement, the Negotiating Agreement for the municipal sector is based on the principle that new agreements should be concluded before the current agreement runs out; however, its provisions on bargaining procedure do not really force the pace of negotiations. Also, it lacks institutions or mechanisms for continuous cooperation on issues that are important for wage formation – these are as important for the functioning of the Industry Agreement as the rules on negotiating procedure.

5.3 Changes in the contents of collective agreements

Although collective agreements on wages are still negotiated at sectoral level, the *substance* of these central agreements has changed dramatically – for some categories of employees with the effect that wages are now set entirely at workplace level. The most far-reaching examples are found among the agreements for white-collar workers in the public sector, but also large blue-collar unions such as the Municipal Workers' Union and the Metalworkers' Union have accepted a decentralization that has resulted in a situation which differs considerably from that at the end of the 1980s. Looking at the number of employees covered, most collective agreements today explicitly aim at – or in practice lead to – individual wages, albeit within a collective framework.

Comparison of a 'typical' central wage agreement from the end of the 1980s and today's agreements illustrates how decentralization has evolved. A typical agreement from the end of the 1980s had the following components:

1. It laid down minimum wages for different categories of employee, based on, for example, occupation, age and seniority.
2. It guaranteed every worker a particular rise based on actual wages. This rise could be determined as a percentage of his or her wage, a specific amount (more favourable to those on low wages) or a combination of both.
3. In addition to the individual guarantees, the parties to the central agreement had often agreed that a given percentage of the total wage bill, or a given amount per employee – a 'wage pool' – be distributed among the workers through negotiations between the employer and the local trade union branch. If the agreement contained such a clause, it usually also contained instructions on how this wage pool should be distributed, for example to workers on the lowest wages.
4. The agreements for categories of employees that had no wage drift regularly contained a 'catch-up guarantee'.

The most extreme examples of the new agreements have the following characteristics:

- They do not lay down any minimum wages.[7]
- They do not establish any guarantees for individual employees. Thus, at least in theory, there may be employees who do not receive any rise at all in a given year.
- They do not even guarantee employees as a group a rise.
- In short: they do not contain any figures at all!

What, then, do they contain? Primarily, they express a set of principles which should govern wage formation and wage setting, and lay down a new procedure for wage setting at local level.

7. Admittedly, this deviates from the principle that all employers have to pay at least a minimum wage stipulated in the collective agreement. On the other hand, the small number of trade unions that have accepted this represent employees with a strong position on the labour market.
8. Framework agreement on wages etc for state employees (RALS 2002–2004) between the Swedish Agency for Government Employers and Saco-S (a negotiating cartel formed by trade unions affiliated to the Swedish Confederation of Professional Associations).

The general idea behind these procedures is that each employer will be forced to adopt a wage policy and create a wage system that is transparent and based on objective factors – whatever they might be. According to some agreements – for example, the collective agreement for graduate employees in the central government sector[8] – the local trade unions are only supposed to negotiate the principles for wage setting – the concrete wages of individual members may be negotiated only exceptionally. After that, managers are supposed to discuss his or her wage with each employee. One remarkable feature of this procedure is that employer and employee are free even to make a binding agreement on the individual's wage. When all these talks have been completed, the employer presents a proposal to the trade union, which can call for negotiations if it finds the outcome unacceptable in individual cases. Thus, where this procedure is consistently applied, the role of the local trade union is limited to *monitoring* the employer's application of the agreed principles.

The first central agreement without figures was concluded in 1992 between the Association for Managerial and Professional Staff, Ledarna, and the employers' organization Almega, affiliated to SAF. However, wages determined partly with regard to individual factors were nothing new to them as white-collar workers in the private sector. The category that has experienced the most dramatic changes are members of trade unions affiliated to Saco and employed by central government. In 1988, state employees were still grouped in 52 salary grades, each divided into six salary classes. The central collective agreement specified exactly how much employees in each of these groups were to be paid. Even if this system had already been undermined in practice when it was formally abandoned in the collective agreement of 1989, it has certainly been a giant step from this rigid system to today's collective agreement, which leaves everything for the local parties to decide.

However, it must be underlined that wage agreements without figures are exceptions. The bulk of today's agreements do not go this far:

- Almost all sectoral agreements still lay down a minimum wage for very young workers or those with their first job in the occupation in question. However, salary grades, seniority and qualifications bonuses and other types of 'scales' or 'steps' have to a great extent been filtered out of central agreements.
- Most sectoral agreements also guarantee every worker some rise, however modest. In some agreements, though, the individual guarantee is merely a default or 'cut-off' provision that applies unless the local parties agree otherwise or cannot reach an agreement within a certain period.
- Most sectoral agreements guarantee the workers as a group a given percentage of the wage bill, either in the form of a traditional, centrally agreed 'wage pool', or through default or cut-off provisions that apply unless the local parties agree otherwise or cannot reach an agreement within a certain period. In the latter case, the theoretical point of departure is that the local parties should decide how much the business in question could afford. Thus, the rise agreed in a specific business can be higher – or lower – than the central agreement guarantees. In reality, of course, such default or cut-off provisions affect the local parties' willingness to compromise.
- While the traditional agreements often gave rather detailed instructions on how the centrally agreed wage pool should be distributed in the local bargaining round, modern agreements merely state some general pay policy principles, which vary from one agreement to another. For example, the first principle expressed in the agreements for the public sector is that wage formation and

wage setting shall be such as to contribute to the employer's achievement of its operational goals. Agreements for the private sector often express a commitment to enhanced productivity, efficiency and competitiveness. One general, common principle is that wages are seen as an instrument for stimulating workers to develop their competence. Another common principle is that every worker should understand on what grounds his or her wage is determined, and what to do to increase it. The – perhaps vain – hope is that thereby every individual will accept his or her wage as 'just'.

5.4 The Agreement between the Swedish Metalworkers' Union and the Swedish Association of Engineering Employers

The collective agreement between the Swedish Metalworkers' Union and the Swedish Association of Engineering Employers (the 'Engineering Agreement') can serve as an example of how the provisions on pay in an agreement for blue-collar workers in the private sector have changed, taking the agreement for 1989–1990 as a starting point.

The agreement for 1989–1990 laid down minimum wages for workers who had reached the age of 16, 17 and 18 years, respectively. In addition, it stated that workers who had worked for the same company for two or four consecutive years should be paid at least 86 or 172 öre,[9] respectively, more per hour than the minimum wage. These provisions on a *minimum* wage are largely the same in today's Engineering Agreement (although, obviously, the amounts are different). The interesting change has taken place in the provisions that concern the *wages actually paid.*[10]

Here, the agreement for 1989–1990 states that, as from 1 February 1990, hourly wages will be raised by 60 öre for adult workers and 48 öre for young workers. Piece rates will be raised by a percentage corresponding to a rise of 60 öre in the average piecework wages at the company in question during the second quarter of 1989. The agreement goes on to lay down corresponding figures for combinations of time-based pay and piece rate or other forms of payment by results.

In addition to these general rises that applied to all employees covered by the Engineering Agreement, it provided for a wage pool to be distributed through negotiation at company level. The instructions on how the pool was to be distributed had a clear equalizing objective. Particular attention was to be given to categories of workers or individual employees at an unfavourable wage level or with an unfavourable wage development, and the solutions sought should seek to avoid substantial differences in pay between different categories of worker. Workers with no wage drift, and especially those paid by the hour, should be given special attention.

Finally, the Engineering Agreement for 1989–1990 contained a kind of catch-up clause and an index clause (see above).

The first evidence of a move towards more individualized wages appeared in the Engineering Agreement for 1993–1994.[11] While the previous agreements had laid

9. 'Öre' is the smallest Swedish currency unit: 100 öre equal 1 Swedish krona.
10. The provisions on wages actually paid are the most significant, as the vast majority of metalworkers are paid more than the minimum wage.
11. The agreement for 1991–1992 was concluded after state intervention and is not representative of the parties' own aims.

down exactly how much (at the minimum) individual workers' wages should increase, the Engineering Agreement for 1993–1994 merely provided for a wage pool to be distributed among workers whose wages exceeded the minimum wage. The part that dealt with wages actually paid contained a new paragraph with the heading 'Wage principles'. The first sentence read: 'Wages shall be differentiated on individual or other grounds'. It was followed by a number of principles intended to guide the local parties when they bargained over distribution of the wage pool. Factors to be taken into consideration included leadership capacity, judgement and power of initiative, economic responsibility, ability to cooperate, and inventiveness and creativity. A worker's wage should increase along with increased responsibility and difficulty and with improvements in his or her performance and capability. Also, market forces would influence wage setting. At the same time, the agreement repeated the instructions that attention should be given to employees with an unfavourable wage level or an unfavourable wage development, and that the solutions sought should try to avoid significant wage differences between different categories of workers.

The fact that the rules on pay had been changed from detailed provisions to general principles was not the only novelty. Equally important was the fact that, for the first time, the wage principles in the metalworkers' collective agreement were exactly the same as those in the collective agreement for white-collar workers in engineering.

However, the metalworkers were not satisfied with how the wage principles were applied at workplaces in the subsequent period. At the same time, they did not want to deviate from the road, once taken. Instead, a further move towards increased responsibility for the local parties was made with the Engineering Agreement for 1998–2000. This was linked to a new agreement on competence development included in the overall settlement.

The new agreement stated that all employees should be given the opportunity for personal development at work in order to be able to take on more skilled and demanding tasks. Special attention should be paid to workers who had left education relatively early. It also stated that the local parties should apply wage systems and terms and conditions of employment that stimulate workers to develop their tasks and competences continuously.

The wage principles in the wage agreement were further elaborated to give the local parties a better basis for their negotiations. After the statement that wages should be differentiated on individual or other grounds, it was emphasized that pay differences must be justified on objective grounds. Every worker should know the grounds on which his or her wage was set and what he or she could do to receive a higher wage. Workers should be able to increase their wage successively as their position became more demanding and through increased experience, more demanding tasks, increased authority, increased responsibility and improved knowledge or competence. Wage systems and wage setting at the workplace should be designed in a way that makes them a driving force for the development of workers' competence and tasks. Thus, wage setting will stimulate increased productivity and competitiveness.

The wage pool was to be allocated on the basis of these wage principles, according to wage systems agreed at company level and in consideration of the agreement on competence development. No reference was made to workers 'with an unfavourable wage level or an unfavourable wage development'.

Apart from the negotiations on wage pool allocation, the local parties were to review all wages in the company twice during the period, and to adjust individual wages based on the worker's development with regard to competence and tasks, in order to achieve the wage structure that they wanted or to apply locally agreed wage systems. Here, they also had to check that every worker had received at least a given minimum raise. The individual guarantee was therefore established as a retroactive check.

The Engineering Agreement for 2001–2003 went further in the same direction. The agreement stated that wage pools were to be allocated on three given dates during the period. However, the local parties could agree on other dates, which means that they would be able to influence the employer's costs. As regards workers 'with an unfavourable wage level or an unfavourable wage development' the agreement said that the issue of competence development was to be specifically taken into consideration. Thus, instead of giving extra money to low paid workers when the wage pool was allocated, as was the rule in earlier agreements, now they should be given an opportunity to develop their competence in order to *qualify* for a higher wage.

To understand the real purport of this evolution one must know that local collective bargaining has always played a very important role in the engineering industry. Before the conclusion of the Industry Agreement, the metalworkers in fact received the largest part of their wage increases through the local negotiations that followed the conclusion of the central agreements. Today, the proportions are reversed. Thus, in one sense, the central agreements have an even greater impact than earlier. This does not change the fact that the norms for distribution to individual workers are much more open in today's central agreements.

5.5 The Agreement between the Municipal Workers' Union and the Swedish Association of Local Authorities

The collective agreement on wages between the Municipal Workers' Union and the Swedish Association of Local Authorities has undergone an even more dramatic change. As late as 1992, the majority of blue-collar workers in the municipal sector were paid according to a pay scale with 60 different steps specified in the central agreement.

As in the engineering sector, a decisive move in a new direction was taken in 1993. The pay scale was abolished, and the central agreement for 1993–1995 declared that, from now on, local authorities would bear significant responsibility for wage formation. The first clause explained the conditions for wage formation in subsequent years. It stated that the Swedish economy was afflicted by a number of severe problems and that the imbalance between costs and revenues in the municipalities was becoming more and more evident. The need for gains in productivity was considerable and, as a consequence, the scope for increases in pay was extraordinarily limited. The wage policies pursued by local authorities should be such as to secure the supply of personnel in both the short and the long term, and enhance the commitment of all employees. Thus, the parties underlined, it was important that the employees regard wages as 'just'.

The only wages specified in the central agreement were minimum wages for workers who had reached the ages of 18 and 19, respectively. Apart from that, the agreement provided for a wage pool of 3% of the total wage bill, to be allocated through local bargaining according to basic principles laid down in the agreement.

These principles were partly identical with those in the Engineering Agreement concluded five months earlier.

Two other provisions completed this radical change in bargaining culture: according to the first, under certain conditions, employers could even agree with individual workers on their wage; secondly, the central agreement authorized the local parties to conclude local collective agreements on merit-based wages and other alternative wage forms.

As in the engineering sector, the transition from detailed central regulation to local wage formation did not proceed without difficulties. The trade union was dissatisfied with how the employers handled their new responsibilities. Consequently, the provisions on 'points of departure', 'joint principles' and 'basic principles for wage formation' were increasingly elaborated in the two subsequent collective agreements, underlining that each local authority had to have a well defined and consistent wage policy, based on clear and distinct principles, well known to the workers in advance. The central parties also agreed to set up a joint working group that would follow and support the local implementation of the central agreement.

In spite of these difficulties, there was never any question of abandoning the road towards decentralization and individualization of wage formation in the municipalities. On the contrary, further steps were taken, including:

- The agreement for 1993–1995 had still guaranteed each worker a minimum raise. In the two agreements that followed, these guarantees were merely cut-off provisions, and the agreement concluded in 2003 contained no individual guarantee at all. Thus, in principle there can be workers who do not receive a raise. However, the central agreements underline that in such cases the employer must talk to the worker and explain what he or she could do to obtain a better outcome in the next bargaining round.
- A novelty in the 1998 agreement was that part of the centrally agreed 'scope' for wage increases could be used for other purposes, for example experiments with working time reduction or competence development.
- Up to 2001 the agreements stated that 'wages shall be differentiated on individual or other grounds', the words 'or other' indicating that wages could be differentiated on a *collective* as well as on an individual basis. Since 2001 this reference to something other than individual grounds has been filtered out of the collective agreement between the Municipal Workers' Union and the Swedish Association of Local Authorities, which now says that 'wages shall be individual and differentiated and reflect obtained objectives and results'. Furthermore, since 2001 the agreement has authorized the local parties to determine the distribution of the centrally agreed scope for wage increases through other procedures than collective bargaining. The 'other procedures' that the central parties have in mind are those described earlier in this chapter, in respect of which the role of the local trade union is restricted to monitoring the employer's application of the wage principles.

However, this does not mean that the Municipal Workers' Union is satisfied with the outcome of decentralized wage formation. The gap between the average wage for municipal workers and that for metalworkers has increased since the beginning of the 1990s and, according to the trade union, part of the explanation is that too many local authorities pay new employees the minimum wage routinely, irrespective of how experienced or qualified they are. Thus in 2003 the Municipal Workers' Union gave notice of premature termination of the collective agreement in force and initiated a strike among its members. Its aim was twofold: first, it called for a substantial rise in the centrally agreed minimum wage and a wage pool that would make it possible to reduce the gap between the average wage for municipal workers and that for metalworkers; secondly, it wanted to introduce mandatory provisions in the central agreement to oblige employers and local trade union branches to agree on local wage systems with starting salaries for different positions. The first aim of the strike was partly obtained, but not the second. However, it is worth noting that the trade union stuck to the idea that wage formation should be left to the local level. Even more, it accepted an agreement without any kind of individual guarantee for workers paid more than the minimum wage.

5.6 Effects of decentralization

The degree of decentralization of wage formation is evident from statistics from the National Mediation Office.[12] It groups the sectoral collective agreements in force in 2003 in seven different categories, based on the degree of local influence over wage formation:

1. Collective agreements that leave wage formation *entirely to the local level*, without any centrally agreed wage margin or individual guarantees covered 7% of employees in the private sector, 32% of state employees and 28% of municipal and county council employees.
2. Collective agreements that leave wage formation to the *local level in the first instance*, but which contain *cut-off provisions regulating a wage pool*, covered 5% of private sector employees.
3. Collective agreements that leave wage formation to the *local level in the first instance*, but which contain *cut-off provisions regulating a wage pool and some form of individual guarantee,* covered 8% of private employees and 68% of state employees.
4. Collective agreements with *a centrally agreed wage pool, but without any individual guarantees* covered 7% of private employees and 72% of municipal and county council employees.
5. Collective agreements with a *centrally agreed wage pool and an individual guarantee* or a cut-off provision regulating the individual guarantee covered 45% of private employees.
6. Collective agreements with a *general pay increase for all plus a wage pool* for distribution at local level covered 18% of private employees.
7. Collective agreements that provided for a *general increase, equal for all workers* covered 10% of private employees.

Thus, in 2003 nearly one third of the employees in the public sector, primarily graduate employees and other white-collar workers, were covered by collective agreements which did not specify figures and that left wage formation entirely to negotiations between individual employer and local trade union branch (or even to individual agreement between individual employee and manager). If you add the third group, agreements in respect of which local wage formation was the

12. Medlingsinstitutet, *Avtalsrörelsen och lönebildningen 2003* (2004), with English summary, pp. 22ff.

rule covered all state employees. Also, all collective agreements for the public sector allowed the local parties to decide how the wage frame was to be distributed.

At the other extreme are central agreements that provide for nothing more nor less than a general increase, equal for all workers. Today, such agreements cover only a very small proportion of blue-collar workers in the private sector. Taken together, almost two thirds of private sector employees are covered by collective agreements that allow the local parties to decide the whole of the wage margin (as wage pools typically are minimum or default provisions) and/or how it is to be distributed.

Collective agreements are instruments for preventing low wage competition and discrimination between workers. Can collective agreements that leave the main responsibility for wage formation to the local parties – in some cases to the extent that the central agreement does not set any wage norm at all – really serve these purposes? The answer is that it is too early to say.

There is little systematic information on actual changes in company wage policies. It is plausible that the changes in sectoral agreements have in fact resulted in more individualized wages. At the same time, it is obvious that it takes time for employers and trade union representatives in workplaces to learn the new procedures, especially in the public sector where the most dramatic change has taken place. It requires a great effort from both parties to build a system based on individual wages that is transparent and in which all differences are well founded and based on objective grounds – that is, a system that can gain legitimacy among the workers covered. Thus, the outcome of decentralization is highly dependent on the strength of the local trade unions.

On the other hand, there are still few areas in which the local trade unions have to rely entirely on their own strength. With some exceptions, the trade unions that have accepted the most far-reaching decentralization are those that organize workers with a strong position on the labour market, who work in occupations or sectors where they do not have to face low-wage competition. However, there are a few examples of trade unions that have misjudged the 'market position' of their members and have called for a return to central agreements with at least a minimum guarantee for each worker. Collective agreements for other occupations or sectors regularly include some type of default or cut-off provisions on the size of the wage margin and/or on a minimum guarantee for each worker. This type of clause reinforces the strength of the local trade unions. In some areas, the local parties can refer the negotiations to a central arbitration board if they cannot reach an agreement. The ultimate protection against low-wage competition is the minimum wages stipulated in the central agreements, which are mandatory under all circumstances. Lately, both the Metalworkers' Union and the Municipal Workers' Union have managed to raise the minimum wages more than the average.

If employer and local trade union do their duty, individual wages will not be synonymous with 'unjust' or discriminatory wages. As regards equal pay, the Equal Opportunities Act obliges all employers with ten or more employees to investigate each year whether there are any unwarranted gender pay differences. Some sectoral agreements contain specific clauses on gender equality according to which the reviews under the Equal Opportunities Act should be coordinated with the general local pay reviews, and for safeguarding that the wages of employees on parental leave will not lag behind. Statistics from the National Mediation Office show that the pay gap on the labour market as a whole has remained largely unchanged over the past ten years, and that the pay differences between men and women in the same occupation are very small.[13] Thus, there is no evidence that the decentralization and individualization of wage formation has led to increased discrimination between the sexes. What is clear, however, is that a system with individual wages makes it much more difficult to *prove* discrimination in individual cases.

Large international companies such as ABB, Ericsson and Volvo have been at the forefront of the employers' campaign for more decentralized and individual wage setting. One of their objectives was to be able to apply the same terms and conditions – including the same wage forms – to blue-collar and white-collar workers. To a great extent, this is now possible due to the changed contents of the sectoral collective agreements. For example, piece rate, which was the traditional wage form for blue-collar workers, is becoming more and more unusual. In the Engineering Agreement for 2004, the provisions on piece rate and hourly pay are no longer included in the body of the agreement but are relegated to a supplement. Instead, monthly pay is the normal form and, as described earlier, the pay principles are identical with those in the agreements for white-collar workers, in which monthly salary is the traditional wage form. At the same time, new types of flexible pay components – in addition to the monthly wage – are introduced for both blue-collar and white-collar workers. Between 1980 and 2000 the proportion of white-collar workers who received some kind of merit-based wage increased from 5% to 17%, although the proportion of this element in their total wage decreased from 23% to 9%. There are very advanced systems for variable pay. For instance, employers try to tie employees to the company by introducing systems in which the variable part of the wage is not paid until the December of the year after it was earned, and only on condition that the employee is still employed by the company.

With the exception of piece rate systems, which are regulated in central collective agreements, systems for variable pay are normally specific to the individual company. As such, they may be regulated in local collective agreements, but they can also be introduced by way of an employer's decision. Still, different bonus schemes are generally regarded by the trade unions as positive, at least as long as they are based on the results of *groups* of workers. Forms of variable pay based on the results on *individual* workers (other than piece rate systems) are regarded with strong scepticism among blue-collar unions.

5.7 Fundamental change in contents but not in form

Looking at the contents of collective agreements one may feel that the Swedish system of collective bargaining and wage formation has experienced a fundamental change since the 1980s. That is correct in the sense that they reflect a completely new approach to wage policies.

However, there has been no fundamental change in the formal system of collective wage formation in Sweden; rather change has taken place within the system. The legislator has modified the provisions on mediation, but trade unions and employers still have full responsibility for the contents of collective agreements on wages.

In fact, even the great shift in the contents of collective agreements is in line with the Swedish tradition, in which trade unions and employers in general recognize each other's interests.

13. Ibid.

6. SWEDEN AND GERMANY: DIFFERENCES AND SIMILARITIES IN THEIR SYSTEMS OF COLLECTIVE WAGE FORMATION FROM A SWEDISH PERSPECTIVE

As regards the Swedish system there is strong ideological and political consensus that the labour market parties should take responsibility for wage formation and wage policy. Our impression is that the state (or other authorities) has a more prominent role in Germany; a fact that can be discerned, for instance, in the possibility of extending collective agreements, which is not present Sweden (see above).

The difference in this respect is perhaps not so evident for the private sector, but clear when we take the whole labour market into account. Here we can refer to what was said earlier about the uniformity of the system encompassing not only blue- and white-collar workers, but also so-called career public servants and civil servants.

Another important difference is the fact that Swedish labour law is based on the assumption that the trade unions are present at both central and local level. This has often been described as being both centralized and decentralized at the same time: that is, a strongly centralized structure is combined with an organizational presence in the workplace. This feature, which is common to the Nordic countries, has often been used to explain the relative success of the Nordic trade union movement in reaching a high membership level and, especially, in being able to maintain it. For example, Kjellberg argues that both one-sided decentralized and one-sided centralized systems tend to have a negative impact on membership figures, while a balanced combination of centralized and decentralized solutions seems, in an international comparative perspective, to offer the best possibilities for success.[14]

One difference between the German and the Swedish collective bargaining systems seems to be that the Swedish system is based on negotiations at local level between the trade union representative and the employer. These negotiations are frequent and the essence of the collective bargaining system. In Germany, the mechanisms for local level negotiations seem to be weaker due to the fact that local trade union organizations are lacking and the dialogue at company level is conducted through the works council.

In Germany, not only trade unions, but also – and primarily – individual employees are parties (on the labour side) to cases heard in labour courts. In Sweden, employees can be parties in the labour court in exceptional cases, but in cases related to the interpretation or breach of collective agreements the trade unions in fact always act. The integration between local and national level can also be discerned in the fact that negotiations at central level concerning the interpretation of the normative part of a collective agreement will normally take place only where local level negotiations have failed. In the same manner the completion of negotiations at central level is an absolute condition for getting access to the Swedish labour court.

One important feature of the Swedish system is the notion of trade union solidarity, which implies that the centralized, unified trade union movement is striving for common goals. One indication of this historically has been the solidarity wage policy; another, the acceptance of solidarity or sympathy trade union action. Sympathy action plays a significant role in the Swedish industrial relations system. It is a means by which the Swedish trade union movement is able to keep up a broad

14. Anders Kjellberg, 'Ett fackligt landskap i omvandling', in Magnus Sverke and Jonny Hellgren (eds), *Medlemmen, facket och flexibiliteten*, pp. 27–49 (Arkiv förlag, 2002).

coverage of collective agreements in different sectors, although there is no 'erga omnes' extension system in use in Sweden.

The lack of 'erga omnes' mechanisms can, on the other hand, be described as a significant difference between the Swedish and the German system.

An initial historical similarity of the Swedish and German collective bargaining systems is that the collective agreement is regarded as a private law contract subject to the general principles of contract law. A significant difference seems to be that the Swedish system has retained this feature, while the German post-war development, with the Constitutional Court deciding on important issues related to the industrial relations system, indicates a certain change in this respect.

There are very strong structural and technical similarities between the Swedish and German legal frameworks regulating collective agreements.

The technical solutions are very similar. In fact, the German legislative efforts of the early twentieth century had an impact on developments in Denmark and Sweden, where the German legal system was generally quite influential.

The structure of the peace obligation is basically similar and so are the fundamental principles of the binding and direct effect of the terms and conditions in collective agreements on individual employment relationships.

Collective agreements are also clearly a well integrated part of the economic and political system in both Germany and Sweden.

7. STRENGTHS AND VULNERABILITIES OF THE GERMAN SYSTEM FROM A SWEDISH POINT OF VIEW

Generally speaking one might assume that the differences in scale between Germany and Sweden might make it slightly easier for the latter to adapt to changes in the economy.

The Swedish system of collective bargaining has always strongly emphasized that the system should promote structural change in the economy. Influential economists such as Rehn and Meidner have developed theories according to which collective bargaining in fact promotes productivity and makes competition based on social dumping and low wages impossible at national level. According to this thinking there should be few obstacles to companies reducing their work force or even closing down; instead, the welfare state should take care of employees' interests. As a result, we find no such institutions as the '*Sozialplan*' in Swedish legislation. That does not mean that companies do not have to pay compensation to laid off or dismissed workers in these situations but that is negotiated between the trade unions and the employer according to rules governing the priority of employees in this respect. Furthermore, there are central agreements or collective arrangements which provide economic protection for employees that have been dismissed or laid off. The difference between Sweden and Germany seems to be that collective solutions based on agreements between the parties are preferred in Sweden, while in Germany the responsibility often lies with the individual employer.

The development of the content of collective agreements has, in our view, had a significant impact on the system's ability to survive. If collective agreements can be flexible procedural tools their value cannot be questioned. The weakness of the German system seems to lie in a combination of lack of legitimacy and inability to adapt to change. On the other hand, the problems in the German economy have been severe and the German debate must be understood in this light.

The shrinking number of employers that are bound by collective agreements is, in our view, an important problem. Still, we believe that the level of trade union affiliation is more important for the legitimacy of collective wage formation.

8. DECENTRALIZATION AND GROWING FLEXIBILITY OF THE GERMAN SYSTEM FROM A SWEDISH POINT OF VIEW

One general challenge facing both Germany and Sweden comprises globalization, internationalization and competition from countries with significantly lower wage levels. Companies are moving their activities from high-cost to low-cost countries.

In Germany there has lately been a strong demand for deregulation of labour law and for more flexibility. The rigidities of the German labour market have been blamed for the problems in the economy.

From a Swedish perspective the interesting question is whether Sweden will face the same development as Germany or has been able to solve some of these problems by using the inherent flexibility in the collective bargaining system, which we have described earlier.

One possible interpretation of the German situation is that Sweden in the coming years will face the same problems as Germany today. One could even compare them with the enlargement of the European Union and claim that Germany had its 'first enlargement' with reunification. If the costs of reunification are one of the reasons for the problems in the German economy, the costs of EU enlargement might lead to similar problems for Sweden.

Variable pay systems have the advantage that wage costs will to some extent follow the economic results of the employer. As already indicated, new forms of variable pay have been introduced in Sweden recently, although it is difficult to assess how widespread they are in the labour market. This trend of flexible wage policy, advocated by international management consultants, is likely to be present also in Germany.

9. CONCLUSIONS

From our perspective the essential structural problem for German collective bargaining is the weakness of its mechanisms in the workplace, where the local trade union organization as such has no role and the works council performs many of the functions which the local trade union performs in Sweden. It is difficult to see how the problem with a dual system for handling issues related to wages and employment conditions in the workplace could be solved otherwise than by rules of coordination, subordination and a clearer division of powers.

From a Swedish perspective it would be strange to propose the introduction of a statutory minimum wage. A statutory minimum wage can be regarded either as some kind of alternative to an erga omnes extension of a wage clause in collective agreements or as a last instance supplement to these mechanisms. In our view a statutory minimum wage is a real alternative only in sectors in which collective bargaining plays no role. We admit, of course, that this perspective is due to the high level of unionization in Sweden, but we think that this argument is relevant also for Germany.

The factors motivating young persons to join a trade union in Sweden seem to be lacking in Germany. In Swedish and international literature the unemployment insurance system is often referred to as a strong factor promoting trade union affiliation. We think that the picture is more complicated and that there are in fact several factors that together might promote the general pattern of wage-earners in Sweden tending to organize. One important reason is the strong trade union presence in the workplace. Here the trade union representatives and shop stewards can help and represent the employees in different situations and conflicts. This representation continues at all levels, even, in the last instance, in the courts. Also, the strong influence that trade unions are able to exercize in different situations according to the law does have an impact. For example, the priority rules can be negotiated by trade unions in situations of reduction of workforce (redundancy) and there are several so-called semi-dispositive rules in Swedish labour law on which the trade unions might agree otherwise in collective agreements. One might also refer to the development concerning collective agreements that was described above. When collective agreements contain only general clauses on wages the decision-making process at local level becomes more important and in Sweden the trade union plays an important role at this level.

Much industrial relations research calls for increased flexibility, based on a range of assumptions and factors (globalization, changed patterns of production, information society, and so on). Although exaggerations and simplifications are well represented in the debate we are convinced that there is an increased need for flexibility at company level. We think that the lack of local trade union presence and decentralized mechanisms is the greatest challenge for the German system. It seems that the works council system has become an obstacle to adapting the collective bargaining system to a more modern framework-agreement design, combined with procedural mechanisms. This specific German problem probably needs a specific German solution. It must also be emphasized that only within this broader framework might collective bargaining be extended to new areas. This is necessary because wage setting is very much a result of external economic developments and the real scope for the negotiating parties is quite limited.

We think that the need to protect wages against low-wage competition is still a valid, reasonable and important argument for sectoral collective agreements. There are, however, clear differences between sectors in respect of how important this aspect is. It seems to be of greater importance in sectors where competition is at national level than in situations in which huge multinational players compete. It is also of importance for competition between subcontractors to big companies. In our opinion the fundamental significance of collective agreements today as a factor restricting social dumping and low wages cannot be denied. In Sweden this is evident in the practice of sympathy industrial action.

In our view there are profound substantive changes going on in the Swedish collective bargaining system. On the surface, these changes are less spectacular than the factors indicating change in Germany (decreasing rate of unionization, changes in the legal framework regulating collective agreements, and so on). These factors presented by German authors have convinced us that a fundamental change is taking place in Germany. Both countries are in the middle of the process of change and so the final outcome is difficult to foresee at this stage. At present the main difference seems to be that the Swedish labour market actors believe that a change can be made within the framework of the existing system, while in Germany the employers in particular seem to think that it is not possible to achieve flexibility within that framework. This is leading them to exit the employers' organizations and seek solutions outside the collective bargaining system.

The trend towards globalization and internationalization is bringing about an increased tendency towards convergence between the Swedish and German systems.[15] For the internationally competing private sector, wage increases are set by comparison with developments in other – especially European Union – countries. On the other hand, development very much builds on national traditions and features. That will be true also in the future.

15. Niklas Bruun, 'The Autonomy of Collective Agreement', pp 1–48, in Roger Blanpain (ed.), *Collective Bargaining, Discrimination, Social Security and European Integration* (Kluwer Law International, 2003).

6. Ideas and suggestions Input for the German debate

Edgar Rose

1. INTRODUCTION

When we decided to produce reports on the collective wage formation systems of five European countries, our intention was not simply comparison. One point of particular interest was the serious problems of collective bargaining in Germany.[1] At the beginning of our comparative work, the experts from other countries were amazed to hear that the German system was deemed to be *in crisis*. In contrast, in France, the Netherlands, Sweden and the UK the collective bargaining systems work in very different ways, but are more or less *stable*. In this context the research perspective was directed towards asking whether there was anything that Germany can learn from other countries concerning the legal and practical development of collective wage formation.

The assumption underlying our investigations was the manifold similarity of all five countries (export-oriented economies, high level of industrialization, developed welfare states, long tradition of workers' representation), so that in all cases the current socio-economic challenges faced by the collective wage formation systems are more or less similar. The culture and legal instruments of collective bargaining, however, differ significantly from country to country. As a result, our comparison made available a great variety of different experiences concerning how to cope with similar challenges. On a more theoretical level, Germany serves as a test case of whether and how collective bargaining systems under pressure can profit from foreign experiences in a process of mutual learning.

The *research procedure* was as follows. To begin with, a report on the German system of collective wage formation (see Chapter 1) and a list of questions emphasizing crucial aspects of the German case were sent to the French, Dutch, Swedish and British experts. In response, similar reports on their collective bargaining systems and comments on the German case were written by the experts in the four other countries (see Chapters 2–5). Finally, in Germany we analysed what messages for the German debate we could identify in these reports and comments. Two possible functions of comparison were envisaged:

1. From the perspective of quite different systems, outside experts may be able to call into question the established views and certainties of the German debate in an unexpected, but well-founded way. So the national analysis of problems may be amplified, modified or even refuted.

---

1. The other special question was whether or not similar challenges may lead to converging legal regulations as a floor for legal harmonization in Europe. This is discussed in Chapter 7.

2. In addition, foreign experts may be able to suggest ideas derived from successful strategies in their own countries that lead to solutions to German problems.

The reports and comments that we received in Germany from the four other countries met these expectations impressively. Each statement has its own, genuinely *surprising message* for the German debate. In this chapter we first discuss the experts' contributions country by country (section 1–4), emphasizing what we regard as the main messages for Germany; second, we summarize the results for further debate on the crisis of collective wage formation in Germany (section 5); finally, we briefly evaluate our method of international mutual learning (section 6).

2. FRANCE

From a German perspective, the basic data on the French system are striking. After years of sharp decline in trade union membership in the 1980s, union density has settled at below 10% of employees, and in the private sector it is below 5%. That is by far the lowest level of unionization among the five countries of our sample. At the same time, the coverage rate of collective agreements in France is among the highest in Europe: in a period of shrinking union membership, the coverage rate increased from 86.4% in 1985 to 93.4% in 1995. This phenomenon has nothing to do with anything like the German practice of incorporating collective agreements in individual employment contracts, a practice which similarly extends the use of collective agreements beyond trade union members. In France, it is *the state* that imposes almost complete collective agreement coverage by massive intervention in favour of collective bargaining. The main instrument of this is the extension procedure, which is widely used to extend collective agreements to employers who are not a member of the contracting parties. A wide range of additional forms of state intervention can be observed over the last 20 years.

These activities of the state are of the greatest relevance for the discussion in Germany where there is extreme reluctance to improve legal support for collective bargaining. The most important measures of statutory intervention in wage formation in France – but which are absent from Germany – are summarized below (for greater detail see Chapter 2):

- In France, trade unions and employers have been legally obliged to negotiate regularly on wages and working time since 1982. This applies not only to the sectoral, but also to the *company level* where the company committee of a trade union enters into negotiations with the employer. Their task is only to negotiate, not to conclude collective agreements. However, the clear shift from sectoral to company agreements in recent decades shows that negotiations usually lead to agreements, particularly at the company level. In addition, it is a legal requirement that annual negotiations be held on matters of equal pay for men and women.
- State intervention on wage formation, however, is not restricted to policies seeking to promote the conclusion or use of collective agreements. A relatively high *statutory minimum wage* (SMIC) that is regularly increased according to legally fixed criteria is paid to about 13% of the working population. The increasing share of employees who receive exactly the minimum wage indicates

its outstanding importance in France. At the same time, the level of wages in French collective agreements is relatively low. At 1,154 euros per month for a full-time job of 35 hours a week (2004), the minimum wage affects more than 80% of French collective bargaining sectors because in these sectors the lowest basic wages in collective agreements are below the level of the statutory minimum wage. The minimum wage therefore has an indirect, but significant influence on collective bargaining results. It is regarded as the main intersectoral instrument of wage coordination in France.[2]

- In France, as in other countries, jobs with low qualification requirements are particularly under pressure. The government has reacted by reducing social insurance contributions on low earnings. Moreover, the introduction of the 35-hour week led to *wage moderation* in general. Whether any compensation was to be paid for wage losses caused by working time reduction was left to negotiations at the company level, where working time agreements may be concluded by trade unions or even by works councils, independently. In many cases, company agreements were made that granted limited compensation on the one hand, but fixed long terms of moderate wage increases on the other.

From the point of view of Germany, which is characterized by a constitutional concept of collective bargaining autonomy with wage formation as its centrepiece, the intensive state intervention in France is very unfamiliar. The most striking aspect is that promotional interventions *in favour* of collective bargaining have been intensified in France in response to the problems of the system. Relatively stable development has been achieved as a result of that strategy. In contrast, the current German debate is completely dominated by demands to *deregulate* existing promotional interventions in collective wage formation, such as the legal extension procedure or the rule that wage bargaining must be conducted by trade unions (not by works councils). The fact that a system of industrial relations like the one in France works well precisely because of a much higher level of state activity clearly favouring collective wage formation must be extremely disconcerting for the German advocates of deregulation.

The *message* from the French experts (Christophe Vigneau and André Sobczak) for the German case starts at this very point (see Chapter 2). To address the crisis of the German system they suggest that the state take on a more active role in favour of collective bargaining rather than try to weaken it, in direct contrast to the views of most participants in the German debate. For example, the French experts explicitly characterize as a problem the rare application of the German extension procedure regarding wage agreements. The established terms of the German debate are turned upside down by French experiences. Moreover, the French case demonstrates a clear alternative to German deregulation plans. It encourages study of the concept of state intervention in detail, including whether it really does work.

However, there are so many differences between the basic conditions of collective bargaining in France and Germany that the transplantability of French policies to Germany is very doubtful. For instance, the French concept of state intervention is strongly supported by society as a whole, which clearly accepts the state's responsibility for fair wages as well as the societal value of collective bargaining. This is shared to a large extent by French employers, who may be attracted to collective bargaining not only by the comparably low wages contained in collective

2. See Hassel (2002), p. 161.

agreements but also by the high militancy of French workers, whether or not they are union members. The dominant attitudes concerning both collective bargaining and the role of the state are completely different in Germany. However, that does not diminish the provocative power of the French concept to contribute new perspectives to the German debate.

All this was unambiguously the case until spring 2004. The new Act on Social Dialogue and Professional Training passed by the French parliament in April 2004 indicates that the direction in which the French system is moving is not so different from German developments. In both countries, there is a process of decentralization and shopfloor negotiations are increasingly encouraged. There is also growing acceptance in France that shopfloor agreements be reached not only by trade union bodies, but also by elected staff representatives. A major difference remains concerning the active role of the state in France and collective autonomy in Germany. Finally, the French Social Dialogue Act of April 2004 seems carefully designed not to weaken collective bargaining: *sectoral* wage bargaining in particular is not touched. Most proposals for legal reform in Germany, however, are clearly designed to undermine *sectoral* wage bargaining. There is still hope, therefore, that the French model will remain instructive for the German debate.

3. NETHERLANDS

In common with France, the Dutch system combines a low union density with a high collective bargaining coverage rate. However, the difference between the two figures is less extreme than in France: a trade union membership of around 25% is enough to achieve a coverage rate of more than 80%. The main reason is the high rate of companies organized in employers' associations. As in France (but not in Germany), these companies have to apply collective agreement provisions to their whole workforce, including those employees that are not unionized. A statutory extension procedure is, again as in France, used intensively by the state. Finally, the Dutch minimum wage of 1,265 euros per month for full-time work is another similarity. Over the last 20 years, however, successive Dutch governments have taken a path that differs significantly from the French one. *Direct* state intervention in collective wage formation has been reduced in the Netherlands. Instead, the state's *indirect* influence on wage policies has been intensified through the promotion of bi- and tripartite social pacts.

The Dutch system of industrial relations has a long tradition of direct state intervention in centralized wage negotiations (see Chapter 4). Numerous political and judicial conflicts in the 1970s and 1980s led to the abolition of most legal intervention instruments. Since 1986, the law has permitted the Minister of Labour to take measures of direct intervention – such as a general wage pause – only in cases of economic emergency. However, no other country has such efficient institutions of wage coordination which are able to guarantee the indirect influence of the state. Efforts to establish such institutions in Germany met with little success, and so they are the main reason why Dutch collective bargaining is of great relevance for the German debate.

First, there is the '*Stichting van de Arbeid*', jointly established by the social partners, that meets regularly with government for consultations. This foundation publishes non-binding recommendations for wage increases, which nevertheless are highly influential. In addition, tripartite concertation is institutionalized in the

Sociaal-Economische Raad, in which one-third of council members represent employers, one-third represent employees and one-third are experts appointed by the government. Both institutions have their headquarters in the same building and most persons sent by associations serve on both bodies (see Chapter 4).

Wage recommendations are not the only instrument available to these bodies. They also set in motion the social pacts typical of Dutch wage formation in times of economic pressure. The current problems of the Dutch economy led to a recommendation from the Stichting van de Arbeid in 2002 to increase wages by 2.5% in 2003. Negotiations in all industries indeed came close to this level. In 2003, a social pact was agreed establishing a two-year wage freeze (see Chapter 4).

A brief look at Dutch law on collective wage formation reveals that it has a lot in common with its German counterpart. The legal effects of collective agreements, the strike law and the legal distribution of competences in a developed dual system of workers' representation are quite similar. It is possibly as a consequence of these similarities that both Dutch and German industrial relations are particularly peaceful and conducted in a spirit of partnership. The strike record in the Netherlands is almost as low as in Germany. The most striking parallel, finally, is the developed social partnership between works councils and employers at the workplace level.

Nevertheless, the neo-corporatist social pacts which are extremely successful in the Netherlands do not work at national level in Germany. The repeated breakdowns of national 'Pacts for Work' offer clear evidence of this. The Dutch expert A.T.J.M. Jacobs believes (see Chapter 4) that German trade unions and employers are less creative in finding win–win solutions than their Dutch colleagues. He attributes this difference not to systemic characteristics but to cultural features: the Dutch 'merchant mentality' fosters compromises with advantages for both parties. Among other aspects that may explain the different outcomes of systems that are so similar in structure he mentions the fact that, compared to the Netherlands, the German trade union movement is strong and unified. Dutch trade union membership may be close to the German, but there is significant union competition in the Netherlands and they face financial crisis. The Dutch trade unions are much more willing to compromise. The outstanding strength of Dutch employers' associations in contrast to the German 'flight' from employers' associations is perhaps an even better explanation. Between 80% and 90% of the Dutch workforce is employed in companies that are members of associations. From such a strong position, associations are able to make the concessions needed to avoid undermining the trade unions. This is very different to Germany where weakened employers' associations try to impress their members with aggressive demands addressed to unions and governments.

The *message* from the Netherlands is very clear. The Dutch system is a perfect model from which to study social pact building in the area of wage formation. When it comes to reaching a compromise to cope with severe economic difficulties, developed institutions based on trust and cooperation between the social partners are a great help. We may conclude that if such institutions are lacking, they must be created and developed laboriously over the long term. Ad hoc action under pressure – tried twice in Germany – is inadequate. Less clear is whether anything from the Dutch experience of pact building can be directly applied to Germany. The chances of learning from the 'Poldermodell' may be limited because it is so much rooted in Dutch culture: in Germany, there is no 'predominantly harmonious atmosphere' like that observed by Jacobs in the Netherlands (see Chapter 4), but often much tension between the German social partners.[3] In any case, it would be interesting to investigate which strategies trade unions have in mind when they agree on far-reaching concessions that are unknown in Germany. It would be interesting to study more intensively the form creative win–win compromises in collective bargaining practice must take to convince trade unions to accept long-term wage pauses.

4. UNITED KINGDOM

While the Netherlands seems most similar to Germany, the UK (among our sample) is without doubt most different. In terms of the legal framework of collective wage formation, indeed, everything in Britain is *different*. Traditionally, British legislators have largely refrained from state intervention in industrial relations; instead, most of the normative framework was created by the participants themselves. For instance, collective representation at shopfloor level is institutionalized by collective agreements and managed by trade union representatives (single channel system). Moreover, the application of collective agreement provisions is usually not guaranteed by law, but by the power and militancy (or otherwise) of trade unions. No legal instrument exists to extend collective agreements to employers who are not directly involved. The British state, however, sets limits on wage formation through a legal minimum wage and equal pay legislation.

In recent decades, there has been increasing state intervention in collective bargaining on specific points (for greater detail see Chapter 3). The widespread practice of closed-shop agreements was ended by the Thatcher government in the 1980s; this was accompanied by legal interventions concerning the right to strike and the internal affairs of trade union organizations (such as secret ballots). Since 1997, the professedly trade union–friendly Blair government has taken selected measures in favour of collective bargaining. A procedure was re-established for trade unions to attain recognition as negotiating partner with an employer under certain circumstances with state support.

Leaving aside the law, there are important *similarities* between the German and British systems of (collective) wage formation (see Chapter 3). In both countries, trade union density has fallen below 30%. In terms of strike frequency, the British level is now similar to the low German one. On the other hand, the decentralization – and, moreover, the deunionization – of wage formation is far more developed in the UK than in Germany: nowadays, collective agreements in British private companies are almost exclusively concluded at the company or shopfloor level, in contrast to 1980 when the majority of workers were still covered by sectoral agreements. The total coverage of all collective agreements decreased from above 70% in the 1970s to 36% in 2001. Especially in the private sector, wage formation through collective agreements is now an exception for about 24% of private employees. Sectoral bargaining has almost disappeared here. Where there is no collective bargaining, wages are usually fixed by unilateral management decisions.

The decentralization and deunionization tendencies in wage formation now observable in Germany have been fully developed in the UK for many years. The British case may therefore offers insights into the future of the German system.

3. Müller-Jentsch (1999) calls it 'conflict partnership'. That describes the contradictory image of German industrial relations: strong claims, hard negotiations, but finally readiness to compromise (usually without strike action).

The British expert Brian Bercusson (see Chapter 3) confronts us with a striking phenomenon.[4] Observers who are worried that the breakdown of collective bargaining in the UK has opened the floodgates to the lowest possible wages and greater inequality and flexibility will be surprized. Real hourly wages in Germany and the UK have increased almost equally since 1980: in fact, because of working time reductions in Germany, the monthly wage increase in Britain is significantly higher. In both countries, wages are fairly homogeneous in different companies in a given industry. The fact that this happens in the UK without sectoral agreements is amazing. Also noteworthy is the fact that in Germany the proportion of performance- or profit-related wages is significantly higher than in the UK. In fact, it is only in the area of wage inequality between different jobs that the adverse prognoses mentioned above have come true: there is a clear trend towards much greater wage inequality in the UK.

These observations seem strongly to contradict the familiar opinion among trade unions in Germany that breakdown of the sectoral agreement system will inevitably end in a downward spiral of lower and more precarious wages. For example, it appears that sectoral wage formation did not disappear in the UK without a replacement. Annual rounds of wage increases simply continued even without collective bargaining. The main points of reference for management decisions on wage increases nowadays seem to be increasing wage rates among competitors. In pursuit of wage increases sufficient to motivate employees and retain key personnel, industry-wide coordination seems the best bet. Employers' associations and consulting firms have taken the role of information agencies. The minimum wage provides a dynamic minimum standard.

Finally, although trade unions in the UK may be weakened, with a union density of about 30% they are still formidable. In some companies, British trade unions may leave wage formation to the management and take care of other matters (comparable to German works councils). Nevertheless, if management wage policy ceases to be acceptable trade unions may intervene.

To summarize, the *first message* from Britain for the German debate is that erosion of the sectoral agreement system may have less dramatic results than expected. The British experience shows that wage dumping is not the only possible development where collective bargaining institutions disappear: even without collective bargaining companies need sectoral standards defining what is a fair and acceptable wage. Accordingly, many German companies which leave employers' associations also continue voluntarily to apply wage structures and levels based on sectoral agreements. For standardization of sectoral wage agreements it is less important how many firms are legally bound; of greater relevance is the ability of the collectively agreed regulations to serve as a strong point of reference in the labour market. At the same time, this calls into question a central argument of many German companies, which argue that they have to leave sectoral bargaining to achieve sufficient wage flexibility. The British experience indicates that in the absence of sectoral bargaining restrictions companies are nevertheless careful in exercising their freedom because the need for sectoral standardization prevails.

Among *other messages* from Britain, German trade unions can observe in Britain that the trade unions' visible interest representation inside companies is more important for trade union survival than full sectoral control of all working conditions.

4. With reference to the research of Schmidt and Dworschak (2003).

Finally, the German legislator may learn that even in a liberal market economy like Britain the introduction of a minimum wage was possible (in 1998), as well as measures (in 1999) to support collective bargaining through a statutory recognition procedure. Proposals like that would be denounced in Germany as an unbearable burden on economic development.

5. SWEDEN

The most striking feature of the Swedish system is not a legal one. It is the extremely *high union density* of more than 80% of all employees, organized in unions belonging to three strong confederations for different groups (blue-collar, white-collar, professional). Taking this into account, the considerable autonomy of the Swedish collective bargaining system can be explained easily. It simply does not need state intervention to work well. Legal extension procedures and a legal minimum wage are unknown. The low state intervention, however, does not create a law-free sphere of self-organization, as in Britain. Instead, the institutions of Swedish collective bargaining have a legal basis: collective agreements are legally binding and employees' representation at shopfloor level is legally regulated as the responsibility of the trade unions (single channel system).

The Swedish trade unions capitalize on their high membership rates to attain almost complete coverage of companies with collective bargaining and workplace representation. This forms the basis of their *unique manoeuvrability*. For instance, Swedish trade unions in the past were able to use all levels of collective bargaining simultaneously or alternately.[5] Recently, collective wage formation has gone through a process of decentralization, so that the sectoral – and increasingly also the company – level now dominates. Industry-wide social partners reach agreement on a more or less precise framework. Almost all concrete questions are regulated at the company level. For Germany, this process of controlled decentralization is the most striking development. The methods employed to provide ample scope for company-level agreements without losing the benefits of sectoral coordination are of the highest interest with a view to addressing similar German problems.

Like other collective bargaining systems, Sweden's has faced significant economic challenges in recent decades (see Chapter 5). High unemployment rates combined with high wage levels in the early 1990s led the government to intervene in collective negotiations and collective action. However, these attempts were almost completely thwarted by the trade unions and employers' associations. Instead, the social partners autonomously implemented far-reaching reform of the procedures and contents of collective bargaining. The main features of this are permanent bipartite self-regulatory bodies of collective bargaining and growing flexibility in collective wage formation.

The so-called 'Industry Agreement' of 1997 between the social partners in manufacturing industry is the key document for the new development (see Chapter 5). It was a framework agreement in which the rules of further collective bargaining were defined autonomously by the bargaining parties. For instance, it contained several regulations aimed at avoiding long-lasting industrial conflicts by setting a fixed schedule for negotiations and – if needed – a mediation procedure. To promote and monitor these and other regulations of the agreement, the Industry Committee

5. See Traxler (2002), p. 115.

was instituted as a bipartite body within the framework of which joint working groups meet regularly. The 'Industry Agreement' was followed by similar agreements for other areas of the Swedish economy. In contrast to the Netherlands no continuous participation is required on the part of the state. The Swedish government played an important role in the launch phase, but the social partners were able to maintain their autonomy by developing their own new bipartite structures.

Before the 'Industry Agreement', decentralization of wage negotiations was already getting under way (for more detail see Chapter 5). In Sweden, it has long been the practice to supplement sectoral agreements through company agreements. The innovation of the 1990s was sectoral level agreements which provide more and more leeway for wage-setting at the company level. Finally, some recent sectoral agreements contain no figures for wage-setting at all, but a set of principles on how to determine wages in company agreements. Other, less radical sectoral agreements still define a minimum wage and guarantee every employee some modest rise, but the traditional pay pool to be distributed at establishment level has been flexibilized for local decision-making. The Swedish experts emphasize the growing importance of sectorally concluded principles replacing clear figures. Usually, these principles aim at objectivity, transparency and – an especially creative feature – the opportunity for each employee to achieve higher wages by developing their skills. Some collective agreements even allow individual wage bargaining according to certain principles.

As a result, the Swedish example gives rise to *two messages* for the German discussion. First, the ability of the Swedish social partners to defend their autonomy when threatened by government plans to make strong legal inroads is exemplary for German associations on both sides. The threats of German politicians concerning major intervention in collective bargaining autonomy have so far failed to produce a joint effort on the part of German trade unions and employers' associations. A concerted program of collective bargaining reform independent of legal intervention – like the Swedish one – could be very helpful in protecting collective bargaining autonomy in Germany.

The second Swedish message is that even the far-reaching opening up of sectoral agreements in favour of decentralized decision-making can be coordinated successfully. As reported, no one in Sweden wants to return to the old dominance of the sectoral level. Also in Germany, according to all participants, the old wage framework agreements urgently require intensive reform that allows – and at the same time limits – wage flexibility. Closer examination of Swedish framework agreements reveals (see Chapter 5) a number of interesting ideas on how a sector may be controlled and coordinated merely through principles and procedures. The Swedish experts Kerstin Ahlberg and Niklas Bruun emphasize (conclusion of Chapter 5) that the German dual channel system, with independent works councils and weak union presence at the workplace, is the essential structural problem giving rise to German weakness. Indeed, duality may be an obstacle to Swedish-style decentralization. Unlike the Swedish company trade union representatives, a German works council would be less able to enforce the principles included in sectoral frameworks. Works councils lack the power of a big union and the right to call for strike action. Moreover, they are often little involved in decisions at the sectoral level, so that their commitment to sectoral coordination is correspondingly low. Finally, many German companies do not have a works council at all. In contrast, the highly organized Swedish trade unions, active at all levels, have the best chance of decentralizing wage formation with perfect coordination and no loss of social protection. The Swedish model of decentralizing wage bargaining is surely not directly transferable to Germany. Anyway, it is worth carefully studying what is probably the most developed model in Europe. In an adapted form it must be possible to transfer some experiences or ideas to other countries.

6. RESULTS

The messages of the four systems for the German debate lead in very different directions. To some extent, they even seem to contradict each other: on the one hand, intensive state action, and on the other, measures to renew collective bargaining autonomy are deemed to be a good response to current problems. There is *one common feature*: decentralization of collective bargaining is an issue in all countries. However, the methods and procedures of decentralization are very different. Collective bargaining systems under economic and political pressure – according to our interpretation – tend to follow their traditional institutional paths and try to mobilize their specific strengths:

- In the French system direct state intervention was extended and improved.
- In the Dutch system indirect state intervention through social pact-building was intensified.
- In the British system the conditions of a free market economy prevail, but loosely framed by a number of few statutory restrictions.
- In the Swedish system omnipresent trade unions enable far-reaching decentralization under the control of autonomous institutions of the bargaining parties.

Clearly, *no one model* could be copied in Germany *in toto*. Each system benefits from specific traditions (the pact-building mentality in the Netherlands) and conditions (high union density in Sweden) which cannot simply be adopted by another country. The main recommendation for Germany rather is that it should try to identify the traditional resources of the German system that could be developed to stabilize it. We have looked at some of them (see Chapter 1, section 5.4): constitutional collective autonomy and the dual system of employee representation. The latter, however, could turn out to be a problem rather than a solution. Indeed, in Germany it has long been customary to shift responsibilities to works councils, which have strong legal rights: this is currently happening in wage formation. However, questions remain concerning what works councils need in order to meet this challenge and what trade unions can do to ensure good cooperation between sectoral and shopfloor levels.

Taking their different environments into account, it would still be a mistake for Germany to reject any of the four neighbouring systems. In detail, each system confronts Germany with its own ideas:

- positive experiences concerning stabilising state intervention;
- successful pact-building;
- the political courage to introduce a legal minimum wage at a high level in times of intensified global competition;
- sufficient self-confidence on the part of the collective bargaining partners to defend their autonomy in a common act of self-regulation.

Impressive unity between social partners and state concerning the *high value* of collective bargaining in most cases lies behind the successful development of traditional institutions and procedures. In no other country in our comparison is there so much political confrontation – in public (not at the negotiation table) – between employers' and employees' organizations as in Germany. In no other country is there so much basic criticism of collective wage formation. At least in France, the Netherlands and Sweden, the economic value of collective wage formation is undisputed by either side and in the public debate. The opposite is the case in Germany where collective bargaining is seen as the most important cause of unemployment by a majority of economists and many politicians. The experiences from abroad presented here may also help us to understand why German unions and employers' associations do not have the courage necessary to regulate the future of collective wage formation autonomously.

One final message is very concrete. It is often argued in Germany by politicians and economists that the labour market is *overregulated*. The comparison with four European countries in respect of collective wage formation, however, reveals almost the opposite. Germany is by no means the front-runner in terms of state intervention in favour of collective bargaining. In one important respect, Germany even has the least restrictive law concerning wages: no other system in our sample allows work to be so badly paid in some areas as the German one. Even in Britain a legal *minimum wage* has been introduced that is significantly higher than some low wages in Germany. The legal minimum wage in France in 2004 was 1,154 euros per month (working 35 hours per week), in the Netherlands 1,265 euros (full time) and in the United Kingdom 840.67 pounds sterling (= 1,226 euros for full time work).[6] There is no statutory minimum wage in Sweden, but collective agreements all over the country provide for a minimum wage. In Germany, however, there are low wages at the bottom of collective agreements below 1,200 euros (full-time) and in some agreements below 1,000 euros.[7] For workers not covered by a collective agreement two-thirds of such collectively agreed wages are in legal terms no problem (see Chapter 1, section 3.3.1). Taking this together with the restrictive criteria for legal extension of collective agreements and the absence of any law promoting the commencement of negotiations between the social partners, it becomes clear that Germany is a case of comparatively low legal intervention in the field of wage formation.

7. FINAL EVALUATION

In the political debate, the experiences of other countries are often mentioned. Frequently, a certain legislative proposal is justified by alleging that the very same scheme has worked well in another country. However, in many cases research reveals that there are various conditions and restrictions to consider, so that transfer of the scheme would be complicated or impossible.

Indeed, we came to realize in the course of our project that mutual learning from comparative studies faces numerous difficulties. For systems of collective wage formation in particular this is true because of their embedding in culture and tradition

6. See Federation of European Employers (2004) (http://www.fedee.com/minwage.html).
7. See Bispinck and Schäfer (2004).

and the considerable complexity of institutions and procedures. On the surface, many aspects of different collective bargaining systems seem similar or – if obviously different – to fall easily into a few categories. However, when investigations go into detail it becomes clear how diverse even the systems of these neighbouring countries in north-west Europe are. These systems appear to differ so much that there is no chance of identifying best practices to serve as a model for other countries. All practices seem to depend on complex preconditions rooted in national culture. The first task is therefore to understand the relevant traditions and institutions. Then, for mutual learning, a second effort is needed which involves the discussion, virtual testing and creative adaptation of various ideas and suggestions derived from foreign experiences. Here the goal is to bridge the gap between major institutional and cultural differences.

Work of this kind requires a lot of time in order to develop a fruitful debate which permits 'trial and error'. In our case, the results were very exciting. Our opinions concerning the situation of collective wage formation in Germany changed dramatically in the process of mutual learning with experts from the other four countries. While we were convinced at the beginning that the German system was undergoing fatal erosion, we learned from positive examples (France, the Netherlands, and especially Sweden) that there might be specific strengths also in the German system, which might stabilize it. We identified two aspects particularly well qualified to serve in this way: 'constitutional collective bargaining autonomy' and the specific division of labour in the dual system of employees' representation. However, not only was our analysis of collective wage formation in Germany improved, but we were also able – thanks to the foreign experiences presented – to challenge some of the most widespread false beliefs in the German debate (for example, the belief that wage formation is unusually highly regulated in Germany). Finally, some proposals for further development of the German system emerged from the comparative research process (for example, joint institutions of social partners or minimum wage legislation). All this is much more than was originally expected. However, *intensive communication* over two years was needed between correspondents in all the countries involved. It took two workshops and several versions of country reports to evolve the necessary understanding. And the discussion of whether our results are valid has still not come to an end. This publication is nothing more – but also nothing less – than another step in that process.

REFERENCES

Bispinck, Reinhard, and Claus Schäfer (2004), 'Niedriglöhne? Mindestlöhne! Verbreitung von Niedriglöhnen und Möglichkeiten ihrer Bekämpfung, Beitrag für die Zeitschrift "Sozialer Fortschritt"': http://www.boeckler.de/pdf/wsi_niedriglohn_2004_05.pdf

Federation of European Employers (2004), 'FedEE Review of Minimum Wage Rates': http://www.fedee.com/minwage.html

Hassel, Anke (2002), 'A New Going Rate? Co-ordinated Wage Bargaining in Europe', in Philippe Pochet (ed.), *Wage Policy in the Eurozone*, Brussels: Peter Lang, pp. 111–30.

Müller-Jentsch, Walther (ed.) (1999), *Konfliktpartnerschaft,* München: Rainer Hampp.

Schmidt, Werner, and Bernd Dworschak (2003), 'Industrial Relations in Britain and Germany Compared: Marks "Benchmarking" a New System of Employment Regulation beyond a Pure Industrial Relations System in the UK?', paper prepared for the 13th World Congress of the International Industrial Relations Association (IIRA) in Berlin, September 2003.

Traxler, Franz (2002), 'Wage Policy, Bargaining Institutions and Monetary Policy: Empirical Findings and Policy Implications for European Monetary Union', in Philippe Pochet (ed.), *Wage Policy in the Eurozone*, Brussels: Peter Lang, pp. 149–73.

7. Outlook – Chances of European harmonization or coordination of collective wage formation

Thomas Blanke

1. INTRODUCTION: EUROPE NEEDS A SOCIAL POLICY INCLUDING TRANSNATIONAL WAGE POLICIES

The European Community was launched in 1957 as a project of *market integration*. Since its beginnings, the European Community has been based on the guarantee of four freedoms, namely the free movement of goods, services, workers and capital. With the founding of the European Union by the Treaty of Maastricht in 1991, the creation of a single European market and the laying down of very restrictive rules for member state fiscal policies in order to establish monetary union it was also evident that the European Union must be based not only on economic but also on *social integration*. The most important step in the direction of so-called Social Europe was taken with the agreement of the European social partners on 'social dialogue' (31 October 1991) as a basis for the Protocol on Social Policy signed at Maastricht in 1992 by most member states[1] and finally inserted in the EC Treaty by the Treaty of Amsterdam in 1997.[2] The new provisions (Art. 136–140 ECT) gave, first, a broad spectrum of legal competences to the European Union in the fields of labour law and social policy that provided for European legislation – partly by qualified majority – by the Council of Ministers. Second, primacy of action in social matters as regards European legislation was given to the social partners at European level. However, it was stated explicitly that this should not apply to wages, freedom of association, the right to strike or the right to lock out (now: Art. 137 par. 5 ECT).

At the latest with Economic and Monetary Union (EMU) it became evident that wage policy could not be excluded from the European social policy agenda.[3] Having lost control of their monetary policy the Eurozone countries must focus on labour costs to sustain economic competitiveness.[4] Our thesis is that Social Europe needs institutions for collective wage formation which are effectively established at a *transnational level*. Particularly the central terms of employment – wages and working hours – must be protected from lower-cost competition on European markets through transnational collective bargaining, or at least close coordination of bargaining processes. That is the only way of avoiding a social downward spiral and protecting employees' participation in the development of European prosperity.

1. This agreement was originally concluded by only 11 of the 12 member states in order to circumvent the firm opposition of the United Kingdom at that time regarding all social matters.
2 See Schiek (2003), pp. 284–92.
3 See Deinert (1999), pp. 86–101.
4 See Traxler (2002), p. 111.

However, such initiatives face numerous obstacles. We identified two major problems in the area of industrial relations institutions and regulations:

1. The *significant national variety* of institutional arrangements. This hinders not only harmonization of the legal frameworks of collective bargaining in Europe, but also effective coordination of national bargaining strategies. One prominent problem, for instance, is that the legal binding effect of collective agreements is regulated completely differently in each country. Embedded in different bargaining cultures the differences between wage policies and bargaining practices are even hard to explain.
2. At the EU level, there is *no legal basis* for transnational collective agreements regulating core working standards. However, even if there were such a base, it would not be very helpful. The European umbrella organizations of employers and employees currently do not have any way of obtaining a mandate for wage bargaining which directly binds union memberships in all countries. The interests and institutional commitments of individual trade unions are too diverse.

In what follows, we will discuss five possible ways of dealing with these problems of divergence. (i) The solution may occur 'from the bottom up' through a spontaneous process of harmonization of national systems initiated by market forces and cross-national learning. (ii) It may occur through EU-wide cooperation in collective bargaining practices. (iii) It may take place 'from the top down' with the development of European bargaining arrangements in the practice of social dialogue, or (iv) by creating an explicit legal basis for collective agreements in European law. Finally, (v) it might be helpful to combine such 'bottom up' and 'top down' effects in an institutionalized process of open coordination.

2. TENDENCIES OF CONVERGENCE

The first assumption proved to be wrong. Our comparison of five European countries revealed clearly that despite similar economic and social challenges, national systems of collective wage formation in Europe show almost *no tendency to converge* (see Chapters 1–5).

The challenges of internationalization, decentralization and individualization are affecting collective wage formation systems in Western Europe in similar ways. However, national systems of collective bargaining are not changing in the direction of increasing uniformity of legal and institutional frameworks.

In contrast, each nation is trying to develop the *specific strengths* of its own collective bargaining system. For instance, data from France indicate a constantly shrinking union membership rate, but at the same time due to state intervention bargaining coverage has risen beyond 90%. In the Netherlands, state intervention was has been reduced in legal terms, but tripartite institutions control wage formation effectively on the basis of recommendations. In Sweden, where labour organisation is very successful and centralized (high degree of unionization and union representatives acting at both industry and company levels) sectoral wage agreements are possible which are very flexible as regards specific company regulations. Germany seems to find its specific strength in giving more bargaining rights to works councils which previously had only formal competences concerning codetermination.

Due to the different structures of national systems of industrial relations and collective bargaining the capacities of national systems to react to specific aspects of common challenges vary widely. It seems that the *trend towards individualization* strongly affects the German and the British systems. In contrast, the French system is protected against this by its high degree of state interventionism. This is obviously also the case in the Netherlands and Sweden which are based on a strong and still dominant tradition of collectivism. The *tendency towards decentralization* from regional level collective bargaining to company level is also common in the European states in question. However, it has a different place in each national structure: for Germany, for example, it is a crucial issue due to its dual system of workers' representation and codetermination. Within this system trade unions have a constitutional monopoly on concluding collective agreements on wages and they traditionally act at regional or multi-company level. If the undertaking became the dominant level for concluding collective agreements it would constitute a fundamental change in the German system as regards the legal and institutional role, legitimacy and function of trade unions on the one hand and of works councils on the other. Therefore the decentralization and so-called '*Verbetrieblichung*' (dealing with something at enterprise level rather than in collective agreements) of collective bargaining on wages indicate a fundamental crisis in the legal and institutional structures of German collective bargaining. Surprisingly, decentralization does not appear to be leading towards a similar crisis in the Netherlands, even if there are structures comparable to those in Germany (the dual system). Industrial relations systems in Sweden, France and the UK are much better prepared to deal with this new challenge due to their single channel systems with acting union representatives at both company and regional level. In France the decentralization process is also supported by the state which has imposed a duty to bargain and has granted wage concessions in implementing the maximum weekly working time of 35 hours. The case of the UK is particularly interesting. It makes clear that the radical dissolution of multi-employer collective bargaining structures does not necessarily lead to the complete disappearance of trade unions. However, it is also clear that the trade unions are changing their role insofar as their representatives within undertakings are increasingly assuming the 'monitoring' role of works councils. The *challenge of globalization and internationalization* is putting increasing pressure on economic competition in all member states. The economically tolerable room for price, wage and taxes differences is diminishing radically and the location of companies and establishments is becoming at the same time more relevant and more flexible. Again, similar challenges are putting national systems of collective bargaining under strain in a different way. National pacts on employment and a growing tendency towards concession bargaining are a common reaction in all member states. However, only in Germany does the mainstream political and economic debate constitute a plea for a fundamental change in traditional structures in a similar way to the UK in the 1970s.

This leads us to the conclusion that on the one hand there are similar tendencies across all countries. Decentralization of bargaining level, forms of negotiated flexibility, possibilities of agreeing on reducing wages in situations of crisis and wage incentive structures are visible everywhere. We also find similar wage increases in most countries. That means that there are similar developments with respect to the outcome of bargaining processes. On the other hand we do not see a convergence regarding the structural differences of national collective bargaining systems.

3. TRANSNATIONAL COORDINATION OF WAGE POLICIES

Since the end of the 1990s, there have been intensified *efforts by the European trade unions to coordinate* bargaining policies, particularly in relation to wage formation, across borders. Four different processes were reported,[5] two at cross-industry level and two at sectoral level. The first prominent example was the Doorn Regional Initiative in which the umbrella trade union organisations of Belgium, Germany, Luxembourg and the Netherlands have been represented since 1997/1998. The group agreed to hold annual meetings and passed a declaration concerning, for example, wage increases. The participating trade unions declared that they wished to reach collective bargaining settlements that corresponded to the sum total of price and productivity increases. This was a clear rejection of competition-oriented wage policies and the associated wage dumping. The ETUC soon followed. In December 2000, the ETUC adopted a resolution promoting the continued coordination of collective bargaining. A guideline was published aiming at several goals, above all:[6]

- nominal wage increases should at least exceed inflation whilst maximising the proportion of productivity allocated to increasing gross wages in order to secure a better balance between profits and wages; and
- any remaining part of productivity should be used in relation to other items in collective agreements, such as qualitative aspects of work where these are quantifiable and calculable in terms of cost.

At the same time, sectoral trade unions began to form cross-border collective bargaining networks at the regional level and the sectoral European Trade Union Federations intensified coordination at the European level.

The main advantage of these approaches to transnational wage coordination is that they accept the great variety of institutions, laws, and practices as regards collective wage formation in different European countries and focus instead on coordinating bargaining outcomes.[7] So far, success has been very limited, however. There are numerous *structural problems*.[8] European cooperation works best between peak organizations; however, they do not have much influence on national wage bargaining. The national trade unions at the sectoral level, in contrast, regard wage bargaining as their central function, so they are usually not willing to subordinate their wage policies to European strategies. Moreover, they are often bound by strong constraints concerning their bargaining options, rooted in national specifics. The pressure produced by interests at national level is clearly dominant. Powerful forces are needed to bring national trade unions in line with European guidelines, but there are no such forces. Indeed, there are no sanctions to apply to national trade unions if they, for instance, refuse to comply with the guideline on wage increases (inflation + productivity). There are therefore prominent cases in which trade unions deviate significantly from European resolutions. A recent example was the Netherlands where wage increases of zero percent were concluded in 2003. Like the Dutch trade unions, many others are committed to social pacts or to national policies which aim at improving the competitiveness of the national economy.

5. See Dufresne (2002), pp. 80–99.
6 ETUC Executive Committee (2000).
7 See Schulten (2004), p. 206f.
8 See Schulten (2004), pp. 207–10.

It is perhaps too early to assert that the efforts of European trade unions to coordinate wage policies have *failed*. The reported difficulties, however, seem to be overwhelming. Indeed, the problems will only increase because decentralisation of wage bargaining (for example, to enterprise level) in many countries will complicate coordination efforts at sectoral level. The best example is Germany where wage increases in 2004 should have been about 2%, according to sectoral collective agreements. In fact, wages were raised by a mere 0.1%.[9] The main reason was that many firms deviated from sectoral agreements to the detriment of employees on the basis of company agreements with trade unions or works councils.

The coordination efforts of European trade unions may therefore go awry. Nevertheless, they include an intensive programme of annual reports and meetings, constituting a process of mutual information and learning to the benefit of all participants. In that way they may contribute to a gradual integration of diverse institutions and practices in the long run.

4. EUROPEAN SOCIAL DIALOGUE

The 'bottom-up' developments mentioned above offer little hope of closer integration of the diverse European wage bargaining systems in the near future. What remains for further discussion are activities directed from the top – namely from the European Union – that might promote transnational harmonization or coordination. At Community level, agreements between management and labour are explicitly regulated in Art. 139, par. 1 ECT: 'Should management and labour so desire, the dialogue between them at Community level may lead to contractual relations, including agreements.' This 'social dialogue', however, is clearly *not directed towards negotiation of wage agreements* binding for individual employment relationships. So far, in almost all cases agreements according to Art. 139 ECT were integrated within the framework of social partner participation in European legislation, establishing loose frameworks of minimum standards, for example, on fixed-term work, part-time work and parental leave. This is because European level trade unions have no power to put pressure on employers' organizations, for example, by instigating strike action. Therefore, only in cases in which the European Commission announced that a given issue would be subject to European legislation if management and labour did not make a proposal were employers' organizations willing to agree on a 'joint request' and to conclude an agreement by means of social dialogue in order to avoid a more restrictive European regulation. Consequently, the compulsory standards established by EC directives as regards social partner agreements appear to be quite low.

Particularly in relation to wage agreements, social dialogue legislation is inadequate. There will be no implementation of 'joint requests' by the social partners (see Art. 139, par. 2 ECT) in that area by European legislation because the European Council has no competence to issue directives on wages (cf. Art. 137, par. 5 ECT). For the same reason, the Commission cannot put pressure on the social partners to agree on wages by announcing legislation. Initiatives concerning European wage agreements must therefore come exclusively from the European social partners themselves. This is not even on the horizon in a situation in which even loose forms of wage coordination between national trade unions are hardly possible. Therefore,

9. See Keune (2004), Tables 4 and 5.

social dialogue is an instrument of European tripartism only in the making of social policy. It is not an instrument of European collective bargaining.

However, this conclusion does not reflect the *essence* of developments overall. In apparent contradiction of what was said above, European social policy may also be said to have become a very strong instrument in developing collective bargaining structures. European social policy – including the social dialogue – has created, since Directive 77/187/EEC of 5.3.1977[10] on acquired rights, an ever growing network of procedures on information and consultation and of collective agreements within companies. One of the major steps in this direction was the European Works Council Directive 94/45/EC of 22.9.1994.[11] So far, nearly all European works councils – about 740, representing more than 60% of the workforce in multinational companies with more than 10,000 employees – have been based on agreements. Concluding further agreements with central management on working conditions is a major activity of works councils. The creation of institutions representing the collective interests of the workforce via collective agreements is becoming the focus of European social policy in the sphere of collective labour law. It also characterizes Directive 2001/86/EC of 8.10.2001[12] on employee involvement in SEs and general framework Directive 2002/14/EC.[13]

The effect of this innovative concept for the creation of procedures and institutions of collective labour law is twofold: (i) it initiates a culture of bargaining and concluding agreements in order to establish European works councils within community-scale undertakings or groups of undertakings; in that way, it creates (ii) a genuine European network of legal practices antecedent to the process of creating national transposition laws. National law, consequently, has to be adapted to the new European legal situation by acknowledging the existence and legal validity of European collective agreements.

To be sure, one must consider that the rights of European works councils as regards *information and consultation* are weak instruments of workers' participation. However, in practice the effectiveness of workers' participation sometimes goes far beyond the formal legal position. In some cases, agreements concluded between European works councils and management also cover aspects of wages and other payments in compensation for loss of workplace or changing working conditions.[14]

As a result, the 'social dialogue' of Articles 138, 139 ECT alone will not produce collective agreements at European level which are binding on individual employment relationships as regards wage formation. However, European social policy in general – including the central instrument of 'social dialogue' – has developed an innovative concept which is generating an increasingly dense network of collective bargaining structures at cross-sectoral, sectoral and enterprise level. Based on agreements between labour and management at enterprise level, there is an emerging practice of signing collective agreements that sometimes also includes wages.

10. OJ L 061/26, 5.3.1977 (now Directive 2001/23/EC of 12.3.2001, OJ L 082/16, 22.3.2001).
11 OJ L 254/72, 30.9.1994; see Blanke (1999).
12 OJ L 294/22, 8.10.2001.
13 OJ L 080/29, 25.3.2002.
14 See most recently the framework agreement between the central management of the General Motors Group and the European Works Council of 7./8.12.2004, reported in: www.euro-betriebsrat.de. Further examples in Klebe and Kunz (1999 and 2001).

5. A CONSTITUTION FOR EUROPE

The new Constitutional Treaty will improve the legal basis for collective bargaining at European level. According to Part II of the Treaty,[15] collective bargaining will acquire *new legal protection* through the Charter of Fundamental Rights. Art. II-88 of the Constitutional Treaty gives workers and employers, or their organizations the right (in accordance with trade union and national laws and practices) to negotiate and conclude collective agreements at the relevant levels and to take collective action, including strikes. This could be used as a legal basis for collective agreements at European level. However, in order to clarify the legal force of such agreements in individual countries, a specific EU legislative act is needed.

The first question arises, Does the EU have the *competence* to pass such an act. One problem might be that according to Art. II-111 par. 2 of the Constitutional Treaty, the Charter of Fundamental Rights does not establish any new power or task.[16] However, in the case of collective bargaining, no new power or task is needed: according to Art. III-210, par. 1f. of the Constitutional Treaty (Art. 137, par. 1 f. ECT), the EU has competence in the fields of representation and collective defence of the interests of workers and employers. Collective bargaining comes under this heading. The exceptions in Art. III-210 par. 6 concern wages, the right of association, the right to strike and the right to impose lock-outs, but not the right to negotiate and conclude collective agreements. Even if one takes into account the fact that the right to take collective action necessarily forms an integral part of collective bargaining and that it is problematic to regulate collective agreements without an integrated guarantee of the right to take industrial action it seems obvious that the EU has the competence to establish regulations on collective bargaining, for example, defining the legal force of European collective agreements. Furthermore, it seems probable that fundamental rights – especially the new constitutional guarantee of the right to collective bargaining and action in Art. II-88 Constitutional Treaty – will serve to extend EU competences in the field of social and labour rights, especially fundamental trade union rights:

> When Member States act within the sphere of EU competence, they must comply with, or at least respect, the fundamental rights in the Charter. The implication that even where there may be no EU competence, the EU must still respect fundamental rights also arguably affects Member States. Even when Member States act outside EU competence, they too must respect fundamental rights.[17]

---

15. Consolidated version approved by the intergovernmental conference on 13 October 2004, published in OJ C 310, 16 December 2004.

16 See, for example, the statement of British Prime Minister Tony Blair to the UK Parliament on 21 June 2004 on the EU Constitutional Treaty: 'The EU Treaty includes, in the Charter of Fundamental Rights, the rights of the citizen under EU law. The Charter expressly rules out establishing any new power or task for the European Union or any change in the powers of the European Union. In each area the rights are expressly limited to those available under existing national law and practices and under existing Union law. So, for example, Article 28 of the Charter says that workers and employers have the right to negotiate and conclude collective agreements at the appropriate levels, but only "in accordance with Union law and national laws and practices". In addition, the Charter contains explanations for each Article making it clear, for example, that "the ... limits for the exercise of collective action, including strike action, come under national laws and practices, including the question of whether it may be carried out in parallel in several member states." The Treaty requires those explanations to be given due regard by the Courts.' See Bercusson (2005).

17 Bercusson (2005).

Second, the European Union is *obliged* to make such regulations as soon as there is collective bargaining at the EU level. As soon as the social partners decide that collective bargaining at the European level is appropriate, it will be a violation of Art. II-88 of the Constitutional Treaty if the Union refuses to establish the European law which is required to render European collective agreements effective. It may be that a more restrictive interpretation of the Charter will become dominant. Art. I-48 of the Constitutional Treaty is relevant in this respect, according to which the European Union recognises and promotes the role of the social partners at EU level, taking into account the diversity of national systems. This clearly provides for additional action, although it is arguable whether 'the role of the social partners' necessarily includes transnational collective bargaining.

Whatever happens, even before the Constitutional Treaty comes into force – after ratification by the member states – there will be no lack of legal grounds for EU action to create a legal framework for European collective agreements. However, the central problem remains: practical preconditions for European wage agreements must be developed. This includes the need for active harmonization of diverging interests and institutional arrangements between countries.

6. THE OPEN METHOD OF COORDINATION

According to Art. III-213 of the Constitutional Treaty, the so-called 'open method of coordination' (OMC) must be applied in matters relating to the rights of association and collective bargaining. This procedure promises *new prospects* for gradually harmonizing (or coordinating) systems of collective wage formation in Europe.

Since the Extraordinary European Council on Employment which took place in Luxembourg in 1997, OMC has been used in the European Employment Strategy (see Art. 128 ECT). At the Lisbon European Council (2000) OMC was further specified. The Treaty Establishing a Constitution for Europe provides for OMC in seven fields of social policy (see Art. III-213), including the 'right of association and collective bargaining' (see letter g). The second sentence of Art. III-213 of the Treaty states that the Commission 'shall act' in these fields of social policy; it does not say 'may', as it does in other policy fields where OMC activities are mentioned in the Treaty (for example, Art. III-250, par. 2: 'may take any useful initiative'). OMC will therefore be compulsory for matters (beside others) relating to collective bargaining between employers and workers. In detail, the Commission shall act 'by making studies, delivering opinions and arranging consultations ... in particular initiatives aiming at the establishment of guidelines and indicators, the organisation of exchange of best practice, and the preparation of the necessary elements for periodic monitoring and evaluation.'

Consequently, national systems of collective bargaining will soon face a new challenge. In a process of defining guidelines, indicators or benchmarks, there must be clarification concerning what the benefits of collective bargaining are and how the performance of collective bargaining systems can be judged. OMC does not entail European standardization of collective bargaining policies or legislation. However, all countries must determine what their collective bargaining aims are and how to distinguish good practices from bad. This would be an important first step towards coordination or harmonization of bargaining systems. Long-term monitoring and evaluation will determine whether variations between national collective bargaining systems are useful, and whether there should be transnational wage agreements, or close coordination of national agreements.

In policy fields where OMC is already applied its *effectiveness* has been much disputed.[18] Since it is 'soft law', no sanctions are available; instead, it achieves its effects by means of indirect pressures.[19] In the area of collective wage bargaining, the determination of guidelines and indicators alone would constitute significant progress for countries in which collective wage bargaining is not willingly accepted (any longer), such as Germany. Moreover, the problem of effective European wage coordination will inevitably become a central part of OMC. Indicators for benchmarking industrial relations were proposed in the 'Report of the High Level Group on Industrial Relations and Change in the European Union': 'Fair and decent terms and conditions of employment' are mentioned at least in second place.[20] In comparison with the wage coordination efforts of European trade unions (see paragraph 2), the coordinated evaluation of collective wage formation in the OMC will have much greater relevance in the political and public spheres.

A process such as OMC represents a significant opportunity to counteract lower-wage competition between European countries. All 'bottom up' and 'top down' effects mentioned above (in paragraphs 1–4) could be *combined* in a institutionalized process of open coordination. However, this also entails a clear risk that policies to achieve fair wages will be set aside in favor of strategies to increase employment. Nevertheless, one point is already clarified in Art. III-213 of the Constitutional Treaty: the goal of the whole procedure is *collective* bargaining, which means that it should strengthen (not weaken) collectivity of bargaining between employers and employees.

---

18 See Goetschy (2003), p. 288f.

19 Trubek and Trubek (2003), p. 18, distinguish five effects generated by OMC: diffusion, shaming, networks, deliberation, learning; see also Rose (2004), p. 225f.

20 High Level Group (2002), p. 38.

REFERENCES

Bercusson, Brian (ed.) (2005), *The EU Charter of Fundamental Rights and the Constitution of the European Union. Postscript*, Baden-Baden: Nomos (forthcoming).

Blanke, Thomas (1999), *EBRG Kommentar*, Baden-Baden: Nomos.

Deinert, Olaf (1999), *Der europäische Kollektivvertrag*, Baden-Baden: Nomos.

Dufresne, Anne (2002), 'Wage Coordination in Europe: Roots and Routes,' in Philippe Pochet (ed.), *Wage Policy in the Eurozone*, Brussels: Lang, pp. 79–109.

ETUC Executive Committee (2000), 'ETUC Recommendation on the Coordination of Collective Bargaining': http://www.etuc.org/EN/Decisions/ecenglish/coordcollbarg/cbrecom.cfm.

Goetschy, Janine (2003), 'The European Employment Strategy and the Open Method of Coordination: Lessons and Perspectives,' *Transfer* 9: 281–301.

High Level Group on Industrial Relations and Change in the European Union (2002), 'Report,' European Commission, Directorate General for Employment and Social Affairs, http://europa.eu.int/comm/employment_social/soc-dial/rapport_en.pdf.

Keune, Maarten (2004), 'The Coordination of Collective Bargaining in Europe' (Annual Report 2004), ETUC: Brussels: http://www.etuc.org/EN/Decisions/ecenglish/coordcollbarg/0412CBCReport%20ENG.c fm.

Klebe, Thomas, and Olaf Kunz (1999), 'Europäische Betriebsräte: Eine praktische und rechtliche Zwischenbilanz,' in Thomas Klebe, Peter Wedde and Martin Wolmerath (eds), *Festschrift Däubler*, Köln: Bund, pp. 823–840.

Klebe, Thomas, and Olaf Kunz (2001), 'Europäische Betriebsräte – Erste Erfahrungen,' in Hellmut Wißmann (ed.), *Jahrbuch des Arbeitsrechts* 38, pp. 55–70.

Rose, Edgar (2004), 'Die "offene Methode der Koordinierung" – Europäisches "soft law" einer wissensorientierten Integrationspolitik,' in Jörg Hammermeister, Bettina Reich and Edgar Rose (eds), *Information – Wissen – Kompetenz*, Oldenburg: bis, pp. 209–229.

Schiek, Dagmar (2003), 'Europäische Kollektivvereinbarungen,' in Wolfgang Däubler (ed.), *Kommentar zum Tarifvertragsgesetz*, Baden-Baden: Nomos, pp. 267–328.

Schulten, Thorsten (2004), 'Gewerkschaftliche Lohn- und Tarifpolitik in Europa – Ansätze, Widerstände und Perspektiven einer europaweiten Koordinierung,' in Eckhard Hein, Torsten Niechoy, Thorsten Schulten and Achim Truger (eds), *Europas Wirtschaft gestalten – Makroökonomische Koordinierung und die Rolle der Gewerkschaften*, Hamburg: VSA, pp. 192–215.

Traxler, Franz (2002), 'Wage Policy, Bargaining Institutions and Monetary Policy: Empirical Findings and Policy Implications for European Monetary Union,' in Philippe Pochet (ed.), *Wage Policy in the Eurozone*, Brussels: Lang, pp. 111–130.

Trubek, David M., and Louise G. Trubek (2003), 'Hard and Soft Law in the Construction of Social Europe,' paper prepared for SALTSA, OSE, UW Workshop on 'Opening the Open Method of Coordination', Florence, 2003: http://eucenter.wisc.edu/OMC/Summer03Conf/trubekTrubek.pdf.

Annex

This annex provides basic data on collective wage formation and related matters for all five countries.

In general, it should be noted that comparisons across countries face numerous problems concerning differences in criteria and measurement. Often, precise data are not available and estimates must fill the gap. In most sources used on the following pages, therefore, the limited reliability of the data is indicated.

List of figures

Figure 1 Collective bargaining coverage rates

Figure 2 Trade union organization rate

Figure 3 Employers' organization rate

Figure 4 Industrial disputes

Table 1 Monthly gross statutory minimum wage rates

Figure 5 Average gross annual earnings in industry and services

Figure 6 Average increases in real wages

Figure 7 Unemployment rates

Figure 1 Collective bargaining coverage rates – covered employees around 2000

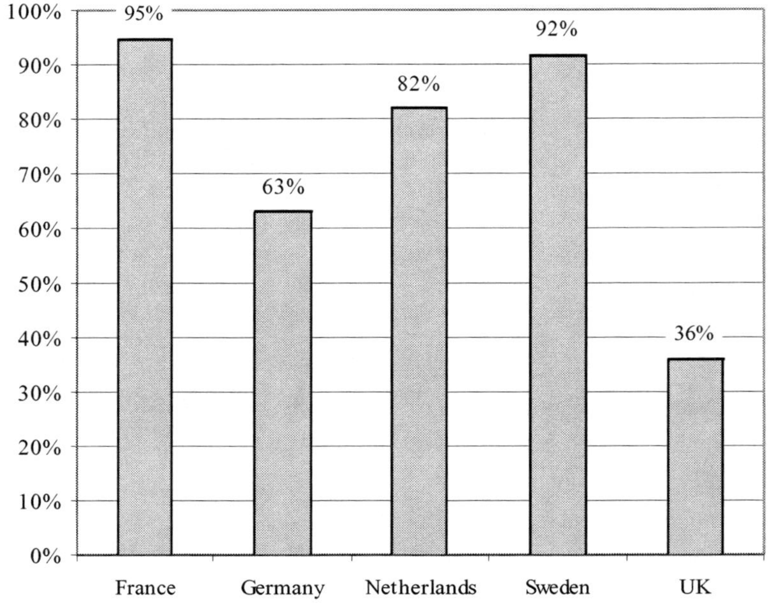

Note: In Germany, about another 20% work at firms where sectoral collective agreements are applied volutarily by individual contract.

Source: European Commission, *Industrial Relations in Europe* (2004), p. 30.

Figure 2 Trade union organization rate, 2001–2002

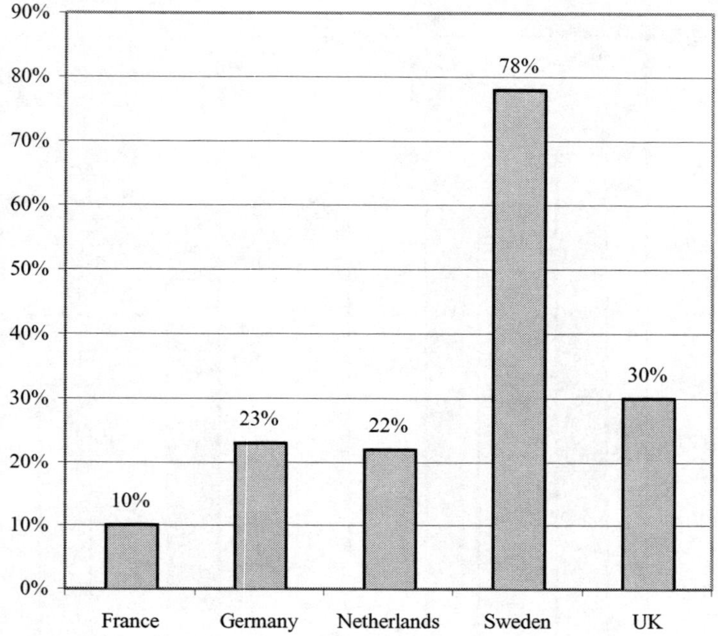

Note: The rate refers to the share of trade union members among active employees. Retired and unemployed union members are not included. Usually, the number of such persons is not known exactly so Figure 2 has been estimated.

Source: European Commission, *Industrial Relations in Europe* (2004), p. 19.

Figure 3 Employers' organization rate, 2000

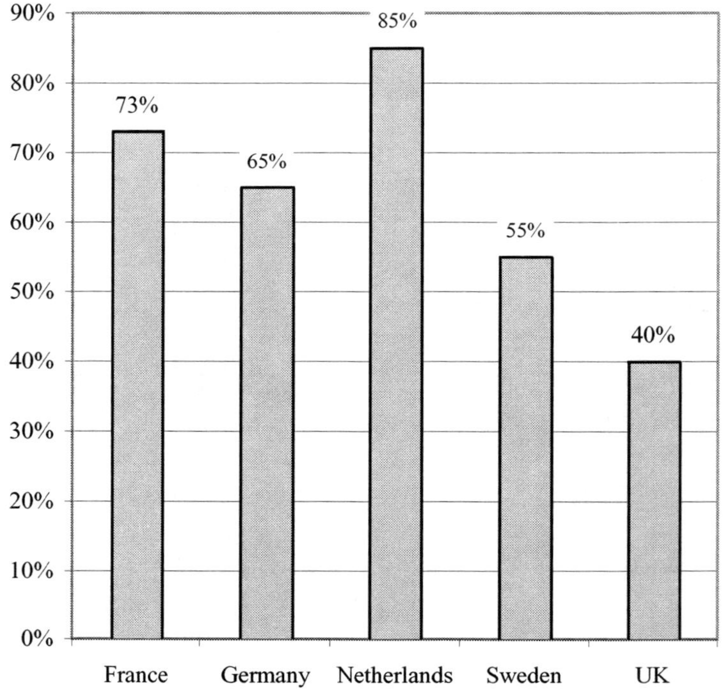

Note: The organization rate of employers is measured as a proportion of the national workforce employed by the member firms. Because there are no official statistics, the data rely on more or less representative surveys and estimates.

Source: European Commission, *Industrial Relations in Europe* (2004), p. 28.

Figure 4 Industrial disputes – days lost per 1000 employees (1990–1998 and 1999–2002)

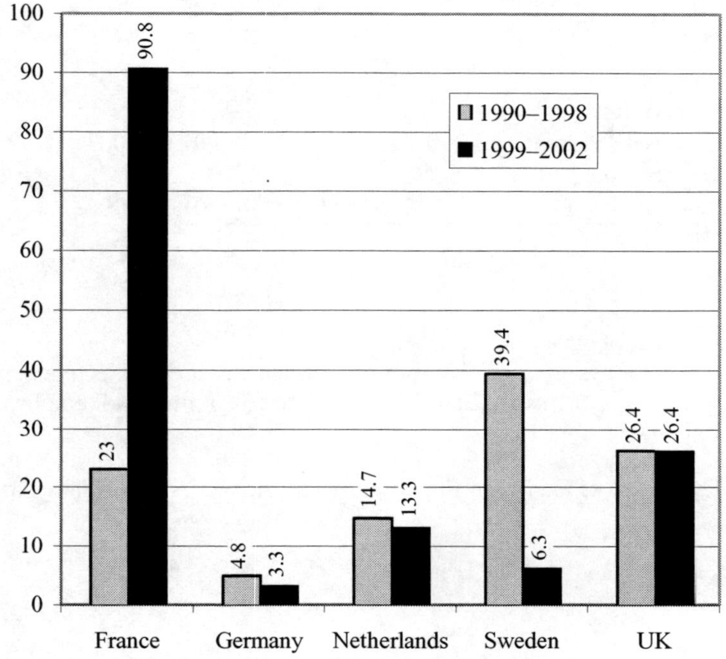

Note: Strike activities differ very much from year to year, so only the average over long periods gives a true impression.

Source: For 1990–1998, Eichhorst et al., *Benchmarking Deutschland, 2001*, p. 158, with reference to data from the ILO *Yearbook of Labour Statistics 1999* and the OECD's *Economic Outlook* (Compendium 2000). For 1999–2002: Eurostat.

Table 1 Monthly gross statutory minimum wage rates

	EUR	Effective date
France	1 154*	25.06.2004
Germany**	No	
Netherlands	1 265	01.07.2003
Sweden***	No	
UK	1 226****	01.10.2004

Note:
* For statutory 35-hour week.
** For construction work there is a minimum wage based on collective agreements.
*** Collective agreements with a minimum wage cover almost all employees.
**** GBP 840.67.

Source: Federation of European Employers (http://www.fedee.com/minwage.html).

Figure 5 Average gross annual earnings in industry and services (EUR)

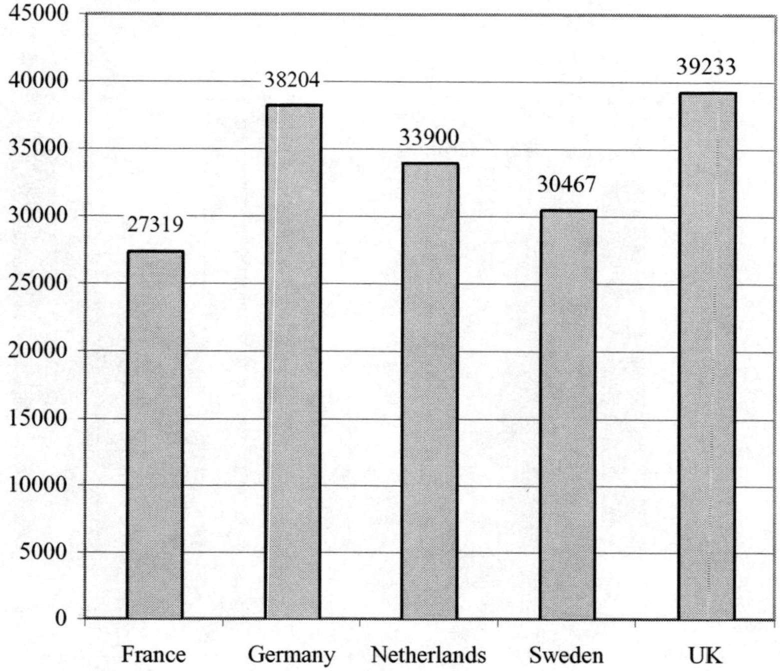

Note: The data concern only full-time jobs in companies with 10 employees or more.

Source: Eurostat Yearbook 2004: p. 144.

Figure 6 Average increases in real wages 1992–1999 (%)

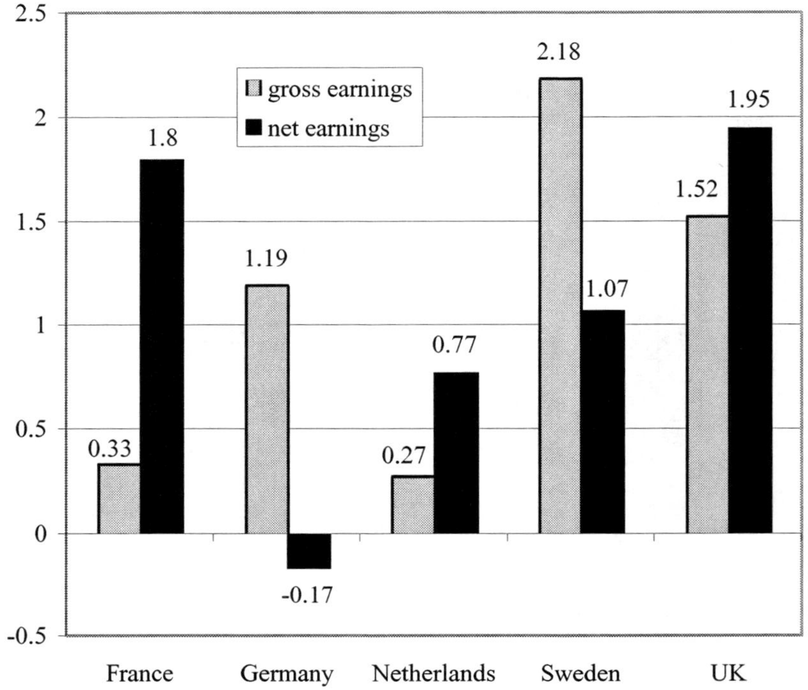

Note: The significant difference between the increase in gross earnings and net earnings in Germany is partly caused by the high reunification costs attached to social security.

Source: Eichhorst et al., *Benchmarking Deutschland, 2001,* pp. 133, 134, refering to data of the OECD Economic Outlook, Main Economic Indicators (Statistical Compendium 2000).

Figure 7 Unemployment rates (annual average; %)

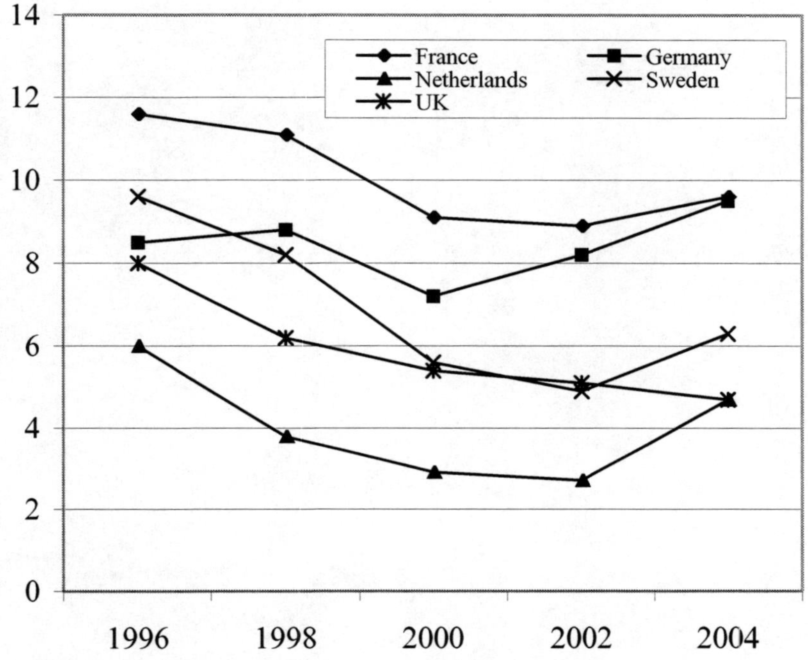

Source: Eurostat.